# Pakistan's Nuclear Doctrine

## Safety, Stability and Strategy

# Pakistan's Nuclear Doctrine

## Safety, Stability and Strategy

R.K. Pandey

**NEHA PUBLISHERS & DISTRIBUTORS**
DELHI

*Publisher*
**NEHA PUBLISHERS & DISTRIBUTORS**
4832/24,Prahlad Lane,S-207 Ansari
Road, Daryaganj, Delhi-110002
Ph.: 43570976, 23278261
Email: nehapubdistributors@gmail.com

**Edition:** 2026



**ISBN:** 978-93-80318-90-5

Laser Typesetting
**JEE-VEE Graphics,** Delhi

**Price:** 1195/-

*Printed*
Vikas Computers, Delhi

# Contents


| | | |
|---|---|---|
| | *Preface* | *(vii)* |
| 1. | Nuclear Doctrine | 1 |
| 2. | Nuclear Weapons of Pakistan | 33 |
| 3. | Pakistan's Nuclear Posture | 66 |
| 4. | Pakistan's Nuclear Diplomacy | 109 |
| 5. | Pakistani Nuclear Strikes on Tactical Targets | 156 |
| 6. | Pakistan's Nuclear Program | 195 |
| 7. | Small Arms Trade and Manufacture in Pakistan | 241 |
| 8. | Nuclear Power in Pakistan | 248 |
| 9. | Nuclear Material Security of Pakistan | 268 |
| | *Bibliography* | 309 |
| | *Index* | 311 |

# Preface

Former Director of Central Intelligence George Tenet reports in his memoirs that A.Q. Khan rebuffed several approaches by Osama bin Laden for access to nuclear know-how, although it was not clear why. Perhaps Khan understood that cooperating with the renowned terrorist leader was a bridge too far as it risked contributing to a scenario of nuclear Armageddon that could cause mass destruction and loss of life in his own country.

While Pakistan has not formally articulated a nuclear doctrine, the senior military officer responsible for the Pakistani nuclear arsenal, General Khalid Kidwai (who is now retired from the military but remains Director General, Strategic Plans Division), outlined in a January 2002 interview the contours of a possible Pakistani nuclear weapons use strategy.

Finally, many in Pakistan believe the US intends to seize Pakistan's nuclear facilities and weapons systems for a variety of political or religious reasons. This issue colours public perceptions of American behaviour so much so that during a January 2010 visit to Pakistan, US Secretary of Defence Robert Gates felt it necessary to state at Pakistan's National Defence University that the US "has no desire to control Pakistan's nuclear weapons." However, US plans to "provide added security for the Pakistani arsenal in case of a crisis," as one American journalist wrote, only exacerbated such fears. Paradoxically, in his memoirs, Musharraf argued that not cooperating with the US against al Qaeda would jeopardize Pakistan's nuclear weapons even more: "It is no secret that the US has never been comfortable with a Muslim country acquiring nuclear weapons and the Americans un-doubtedly would have taken the opportunity of an invasion to destroy such weapons."

As the book addresses this crucial issue quite deftly, it is hoped that it would prove to be a source of great information for the reader. It an essential reading for the students taking courses on this book.

—*Auther*

# 1

# Nuclear Doctrine

While Pakistan has not formally articulated a nuclear doctrine, the senior military officer responsible for the Pakistani nuclear arsenal, General Khalid Kidwai (who is now retired from the military but remains Director General, Strategic Plans Division), outlined in a January 2002 interview the contours of a possible Pakistani nuclear weapons use strategy.

He said Pakistan would launch nuclear weapons only "if the very existence of Pakistan as a state is at stake."

Kidwai went on to say, "Nuclear weapons are aimed solely at India." Explaining that if usual deterrence fails, nuclear weapons would be unleashed under the following circumstances:

- India attacks Pakistan and conquers a large part of its territory;
- India destroys a large part of either Pakistan's land or air forces;
- India attempts the economic strangulation of Pakistan;
- India pushes Pakistan into political destabilization or creates large-scale internal subversion in Pakistan.

Pakistan refuses to adopt a "no-first-use" doctrine—suggesting that Pakistan might use its nuclear weapons even if India did not use them first.

Some analysts believe that if Indian forces crossed the N-5 highway connecting Lahore to Karachi, Pakistan might escalate a conventional conflict into a nuclear one.

## PAKISTAN'S STRATEGIC CHALLENGES

In less than seventy years, Pakistan fought four major wars, lost significant territory to a secessionist movement, served as a frontline for a superpower proxy confrontation, and endured major militant insurgencies and terrorist campaigns. Natural disasters in 2010, continued extremist violence against the state and its citizens, and US demands to support operations in neighboring Afghanistan highlight the prominence of Pakistan's armed forces in the life of the country. Drawing even more attention, Pakistan's engagement in a regional nuclear arms race tests the limits of the global non-proliferation regime and significantly raises the stakes in a future war.

This grim security picture, along with periods of turbulent civilian rule and internal unrest, has historically empowered the military to take what it considered necessary action to defend the Pakistani state.

## KEY CONCERNS ABOUT PAKISTAN'S NUCLEAR PROGRAM

Since a conflict with India would be a high-stakes challenge for Pakistan, observers remain concerned with Pakistan's nuclear program due to the possibility of a nuclear confrontation. After all, India and Pakistan are willing to engage in limited conflict with each other despite the possibility of nuclear war. Indian leaders are acutely aware of this precarious position as well. India's former Chief of Army Staff in November 2009 stated that, "the possibility of a limited war under a nuclear overhang is still a reality, at least in the Indian subcontinent." Concerns about an Indian attack on vulnerable Pakistani command-and-control systems might lead Pakistan's military to decentralize nuclear launch authority to enable a response in the event of a surprise first-strike. Such a move would also increase the chances of inadvertent escalation during times of military uncertainty.

To reduce nuclear dangers, Pakistan and India in 1999 agreed to a number of nuclear confidence-building measures such as notification prior to the testing of ballistic missiles and the annual exchange of a list of nuclear facilities that are not to be attacked during a war. Yet the risk of a wider conflict—triggered, perhaps, by a terrorist attack—suggests that a nuclear war in South Asia remains a calamitous possibility.

Despite the military's extensive vetting system, the "insider threat"— perhaps from low-level personnel working on nuclear sites—is an ongoing challenge to Pakistan's nuclear security. An assault and takeover of even a single nuclear device or facility, a fear heightened by recent suicide bomb attacks on Air Force bases reportedly serving as nuclear weapons storage sites, also remains a persistent threat to the nation and to neighboring countries.

It is believed that as a response to the threat of an Indian attack, Pakistan dispersed its weapons to several low-profile sites, thereby increasing the challenge of securing these weapons. Similarly, the imperative to protect its weapons would likely lead the Pakistani military to transport these in small, secret convoys—potentially at greater risk of capture from an insider. *The "insider threat" is discussed in more detail in the second report in this series.*

Furthermore, Pakistani scientists have sold off-the-shelf nuclear technologies to the highest bidder in the past, raising significant proliferation worries. It remains unclear whether the Pakistani military leadership was aware or truly ignorant of the transfers carried out by A.Q. Khan to Iran, North Korea, and Libya. The fact that such a robust network existed over the course of some twenty years and was run from within the country's nuclear program nonetheless indicate that Pakistan's nuclear weaponry may not be as secure as its leaders claim.

Finally, many in Pakistan believe the US intends to seize Pakistan's nuclear facilities and weapons systems for a variety of political or religious reasons. This issue colours public perceptions of American behaviour so much so that during a January 2010 visit to Pakistan, US Secretary of Defence Robert Gates felt it necessary to state at Pakistan's National Defence University that the US "has no desire to control Pakistan's nuclear weapons." However, US plans to "provide added security for the Pakistani arsenal in case of a crisis," as one American journalist wrote, only exacerbated such fears. Paradoxically, in his memoirs, Musharraf argued that not cooperating with the US against al Qaeda would jeopardize Pakistan's nuclear weapons even more: "It is no secret that the US has never been comfortable with a Muslim country acquiring nuclear weapons and the Americans un-doubtedly would have taken the opportunity of an invasion to destroy such weapons."

## *Counterinsurgency*

The Pakistani military has primarily directed its resources towards countering the threat of its strategic nemesis, India. As a result, it was less prepared to quell the insurgencies that developed in Pakistan's FATA following the fall of the Taliban in Afghanistan. Although Pakistan has a long history of frontier warfare and low-level conflict in its tribal regions, the knowledge gleaned from that experience was not prioritized or disseminated in military training. Many of the first units going into the FATA and Swat Valley had difficulty shifting from a focus on large-scale mechanized warfare to one that emphasized smaller units, more precise air and artillery support, greater concern for civilian casualties and infrastructural damage, and a dominant and persistent military and government presence.

Since 2008, however, the military's effectiveness in counterinsurgency operations has improved significantly. The process by which the military increased its counterinsurgency capacity has been an adaptive one in which lessons learned on the battlefield gradually evolved into a set of standard practices taught at the training facilities that prepare Pakistani units for tribal area operations. These tactics, techniques, and procedures continue to evolve. However, insurgent organizations in the tribal agencies have adapted their tactics as well. As it stands today, both sides often claim victory before their gains are fully secured. Military units are effective in battle and capable of executing their missions tactically; the problem lies in the larger issues of governance, reform, and civilian aid and reconstruction.

The Pakistani military's dominant presence in Pakistani society is often matched by an equally underdeveloped civilian government. In the tribal areas, this is manifested in the difficulties Pakistan has had in bringing economic and infrastructural development to the region. Although Pakistan's military follows its own distinct brand of counterinsurgent doctrine, it does recognize the value of securing civilian populations, providing better governance, and developing the local economy; yet the inability of the civilian government to accomplish these goals hinders the military's ability to end its counterinsurgent campaigns.

As a result, the Pakistani military has been forced to continuously recapture territory it has already held. It has also been reticent to move into North Waziristan, a bastion of insurgent organizations that operate in both Pakistan and Afghanistan. Although the Pakistani military is now a relatively effective counterinsurgent-capable organization, the lack of civilian government capacity continues to prevent any long-term reform from occurring in the tribal areas. Until civilians are able to govern effectively, the stalemate between the Pakistani military and the organizations it fights on a daily basis will likely continue.

The second report in this two-part series will discuss in greater detail how the Pakistani military's counterinsurgency tactics have changed, and highlight how counterinsurgency is one of many areas in which Pakistan and its military would benefit from a capable and credible civilian partner.

## INTERNAL THREATS

*Secessionists:* Separatist movements have long threatened the Pakistani state and held a special significance for the armed forces. The secession of East Pakistan (modern-day Bangladesh) in 1971 was traumatic for Pakistan's armed forces and cemented the military's identity as the guardian of national unity. Many recently-retired senior military officials and COAS Kayani himself served as junior officers during this conflict, including Pervez Musharraf, who called it "the saddest episode in Pakistan's history." In the aftermath of the 1971 experience, the military found its state torn in half, its army shamed before its archrival, and its influence within Pakistani society challenged by a viable and assertive civilian political movement.

The 1971 experience, as well as the long-simmering insurgency in Balochistan, heightened the military's sensitivity to separatist movements. Consequently, Afghanistan's claims to territory across the Durand Line have been particularly inflammatory to Pakistan's military. Pakistan's support of the *mujahideen* and its early backing of the Taliban were, in part, motivated by Pakistan's desire to support Pashtun leaders whose aspirations were limited to Afghanistan, in contrast to those who call for a so-called "greater Pashtunistan" in uniting tribes divided by the current borders. Similarly, calls for Baloch independence have been met with stern responses by the military. This is particularly true because of a persistent suspicion by Pakistani officers that India and Iran seek to weaken Pakistan by empowering these separatist movements.

## Internal Cohesion

Conflict within Pakistan is not limited to political separatist movements. Pakistan is an economically, ethnically, and politically diverse nation, with all of the attendant tensions that can be found when a relatively new political structure is built on top of complex societal fissures. Tensions along these divisions have at times led to violence and intervention by the military. For example, during the 1990s the Mohajir-Sindhi rivalry turned violent in Karachi, and the Army was dispatched to stop the fighting. In mid-2010, the Mohajirs and Pashtuns in Karachi began fighting each other, necessitating the deployment of Sindh Rangers to quell the bloodshed.

Religious conflict also poses a significant challenge within Pakistan. Assassins killed the governor of Punjab in January 2011 and a cabinet minister in March 2011, both of whom spoke out against Pakistan's controversial blasphemy laws. There were a series of politically motivated attacks against the Shia minority over the past decade, particularly around the holiday of Ashura. Other conflicts over Islamic identity include laws enacted during the Zulfikar Ali Bhutto era that prevent the Ahmadi religious community from describing itself as Muslim. However, perhaps the broadest religious divide is between a largely secular political elite and an increasingly religious and conservative public. Particularly since the Zia period, the military has sought to find the proper balance between the relatively secular demands of its role as defender of the Pakistani state and the Islamic identity of the force and its members.

The latter point significantly concerns policymakers in the US and elsewhere. Nonetheless, the officers interviewed for this report held that their personal religious convictions are separate from their roles and responsibilities as members of the military. While these opinions are not conclusive, these interviews reinforce the argument made by many Pakistani officers that Western observers consistently misunderstand the role of Islam in the armed forces. *The question of religious radicalization in the Pakistani military is addressed more comprehensively in the second report in this series.*

### Militant Islam

A relatively new threat—in terms of its methods, goals, and ideology—to the Pakistani state has been the rise of domestically-focused militant Islamic groups, particularly the *Tehrik-e-Taliban* (TTP). While other militant groups have similarly attacked military personnel, the fierceness of the strikes carried out by the TTP raised their profile in the eyes of senior leaders. The TTP has carried out suicide attacks not only on the Pakistani state, but also against the Pakistani military. Perhaps the most shocking of these episodes were the October 10, 2009, assault on the Army General Headquarters (GHQ) in Rawalpindi. the deadly attack on officers and their families at a mosque, and the May 2011 attack on the Pakistan Naval Station Mehran in Karachi.

Other groups also threaten military personnel. In November 2008, an al Qaeda/Harkat-ul Jihad Islami leader murdered a former head of Pakistan's elite Special Service Group (SSG), and in October and November 2009 other militants tried to kill three serving brigadiers. Suicide attackers also targeted regional headquarters of the Directorate for Inter-Services Intelligence (ISI) in Lahore and Peshawar in May and November 2009, respectively.

## EXTERNAL THREATS, INCONSISTENT PARTNERS

### China

The People's Republic of China (PRC) plays a critical role in assisting Pakistan in a wide-ranging relationship that encompasses conventional arms sales, nuclear assistance, and military exercises. Pakistani leaders routinely describe China as its closest foreign ally and its bilateral relationship as an "all-weather friendship" and a "comprehensive partnership."

The Sino-Pakistan relationship dates back to the PRC's founding, when Pakistan was one of the first countries to recognize Mao Zedong's government in Beijing after the 1949 victory of Communist forces. Separate Chinese and Pakistani conflicts with India in the 1960s further cemented ties between the two countries. The Sino-Pakistan relationship is primarily anchored in a shared wariness toward and history of war with India. Military ties remain deep, based on a shared desire to ensure "regional stability"—prompting Indian concerns—as well as Chinese commercial interests and Pakistani defence requirements. For example, during the US suspension of military assistance in the 1990s, China was Pakistan's largest supplier of conventional arms.

Furthermore, China provided crucial assistance to Pakistan's nuclear program. Beijing provided technology and training to Islamabad, including the design and triggering mechanism it used in its own nuclear weapons test in 1966.23 In the early 1980s China sent scientists to Pakistan's secret nuclear facilities and provided uranium hexafluoride (UF6), a critical precursor to enriching uranium, to jumpstart Pakistan's uranium centrifuge process. Illustrating this cooperation, US operatives in the 1980s discovered blueprints of a Chinese-designed atomic weapon in Pakistani nuclear scientist A.Q. Khan's luggage.

Chinese arms transfers have often "filled the gaps" during periods of sanctions by the United States. Recent years have seen an increase in arms transfers between China and Pakistan; the two nations are currently jointly producing the JF-17 multi-role combat aircraft and the K-8 Karakorum jet trainer. Pakistan also acquired the first of four Chinese Airborne Warning and Control Systems (AWACS) in December 2009. In a landmark agreement, Pakistan will reportedly be China's first customer in purchasing some thirty-six J-10s—one of China's most advanced fighter aircraft. On the naval front, Pakistan purchased four F-22 frigates from China. The first of three frigates was delivered in 2009; China will assist in building the others in Pakistan. Joint production also includes the al Khalid tank—the mainstay of the army. China also helped build

Heavy Industries Taxila, the centre of the army's engineering industry. This emphasis on joint production and building indigenous capacity earned China considerable goodwill with the Pakistani military.

That said, some analysts observe that Pakistan's military leaders find Chinese weapons generally inferior to Western weapons systems. As Fazal-ur-Rahman, a China expert at the Institute for Strategic Studies in Islamabad, argued: Their technologies are not original technologies. They are borrowing from other countries. It is not state of the art. It is not the best option for Pakistan. You can't use their equipment as a force multiplier.

Western weapons systems—and not Chinese ones—are considered much more useful for fighting India. A Pakistani analyst and a US official both note that the Pakistani military prefers "American toys" rather than Chinese weapons. Furthermore, some Chinese military systems also seem to have some dangerous flaws. For example, the Pakistan Air Force was obliged to replace the ejection seats in Chinese-manufactured jets because they were believed unreliable, not meeting Pakistani safety standards. While a critical supporter and Pakistan's "best bet," China is not seen as a "force multiplier" at the same level as is Western support.

In addition to their conventional and nuclear relationship, China and Pakistan's militaries have conducted multiple joint military exercises. The People's Liberation Army (PLA) and Pakistan's army conducted major "Friendship Exercises" in 2004 and 2006.35 In October 2003, China selected Pakistan to engage with in its first-ever naval bi-national search-and-rescue exercise; in November 2005 both countries conducted another such exercise. In March 2007, China held the "Peace-2007" joint maritime training exercise in the Arabian Sea with seven other countries, including Pakistan.

In recent years, Pakistan's security situation and military operations in the tribal areas prominently factored in bilateral discussions. Notably, China was concerned with militancy in its western provinces and with ensuring regional stability vital for its domestic economic development. Thus, in 2007, Pakistan and China signed an extradition treaty to make combating cross-border militancy easier. Pakistan also recently sent Chinese nationals accused of extremist behaviour back to China for prosecution. In 2009, Pakistan's main Islamist party, Jamaat-e-Islami, even signed a Memorandum of Understanding (MOU) with the Chinese Communist Party, which, among other issues, supported China's position on its Xinjiang Uyghur Autonomous Region. The leader of *Jamaat-e-Islami* went so far as to travel to China three times to allay fears that Pakistan's Islamist parties were supporting Chinese militants. In short, Pakistan's relationship with China across a range of security activities is strong, enduring, and central to its foreign policy. The only comparable partnership is Pakistan's turbulent relationship with the United States.

### Afghanistan

Pakistan has three interests in Afghanistan primarily shaped by its preoccupation with the threat from India. First Pakistan's geography limits its military's ability to strategically retreat in the event of a full-scale Indian invasion, but maintaining a friendly regime in Kabul gives Pakistan the potential to achieve "strategic depth." This fallback option is an openly acknowledged element of Pakistani strategy. However, while rhetorically the concept of strategic depth is an option, it seems unrealistic that the Pakistani army, if completely chased from Pakistan territory, would have the strength or logistical capability to mount an effective counterattack. Rather, the term strategic depth is shorthand for ensuring that Afghanistan does not pose a threat to Pakistan on its western border in the event of a war on the subcontinent, freeing much-needed forces to match India on its eastern border.

Second, worse than an unfriendly regime in Afghanistan would be a pro-Indian government, which could, from the Pakistani military perspective, allow the state to be encircled by its enemies. India's diplomatic and humanitarian efforts in Afghanistan since 2001 have fed multiple conspiracy theories in Pakistan, including one that describes "tens of billions" of dollars spent and "hundreds" of Indian consulates being established within the country. In reality, India has only one embassy and four consulates in Afghanistan and describes its activities as focused on development projects, publicly pledging $1.2 billion in aid to help rebuild the war-shattered country. Still, even this scale of Indian activity stokes the suspicions of the Pakistani military and public.

Finally, Afghanistan presents Pakistan with a historic challenge as it never officially accepted the Durand Line, the border between Afghanistan and British India drawn during the 1890s by the British colonial government. This ongoing dispute, along with Afghan claims on Pashtun and Baloch regions within Pakistan proper, are a source of concern to a Pakistani military shamed by the loss of significant portions of the country in 1971.

Pakistan has attempted to manage the strategic risks in Afghanistan by backing groups aligned with Pakistan's interests. Under Benazir Bhutto's government in the 1990s, Pakistan supported the Taliban—a Pashtun group that satisfied Pakistan's basic security needs in Afghanistan and did not make aggressive claims to leadership over Pashtuns in Pakistan. After the September 11, 2001 al Qaeda attacks against New York City and Washington DC, this strategic calculus changed. The United States applied significant pressure on Islamabad, and Pakistan's public and direct support for the Taliban in Afghanistan dropped off sharply. The rapid victory by the US-backed Northern Alliance came at the cost, however, of upsetting the balance between the Pashtuns in the south of Afghanistan and the northern communities that came to dominate Hamid Karzai's government.

This perceived imbalance, combined with the aforementioned concerns about retaining influence and strategic depth in Afghanistan, allegedly led elements within the Pakistani security establishment to provide some level of support to groups like the Haqqani network and militants commanded by Gulbuddin Hekmatyar. While this report contains no direct evidence to either confirm or deny these allegations, it should be noted that support for insurgent groups would be consistent with an attempt by Pakistan to secure its interests in Afghanistan long after US forces withdraw from the region.

### India

India is Pakistan's principal strategic competitor and has been the single largest factor in the development of the Pakistani military's conventional and nuclear capabilities. The two nations share a 2,900 km (1800 mile) border and have fought numerous conflicts for control of the disputed territory of Kashmir and over the secession of East Pakistan (now Bangladesh).

While Pakistan is the 36th largest country in the world in terms of total land area, it has numerous geographic vulnerabilities. For example, it is so narrow at its midpoint that an Indian advance of 300-400 kilometers—the range of Indian tanks prior to refueling—could effectively cut the country (and its forces) in half. Furthermore, Pakistan's lines of communication—most importantly the highway that runs between Lahore and Karachi—run perpendicular to a probable Indian advance and could be easily severed if Indian forces gained ground. Many of Pakistan's major population centres, like Lahore, also lie within relatively easy striking distance of the border.

India is more powerful than Pakistan by almost every metric of military, economic, and political power—and the gap continues to grow.

Pakistan's fragile economy increasingly plays a part in the country's long-term strategic competition with India. The economic gap between India and Pakistan dramatically widened over the last thirty years, allowing India's defence expenditures to rapidly outpace Pakistan's, at a lower and decreasing share of GDP. 8 At the same time, India's economic rise has granted it increasing prominence on the world stage while Pakistan has been derided as an economic basket case.

With 1.3 million men and women in uniform, India's armed forces are over twice the size of Pakistan's 617,000-strong armed forces. India also has an additional 1.1 million reservists, compared to Pakistan's 500,000.11 In practical terms, while Pakistan's military could perhaps stem an Indian offensive for a few weeks or months, India's ability to commit more men and resources to the fight would likely ultimately undermine Pakistan's defences in a prolonged conventional engagement. From the Pakistani perspective, therefore, India remains indisputably its primary conventional threat (any specific Indian plans to attack notwithstanding.)

The Pakistani military, realizing the danger of losing territory in a war against India, has developed a "Riposte" strategy. "Riposte" calls for Pakistani "strike" corps to take the initiative in a war with India, pushing deep into Indian territory while other corps hold back the initial Indian advance. This bold action against a numerically superior enemy relies upon initial momentum and the assumption that the international community will buttress their efforts by stepping in within a few weeks to urge a ceasefire—effectively halting both armies from advancing farther into each other's territory. Under such a scenario, Pakistan could then trade territory gained for concessions from India.

Ideological extremists exacerbate this already tense relationship, threatening to drive the countries to war. After Pakistan-based terrorist groups carried out deadly attacks on Indian soil—including a suicide attack against the Indian Parliament in 2001—the Indian government articulated an increasingly aggressive military doctrine. Under the Hindu-nationalist BJP government, the Indian military in 2004 supposedly implemented a "*Cold Start* doctrine," positioning quick-strike military units near the Pakistani border. However, despite provocations by Pakistan-based terrorist groups such as the *Lashkar-e-Taiba* (LeT) attack in 2008 on Mumbai landmarks that killed over 160 people, India has not risked a large military campaign against Pakistan.

It remains unclear whether *Cold Start* indeed existed or exists as a viable plan, or was an elaborate bluff by the Indian government. On the one hand, statements in late 2009 by former Indian Army Chief Deepak Kapoor on India's preparations to fight a two-front war against Pakistan and China fuel Islamabad's suspicions about Delhi's intentions. On the other, leaders like India's Army Chief V.K. Singh denied its existence in December 2010, stating that "we don't have anything called 'Cold Start.'"

Tests of nuclear weapons by both India and Pakistan in 1998 significantly altered the strategic calculus of the Pakistani military. The impact of nuclearization on the likelihood of conventional war between Pakistan and India has significantly raised the potential costs of escalation. Worryingly, a misinterpretation of the relatively muted Indian response to the 2008 Mumbai attacks might encourage the belief held by some Pakistani policymakers that their nuclear capabilities act as a deterrent from massive retaliation in both border skirmishes and attacks by Pakistan-based terrorist organizations. It remains unclear whether this belief is grounded in a complete understanding of India's strategic posture. At a minimum however, given conventional military disparities, nuclear weapons and a willingness to use them remain Pakistan's primary deterrent against India.

## *Iran*

Historically Pakistan and Iran have been relatively amicable neighbours; Iran was the first country to recognize the newly-created state of Pakistan in 1947. Economically, the two nations have mutually benefitted from the relationship; annual trade between Pakistan and Iran exceeds $1 billion. Pakistan stated that it will purchase natural gas from Iran despite the increasing sanctions on the regime in Tehran; the two countries signed an agreement in 2009 to build a large gas pipeline together. Infamously, Iran also received nuclear technology from Pakistan through the A.Q. Khan network during the 1980s and 1990s.

However, several security issues complicate the relationship. Iranian President Mahmoud Ahmadinejad recently accused Pakistan of supporting *Jundallah*, the group believed responsible for several suicide attacks against Iranian Revolutionary Guard Corps officers and other Iranian sites in cities near the Iran-Pakistan border. According to Iranian officials, *Jundallah* carried out a mid-December 2010 suicide bombing outside a mosque in the Iranian city of Chabahar that killed 39 people, and then fled across the Pakistan border to safety. Anti-Shia violence within Pakistan antagonizes the Shi'ite majority in Iran. Mutual suspicions also hamper opportunities for Pakistan and Iran to jointly confront the Baloch insurgencies faced by both nations.

Prior to the September 11, 2001 attacks, Iran worked against Pakistani interests by supporting the Northern Alliance aganst the Pakistan-backed Taliban. In a surprising reversal, both crude and sophisticated Iranian weapons were found headed for the Taliban in Afghanistan, raising concerns about Iranian support for that group. Finally, given the contentious relationship between Saudi Arabia and Iran, the close historical ties between Riyadh and Islamabad continue to irritate Tehran.

### The United States

Although the United States does not share a border with Pakistan, it remains a central actor in Pakistan's external relations and domestic political debates. Pakistan's relationship with the US and with its military, in particular, has fluctuated significantly since the 1950s. This has led many in the Pakistani military—and many more in Pakistani society—to consider the US at best as an unreliable, transactional "fair weather friend." The complexity of the relationship can be summed up in two statistics: First, Pakistan is one of the largest recipients of US military and non-military aid in recent years, including the $7.5 billion in development funding committed in the Kerry-Lugar-Berman bill, and one of the largest purchasers of US weaponry, signing sales agreements worth some $3.5 billion in 2006.[62] At the same time, however, almost 60 percent of Pakistanis view the US as "an enemy of their country" according to a Pew Global Attitudes poll conducted in mid-2010. Furthermore, 65 percent are concerned that the US could become a military threat to Pakistan. While on average less anti-American than the general population, many in the Pakistani military remain skeptical of US intentions and concerned about the level of US activity within their borders. This skepticism was dramatically exacerbated by the US raid on Osama bin Laden's compound in Abbottabad, Pakistan.

Since 2001, the US has provided Pakistan with more than $11 billion in military aid, mainly intended to fight terrorism. However, most US weapons sold to Pakistan could easily be used in a future conflict with India. Advanced F-16 aircraft, Harpoon anti-ship missiles, and P-3 Orion anti-submarine aircraft provide Pakistan with a means of countering some of India's significant military advantage. Furthermore, US-provided TOW anti-armour missiles, Sidewinder air-to-air missiles, and 155mm howitzers could be employed against India should large-scale conflict erupt. In addition, much of the arms relationship between the US and Pakistan has involved maintenance and upgrades on equipment bought in the past, such as older F-16s. Some analysts even suggest that A.Q. Khan's black market network was initially created in part to supply the Pakistani military with spare parts for its American equipment during periods of sanctions.

Pakistan's access to US weapons systems is nonetheless bounded by the US desire to maintain good relations with India. This position is further complicated by Pakistan's nuclear program outside the Non-Proliferation Treaty (NPT). America's recent cooperation with India on its civilian nuclear program particularly upset many Pakistanis, especially since no similar deal is likely to be forthcoming for Pakistan in the foreseeable future. Other more direct US actions, such as drone strikes against suspected militants, even when tacitly approved by Pakistan's military establishment, are extremely unpopular with the Pakistani public. The perceived unreliability of the US to supply weapons and spare parts over the long term has pushed Pakistan to increase its domestic capacity, diversify its arms suppliers, and develop a closer relationship with China.

The US-Pakistan relationship continues to be contentious because of conflicting regional interests. In 2010, the US pressed Pakistan to move more robustly against extremist elements in North Waziristan and other areas of Pakistan, despite the army's stated desire to tackle this militancy on its own timeline. This pressure increased in the wake of a failed 2010 bombing in New York City's Times Square—a plot with links back to the region.

The January 2011 shooting of two unarmed men in Lahore by CIA contractor Raymond Davis deepened tensions between the US and Pakistan. Following the killings, Chief of Army Staff (COAS) General Ashfaq Parvez Kayani demanded that the US withdraw approximately 335 CIA officers and contractors and Special Operations forces from the country, as well as halt CIA drone strikes in the Federally Administered Tribal Areas (FATA).

The US killing of Osama bin Laden strained US-Pakistani relations even further. The raid sullied the reputation of the military within Pakistan and raised fears that India could exploit the same types of vulnerabilities that allowed the US forces to enter the country undetected. The operation also stoked anti-Americanism within the military and undermined confidence in the leadership of a (COAS) believed to be "too close" to the US. The consequences of this action were still unfolding as this report went to press.

## PAKISTAN'S RESPONSE TO THE PROLIFERATION THREAT

Then-Under Secretary Burns testified in July 2007 that the Bush Administration has "told the Pakistani government that it is its responsibility... to make sure" that neither the Khan network nor a "similar organization" resurfaces in the country. Since the revelations about the Khan network, Pakistan appears to have increased its efforts to prevent nuclear proliferation. But whether and to what extent these efforts have been successful is not yet clear. It is worth noting that, because Khan conducted his proliferation activities as a government official, they do not necessarily indicate a failure of Islamabad's export controls.

Pakistani officials argue that Islamabad has taken a number of steps to prevent further proliferation of nuclear-related technologies and materials. For example, Islamabad adopted in September 2004 new national export controls legislation which includes a requirement that the government issue control lists for "goods, technologies, material, and equipment which may contribute to designing, development, stockpiling, [and] use" of nuclear weapons and related delivery systems. According to a February 2008 presentation by Zafar Ali, Director of Pakistan's Strategic Export Controls Division (SECDIV), the lists, which were issued in October 2005 and are to be periodically updated, include items controlled by multilateral export control regimes, such as the Nuclear Suppliers Group, the Australia Group, and the Missile Technology Control Regime. The export controls legislation also includes a catch-all clause, which requires exporters to notify the government if they are aware or suspect that goods or technology are intended by the end-user for use in nuclear or biological weapons, or missiles capable of delivering such weapons.

The legislation includes several other important elements, such as end-use and end-user certification requirements and new penalties for violators. Since its adoption, Pakistan has established the SECDIV and an associated Oversight Board. The SECDIV is responsible for formulating rules and regulations for implementing the legislation. The board is comprised of officials from multiple agencies and is headed by Pakistan's Foreign Secretary.

Islamabad says that it has also taken several other steps to improve its nuclear security. For example, the government announced in June 2007 that it is "implementing a National Security Action Plan with the [IAEA's] assistance." That same month, Pakistan also joined the U.S.- and Russian-led Global Initiative to Combat Nuclear Terrorism. As noted above, the December 2007 National Command Authority Ordinance also includes measures to prevent the spread of nuclear-related materials and expertise.

Pakistani officials participating in an April 2007 Partnership for Global Security workshop argued that Islamabad has improved the reliability of its nuclear personnel by, for example, making security clearance procedures more stringent. However, the officials also acknowledged that Islamabad still needs to do more to control its nuclear expertise. Similarly, Admiral Mullen stated May 14, 2009, that the country's personnel reliability system must "continue to improve." Some reports about the early January 2011 shooting of Salmaan Taseer, the governor of Punjab province, have raised questions about Pakistan's ability to vet security personnel properly.

The United States has also provided export control assistance to Pakistan. Burns described several such efforts in his July 2007 testimony. And according to an October 2007 U.S. Government Accountability Office report, Islamabad was during FY2003-FY2006 the second-largest recipient of bilateral U.S. assistance designed to improve target countries' export controls. Pakistan received such assistance from the Departments of State, Energy, and Homeland Security.

Under Secretary of State for Arms Control and International Security Ellen Tauscher told the Senate Foreign Relations Committee that the Obama Administration does not support conditioning aid to Pakistan on permitting direct U.S. access to Khan, arguing, in part, that the United States has "obtained a great deal of information about the Khan network without having direct access to A.Q. Khan."

### *Pakistan's Civil Nuclear Program*

Pakistan also has a civil nuclear power program, with two reactors currently operating—the Karachi Nuclear Power Plant, which went critical in 1971, and the Chasma Nuclear Power Plant, which went critical in 2000. Prime Minister Gilani announced May 12, 2011, that a second nuclear reactor at Chasma, constructed with Chinese assistance, had become operational. Beijing has also apparently agreed to construct two additional power reactors at Chasma, according to both Chinese and Pakistani officials. Pakistan Atomic Energy Commission Chairman Ansar Parvez stated May 12, 2011, that concrete has been poured for one of these reactors and that ground breaking for the other reactor would take place the next month. The first reactor is to come on line in 2016, with the next to follow 10 months later. Acting Assistant Secretary Van Diepen stated July 22, 2010, that such a sale would appear to be inconsistent with current Nuclear Suppliers Group (NSG) guidelines. Additionally, Pakistan and China are reportedly close to finalizing an agreement for Beijing to construct a third, larger, reactor in Pakistan. As noted, the NSG changed its guidelines in 2008 to allow nuclear trade with India. Secretary of State Clinton suggested July 20, 2010, that the United States does not currently support a similar change for Pakistan. Assistant Secretary of State Robert Blake reiterated Van Diepen and Clinton's positions March 18, 2011.

Pakistan is also operating two research reactors—Pakistan Research Reactor 1, which went critical in 1965, and Pakistan Research Reactor 2, which went critical in 1989. Pakistan Research Reactor 1, which was originally supplied by a U.S. firm, was converted from using highly-enriched uranium (HEU) to low-enriched uranium fuel in 1992. A "small amount" of the HEU fuel remains in Pakistan.

### *Issues for Congress*

Legislation introduced during the 111 Congress appeared designed to influence Islamabad's nuclear stability and policies regarding the Khan network. March 12, 2009, stated that U.S. military assistance could be provided to Pakistan only if the

President were to certify that Islamabad is both making A. Q. Khan available to the United States for questioning and "providing adequate assurances to the United States Government that it will monitor Khan's movements and activities in such a manner as to prevent his participation in any efforts to disseminate nuclear technology or know-how." This chapter would have allowed the President to waive restrictions on U.S. assistance imposed pursuant to the proposed legislation if the President were to certify to Congress "that it is in the national interests of the United States to do so."

H.R. 2481, the United States-Pakistan Security and Stability Act, which was introduced May 19, 2009, would have required the President to "develop and transmit to the appropriate congressional committees a comprehensive interagency strategy and implementation plan for long-term security and stability in Pakistan." The strategy was to include a "description of how United States assistance" authorized by the bill would be "used to achieve the objectives of United States policy toward Pakistan," including enabling Islamabad to "maintain robust command and control over its nuclear weapons technology." The bill would have authorized foreign assistance for Pakistan, including funds for improving the government's counter-insurgency capability.

In addition, legislation to authorize various forms of U.S. assistance to Pakistan contains provisions related to Islamabad's nuclear program. S. 1707, the Enhanced Partnership with Pakistan Act of 2009, which became law (P.L. 111-73, 123 Stat. 2060) on October 15, 2009, authorizes various forms of U.S. assistance to Pakistan, including strengthening democratic institutions and law enforcement, as well as supporting economic development, education, human rights, and heath care. Section 203 (c) of S. 1707 requires the President to certify that Pakistan is "continuing to cooperate with the United States in efforts to dismantle supplier networks relating to the acquisition of nuclear weapons-related materials, such as providing relevant information from or direct access to Pakistani nationals associated with such networks." It also requires a Semi-Annual Monitoring Report that is to include a detailed description of Pakistan's nuclear non-proliferation efforts and an assessment of whether assistance has directly or indirectly aided the expansion of Pakistan's nuclear weapons program, whether by the diversion of United States assistance or the reallocation of Pakistan's financial resources that would otherwise be spent for programs and activities unrelated to its nuclear weapons program.

In response to concerns expressed in Pakistan over the intent of the bill, a "Joint Explanatory Statement" was submitted for the Congressional Record by Senate Foreign Relations Committee Chairman John Kerry and then-House Foreign Affairs Committee Chairman Howard Berman. The statement emphasizes that "the legislation does not seek in any way to compromise Pakistan's sovereignty, impinge on Pakistan's national security interests, or micromanage any aspect of Pakistani military or civilian operations." Regarding reporting requirements on nuclear nonproliferation cooperation, the statement says:

The many requirements of this report are intended as a way for Congress to assess how effectively U.S. funds are being spent, shortfalls in U.S. resources that hinder the use of such funds, and steps the Government of Pakistan has taken to advance our mutual interests in countering extremism and nuclear proliferation and strengthening democratic institutions.

There is no intent to, and nothing in this Act in any way suggests that there should be, any U.S. role in micromanaging internal Pakistani affairs, including the promotion of Pakistani military officers or the internal operations of the Pakistani military.

S. 1707 represented a compromise between two bills, H.R. 1886, the Pakistan Enduring Assistance and Cooperation Enhancement Act of 2009, and S. 962, the Enhanced Partnership with Pakistan Act of 2009. H.R. 1886 would have placed conditions on U.S. security assistance to Pakistan; it stated that no U.S. military assistance could be provided to Pakistan if the President had not made a series of determinations, one of which is that the government "is continuing to cooperate with the United States in efforts to dismantle supplier networks relating to the acquisition of nuclear weapons related materials, including, as necessary, providing access to Pakistani nationals associated with such networks." The bill also required a report to Congress which would have included a "description of Pakistan's efforts to prevent proliferation of nuclear-related material and expertise" and an "assessment of whether assistance provided to Pakistan pursuant to this Act has directly or indirectly aided the expansion of Pakistan's nuclear weapons program." The committee report underlined ongoing concerns about getting full information about the activities of the Khan network and development of Pakistan's own nuclear arsenal:

Pakistan's history of nuclear development and Dr. Abdul Qadeer Khan's establishment of a nuclear proliferation network remain a source for concern to many in the United States, particularly since the Committee understands that representatives of the United States have not interviewed certain individuals involved in the network.

The Committee believes the United States should continue to engage the Government of Pakistan on the network, and should, as necessary, obtain direct access to the individuals covered by this subsection, including Dr. Khan. The Committee also maintains strong concerns regarding recent reports of Pakistan expansion of its nuclear arsenal. Given the expanding threat of Pakistan's domestic insurgency, the Government of Pakistan's further development of nuclear materials appears inconsistent with its immediate security threats and is unhelpful in the context of efforts to strengthen U.S.-Pakistani relations.

S. 962 would have provided aid to Pakistan but did not include conditions regarding the nuclear nonproliferation or nuclear weapons activities. The Senate report (S.Rept. 111-33), however, stated that "[a]ny use of funds contained in this legislation for the purpose of augmenting Pakistan's nuclear weapons program would be directly contrary to Congressional intent."

It is worth noting that Pakistani officials have expressed interest in concluding a nuclear cooperation agreement with the United States, which would require congressional approval. Prime Minister Gilani told a visiting congressional delegation in June 2011 that such cooperation "would help build a positive image of the U.S. in the country."

## DEFENCE DOCTRINE OBJECTIVES

The objectives of India's national defence doctrine vis-a-vis *China* are twofold and simple:

- How to prevent a repeat of 1962, by maintaining an adequate level of conventional military capability to deter any Chinese temptation to enforce its territorial claims against India by force?
- How to maintain a credible nuclear deterrent against it?

The objectives vis-a-vis *Pakistan* are manifold and much more complex:

- How to find a controlled retaliatory response to Pakistan's proxy war without allowing the response to degenerate into a war involving the use of nuclear weapons?
- How to neutralize the Pakistani attempts to intimidate and demoralize the Indian population through over-projection of its nuclear and missile capability and irresponsible nuclear rhetoric?
- Whereas any war with China will most probably be fought in Indian territory, any war with Pakistan will be in Pakistani territory. How to prevent India's overwhelming conventional superiority from pressing the panic button in Pakistan's military leadership and triggering off a nuclear response?
- How to achieve India's military objectives in the shortest time possible before international intervention comes in the way of the further conduct of the war?

In response to these questions, a number of possible options have figured in the debate on national security in recent months. Among the various options and suggestions considered were:

- Greater transparency about India's nuclear and missile capabilities to reassure our own population and to have a sobering effect on Pakistan's adventurist generals.
- A public announcement of India's nuclear command and control mechanism.
- Discarding India's no first use of nuclear weapons policy.
- India's readiness and ability to fight a limited conventional

war without allowing it to escalate into a nuclear confrontation.

- A counter-terrorism doctrine to exploit Pakistan's vulnerabilities through covert action to make it pay an increasingly prohibitive price for its proxy war.
- Cooperative action through other concerned powers to prevent Pakistan's weapons of mass destruction capabilities from falling into the hands of its terrorists.

The announcement by the government of India of India's nuclear command and control mechanism and the contours of its nuclear doctrine on January 4 was the necessary first step in this direction. The no first use policy has been reiterated, but in a nuanced form by underlining that India's nuclear capability is meant to deter not only a nuclear strike, but also a strike with chemical or biological weapons. India's capability and determination for a massive retaliatory response has been reiterated. However, the nuclear doctrine by itself will not complete the national security doctrine unless it is supplemented by a counter-terrorism doctrine to enable India to exercise its right of active defence against the Pakistani use of terrorism as a weapon to achieve its strategic objectives. Such a doctrine should have a mix of carefully-controlled overt and extensive, sustained and deniable covert actions. The national security managers should now devote themselves to this task. It brooks no delay.

## UNDERSTANDING CHINA'S NON-PROLIFERATION VIEWS

China has traditionally viewed multilateral control regimes to be discriminatory and a means of control over third world states by western powers. "Even as it criticized international non proliferation regimes, however, the Chinese leadership professed an opposition to nuclear weapon states sharing the bomb with non nuclear weapon states and proclaimed that China would assist other countries' nuclear energy programs but not weapons programs." China's progression into accepting these multilateral regimes, and gaining membership to them in contemporary times reflect its progression in policy, wherein it accepts some of the elements of the international order which gives legitimacy to its status as a great power Its interest in maintaining non proliferation double standards is linked to its great power status, especially one as being the sole accepted nuclear power in Asia. It also ties into the strategic outlook of China, on what it deems to be its interests and what it views as inconsequential irritants. For example, it is argued by T.V Paul, that "South Asia and Middle East are less vital to China than is East Asia. China has been uncomfortable with the North Korean nuclear efforts and Beijing shares the desire of the US and Japan that the Korean peninsula remains non nuclear." Former US Air Force Secretary Thomas Reed articulates China's thinking on proliferation in the following words, "China in about 1982, under Deng Xiaoping, decided to proliferate nuclear technology to communists and Muslims in the third world. They did so deliberately with the theory that if nukes ended up going off in the western world from a Muslim terrorist, well that wasn't all bad. If New York was reduced to rubble without Chinese fingerprints on the attack, that left Beijing as the last man standing. That's what the old timers thought." He adds that, while this represented the old school of thought, the new generation of Chinese leaders realizes the limitations of such a policy, and has therefore tempered their nonproliferation views.

Chinese Vice Foreign Minister, Wang Guangya in an op ed dated October 16, 2002, elucidated China's 'non proliferation policy and practice', stating "China has consistently stood for the complete prohibition and thorough destruction of all kinds of WMD and firmly against the proliferation of WMD and their delivery systems. For this, China has over the years been an active participant in international non proliferation efforts." He adds "we have steadfastly pursued a policy of not advocating, encouraging or assisting any other country in developing weapons of mass destruction and made our contribution with concrete deeds to the international non proliferation process." Furthermore, in closed door interactions with senior Chinese scholars and former military officials, the Chinese have continued to maintain their deniability in supporting Pakistan's nuclear weaponization program.

However, proliferation links to China have allegedly influenced major international policy matters in the international stage. One of the regions in addition to South Asia is West Asia. This can be attributed to the China US rivalry for resources in the region, especially since China's growing economy becomes increasingly dependent on fossil fuels in addition to alternative energy resources. By proliferating, nuclear and missile technology, it seeks to leverage against the United States in these regions. The expectation in Beijing is that the supply of these materials to the Middle Eastern countries will increase Chinese influence, thereby reducing American influence.

### *Why Proliferate to Pakistan?*

China's proliferation to Pakistan achieves twin strategic objectives of encirclement of India, and a proliferation buffer, wherein Pakistan in turn further proliferate Chinese nuclear technology, giving China leeway in investigations.

According to Robert Ross, China continues its support for Pakistan by supplying nuclear and missile technology because "China views a credible Pakistani deterrent as the most effective way to guarantee the security of its sole ally in Southern Asia against Indian power." This argument is also postulated by T.V Paul, that "China wants to limit India's power capabilities to South Asia and thereby constrain New Delhi's aspirations to become a major power in Asia. India's emergence as a peercompetitor in Asia would upset China's predominant position in the region. However, if acute conflict and an intense arms race between India and Pakistan persist, India would continue to be bracketed with its smaller regional rival Pakistan and not with China." Proliferation to Pakistan, also offers China a certain leeway in their doctrinal stance of No First Use, since Pakistan does not subscribe to that element. China can make use of its proxy in instigating a nuclear conflict in South Asia, wherein the affected parties would be Pakistan and India, with China attempting to emerge unscathed. For China, using Pakistan as an extended deterrence proxy was much more practical than merely extending its nuclear umbrella onto Pakistan. This would likely explain the Chinese aversion to Pakistani Foreign Minister, Shamshad Ahmed's request in 1998, to guarantee nuclear protection should India attack. While growing

Indian aspirations in the region are clearly opposed by China, the original reason for the Sino Pak relationship was largely economic.

According to Mao Zedong's calculations, Pakistan was nothing but China's easy access to the Atlantic and the Indian Ocean It was to be the route for Chinese access to Middle Eastern oil, and resources to Africa, and therefore there was a need to build upon an economic and military relationship with the country. This argument is bolstered through the fact that China has been deeply involved in building of a deep water naval port at Gwadar, Balochistan, and has consistently advocated Pakistan as a trans national corridor for Middle Eastern energy transport to its mainland. The nature of the China Pakistan military/nuclear alliance makes it beneficial for China to extend its nuclear proliferation tentacles worldwide through proxies; thereby holding a level of plausible deniability in international forums. This is exemplified in the case of proliferation rogue states of North Korea, Iran and Libya, wherein Chinese nuclear components have been found, courtesy the proliferation ring run by A.Q Khan Laboratory's. Therefore, China can use Pakistan as a scapegoat for any eventual international sanction, gambling on Pakistan's geo strategic importance for furthering its own interests beyond the region.

### *International Implications of the Alliance*

A consequence of the China Pakistan nuclear trade has been further proliferation from Pakistan to additional states, thereby weakening the non proliferation regime, and indirectly furthering Chinese strategic interests in these countries. The implications for regional peace and stability in South Asia are also critical, since Pakistan continues to hold ambiguous red lines on its nuclear doctrine, allowing it to extend a nuclear umbrella over terrorist groups based in Pakistan, operating against India. Pakistan's nuclear links to North Korea were first reported in October 2002, when press reports suggested that nuclear materials and technology for uranium enrichment were transferred to North Korea since 1997.44 In July 2011, A.Q Khan made further revelations on the nuclear trade between Islamabad and Pyongyang, alleging that $3.5 million was paid to senior Pakistani officials to facilitate the agreement.

Collaboration with North Korea for missiles was acknowledged by Benazir Bhutto, who said "When I went to North Korea, AQ Khan told me we could get their (missile) technology (so) that we can compare (it) to our own. So I took (it) up with Kim Il Sung...December '93 I talked to him, he agreed...and it was in cash, they needed money and so it was done for cash, with no exchange of nuclear technology. Exchanging nuclear technology for missiles was never even discussed during my visit."

It remains unclear whether the government was in the know about nuclear transactions. However, the spread of the network to countries including Libya, Iran and allegedly to Myanmar, make it difficult to accept that the Pakistani government or Army headquarters was completely unaware of these transactions.

Especially in the realm of nuclear transfers to North Korea, as pointed earlier, China would have been aware of the ongoing transfers, owing to the sensitivity of its interests there. The fact that China did not broach this topic with Pakistan, and on the contrary continued its nuclear relationship with Pakistan, leads this author to believe that China tacitly approved of these transfers. Similarly, the implications of Pakistan furthering Chinese products to West Asia can be seen in how Pakistan is trying to play both sides of an ideological divide, by having contributed to the Iranian nuclear program, and having a suspected tie up with Saudi Arabia to arm them with nuclear warheads too.

In an interview, A.Q. Khan lauds Iran, saying "If Iran succeeds in acquiring nuclear technology, we will be a strong bloc in the region to counter international pressure", adding that "Iran's nuclear capability will neutralize Israel's power." Khan, having been associated with the nuclear program, would be well aware of the strategic implications of the ideological divide between Saudi Arabia and Iran. It is alleged that Saudi Arabia also played a role in supporting Pakistan's nuclear ambitions, in return for an extended nuclear umbrella against Iran. This is the reason argued for Pakistan's rapid fissile material productionto cater for its own demands, and those for West Asian deterrence. The Chinese ambivalence in pushing for sanctions on Iran, and its missile transfers to Saudi Arabia, add to these suspicions of collaboration.

## NUCLEAR DETERRENCE WILL BE USED IN LOCAL WARS

The local wars that broke out after World War II were mostly carried out under the conditions of nuclear deterrence if the Western powers were involved in them. During the Korean War, U.S. Commander-in-Chief MacArthur once threatened a sudden attack of atomic bombs on China's northeast and coastal strategic targets. After Eisenhower came to power, he again ordered the Pentagon to formulate a nuclear program aimed at China. During its war of aggression in Vietnam, the United States also made nuclear threats and was prepared to resolve the issue with nuclear weapons. After the armed conflicts on Zhenbao Island between China and the Soviet Union in 1969, Brezhnev considered initiating a nuclear attack on China in an attempt to ruin China's nuclear facilities. In the Malvinas Islands War, Britain carried tactical nuclear weapons on its huge fleet and was prepared to use them if its conventional operations failed. In particular, the multinational coalition troops headed by the United States used extremely advanced high-tech weapons in the Gulf War, and although they held the trump card, they still deployed 800 to 850 tactical nuclear weapons on three sides of Iraq.

What is more, U.S. troops considered using radio flash bombs but, because of political considerations, they were not approved by U.S. President Bush. In response to Saddam's repeated threats to use chemical weapons, the British Government warned again and again that its troops would retaliate by using tactical nuclear weapons should Iraq resort to using chemical weapons. Bush also hinted that he would give field commanders freedom when necessary. These countries threatened to use nuclear weapons in conventional wars because they believed that with nuclear weapons in hand, psychologically they would be able to hold a dominant position, which would enhance troop morale and frighten the enemy on the one hand, and restrict the enemy's use of some conventional means on the other, thus changing the direction of the war. These past events should not be forgotten. At present, nuclear deterrence is still a strategic pillar of military power. U.S. President Clinton thinks that the United States must build up military muscle that suits the new age, and this military muscle must have the capacity of nuclear deterrence. Nuclear deterrent force is an effective form of security. The 1993 defence report submitted by the U.S. Defence Department to Congress proposed that an all directional global defence system of strategic nuclear deterrence to prevent limited nuclear attacks should be set up, under which the former nuclear deterrent strategy chiefly aimed at the Soviet Union should be readjusted to an all-direction and multilevel nuclear deterrent strategy aimed at both the former Soviet Union and other regions.

On September 25, 1995, President Clinton ordered the Energy Department to maintain the three major nuclear weapon laboratories to ensure that U.S. nuclear deterrent capacity remains effective. Russia set up a defence ministry in March 1992, then founded its nuclear strategic forces and made the development of strategic nuclear weapons a top priority in the future development of eight technical weapons.

President Yeltsin said that a strategic nuclear force was the foundation of Russia's military strength. In November 1993, giving sanction to the new Russian military theory, he officially abandoned the Kremlin's 11-year-old commitment that in a conflict it would not be the first to use nuclear weapons. In its 1992 defence report, France claimed that it merely wanted to have the "most rudimentary" nuclear deterrent for as a way to cope with various kinds of unexpected events and check possible encroachments on its interests by potential enemies.

In the meantime, France announced that it is continuing to focus on the development of a submarine-launched strategic nuclear missile system to ensure the reliability of its nuclear deterrent strategy. At his first news conference after assuming office as president on June 13, 1995, Chirac declared that France would resume its nuclear tests in the South Pacific. The French Defence Minister maintained that President Chirac had made a "very serious decision." British Prime Minister Major said, "As far as Britain is concerned, laying down the nuclear shield in whatever manner is an indiscreet move. Britain holds on to its views that as long as the CIS countries are still in possession of nuclear weapons, Britain should retain its own. The number of British nuclear weapons will not be determined by that of other countries, but by whether or not they are sufficient to make potential enemies feel incapable of sustaining their losses."

Deterrence and actual combat are complementary and closely interrelated. Generally speaking, the military strategy of all countries has a dual character of deterrence and actual combat. Before a war breaks out, a country will, by way of military deterrence, try to make the opposite side refrain from launching an attack rashly, so as to provide a powerful backing for its own political, economic, and diplomatic activities. Once military deterrence does not work, it will strive to win a victory through actual combat, so as to remove obstacles to its political, economic, and diplomatic activities.

Militarily, the immense effect of nuclear weaponry is that it can serve as a deterrent force and, at the same time, as a means of actual combat. Some countries, even those of the Third World, also consider possession of limited nuclear strength to be a significant way to contend against the deterrence of big powers or to deter one another in order to make up for the deficiency of their conventional forces. Military history after World War II has principally centred on the two superpowers that applied nuclear deterrence to each other and contended with each other for nuclear hegemony. After one of the superpowers disintegrated, a "crowd of heroes" rose up. As a result, conflicts that were in the past covered up by the Cold War surfaced with each passing day, and the collision and coalition of various political forces intensified simultaneously. Some regional powers were not weakened by the superpowers' relaxed control over them. On the contrary, they will, perhaps, go their own way even more wilfully on the issues of possessing and using nuclear weapons. Both the United States and Russia believe that future nuclear threats will primarily stem from small nuclear nations in certain regions. Hence, the world situation of nuclear deterrence will be transformed from the previous global nuclear deterrence and confrontation between the United States and the Soviet Union to multiple and regional nuclear deterrence and confrontation. In future high-tech local wars, the struggle between nuclear deterrence and counter nuclear deterrence will be even more complex.

We are materialists, so when we study an issue, we must proceed from the objective reality rather than from a subjective wish and, through investigation and study of objective reality, we derive our principles, policies, and measures. The study of issues concerning warfare can be conducted in the same way. Comrade Mao Zedong said a long time ago:

Investigation and study are very important. When we see someone hold something in his hand, we should look into the matter. What is he holding in his hand? It is a knife. What is the use of a knife? It can kill a person. Whom will he kill with the knife? He will kill the people. After probing into these matters, we should further the investigation: The Chinese people also have hands, and they can hold knives too. They can forge one if they have none....

We love peace. China's development and possession of a small number of nuclear weapons is entirely for self-defence. Since the very first day when China had nuclear weapons in 1964, it solemnly proclaimed that it would never be the first to use nuclear weapons at any time and under any circumstances. China also made the commitment that it would never use or threaten to use nuclear weapons toward nuclear-free countries or regions. At the same time, we clearly understand that only by relying on the arduous work of the people all over the world can the objective of genuinely eliminating nuclear wars and genuinely obtaining world peace be realized: "It is a universal truth since ancient times that proficiency in warfare is not tantamount to bellicosity." The stronger our national defence muscle and the more sufficient our preparations for high-tech warfare under the condition of nuclear deterrence, the smaller the possibility of the outbreak of nuclear war.

We wish that the day will come when the nuclear shadow will disappear from the blue sky and the people the world over will live under the sunshine of genuine peace. To hail the early arrival of this day, we should work with greater stamina and diligence.

# 2

# Nuclear Weapons of Pakistan

Chronic political instability in Pakistan and Islamabad's military efforts against the Taliban and al-Qaeda have raised concerns about the security of Pakistan's nuclear weapons. Some observers fear that Pakistan's strategic nuclear assets could be obtained by terrorists or used by elements in the Pakistani government. Chairman of the Joint Chiefs of Staff Admiral Michael Mullen described U.S. concern about the matter during a September 22, 2008, speech:

To the best of my ability to understand it—and that is with some ability—the weapons there are secure. And that even in the change of government, the controls of those weapons haven't changed. That said, they are their weapons. They're not my weapons. And there are limits to what I know. Certainly at a worst-case scenario with respect to Pakistan, I worry a great deal about those weapons falling into the hands of terrorists and either being proliferated or potentially used. And so, control of those, stability, stable control of those weapons is a key concern. And I think certainly the Pakistani leadership that I've spoken with on both the military and civilian side understand that.

Officials have generally expressed confidence in the security of Pakistan's nuclear weapons. President Obama addressed this issue in an April 29, 2009, press conference, stating, "I'm confident that we can make sure that Pakistan's nuclear arsenal is secure, primarily, initially, because the Pakistani army, I think, recognizes the hazards of those weapons falling into the wrong hands. We've got strong military-to-military consultation and cooperation." He also recognized the sensitivity of the issue for Pakistan, saying, "[w]e want to respect their sovereignty, but we also recognize that we have huge strategic interests, huge national security interests in making sure that Pakistan is stable and that you don't end up having a nuclear-armed militant state." Declining to engage in "hypotheticals" when asked if the United States is ready to secure the nuclear arsenal if the Pakistani government could not do so, President Obama said he felt "confident that that nuclear arsenal will remain out of militant hands." More recently, Department of State spokesperson Mark Toner told reporters May 26, 2011, that "the safeguard and security of Pakistan's nuclear weapons are of concern, but... it's an issue that we discussed with the Pakistani government, and we're sure that they're under safeguard." Toner also stated November 9, 2011, that the United States "continue[s] to have confidence in the government of Pakistan that they both understand the threat to their nuclear arsenal, the varied threats to their nuclear arsenal, that they're taking appropriate steps to safeguard them."

Then-Director of National Intelligence Dennis Blair told the House Permanent Select Committee on Intelligence February 3, 2010, that "from what we see of ... measures that they take," Pakistan is keeping its nuclear weapons secure. Lieutenant General Burgess, Director of the Defence Intelligence Agency, stated in March 10, 2011, testimony before the Senate Armed Services Committee that "Pakistan is able to safeguard its nuclear weapons, including protecting important segments of its nuclear program in underground facilities," but added that "vulnerabilities still exist."

The collapse or near-collapse of the Pakistani government is probably the most likely scenario in which militants or terrorists could acquire Pakistani nuclear weapons. General David H. Petraeus, the former Commander of U.S. Central Command, testified March 31, 2009, that "Pakistani state failure would provide transnational terrorist groups and other extremist organizations an opportunity to acquire nuclear weapons and a safe haven from which to plan and launch attacks." More recently, Gary Samore,

National Security Council Coordinator for Arms Control and Non-Proliferation, stated in an April 2011 interview that

The Pakistani government takes the nuclear security threat very seriously, and they've put a lot of resources into trying to make sure that their nuclear facilities and materials and weapons are well secured. There's no lack of recognition that this is a very important issue, and there's no lack of incentive on the part of the Pakistani government to maintain control. What I worry about is that, in the context of broader tensions and problems within Pakistani society and polity—and that's obviously taking place as we look at the sectarian violence and tensions between the government and the military and so forth—I worry that, in that broader context, even the best nuclear security measures might break down. You're dealing with a country that is under tremendous stress internally and externally, and that's what makes me worry. They have good programs in place; the question is whether those good programs work in the context where these broader tensions and conflicts are present.

Additionally, former Pakistani President Pervez Musharraf told CNN May 26, 2011, that "[i]f Pakistan disintegrates, then it can be dangerous. Otherwise, if Pakistan's integrity is there, and which I'm sure it will be there as long as the armed forces of Pakistan are there, there is no danger of the nuclear assets or strategic assets falling in any terrorist hands."

Pakistani efforts to improve the security of its nuclear weapons have been ongoing and include some cooperation with the United States; Musharraf told a journalist that Islamabad has "given State Department nonproliferation experts insight into the command and control of the Pakistani arsenal and its on-site safety and security procedures." Since the 1998 Pakistani and Indian nuclear tests, the international community has increased attention to reducing the risk of nuclear war in South Asia. The two countries most recently came to the brink of full-scale war in 1999 and 2002, and, realizing the dangers, have developed some risk reduction measures to prevent accidental nuclear war. Islamabad has also developed its command and control systems and improved the security of its military and civilian nuclear facilities. Since the 2004 revelations of an extensive international nuclear proliferation network run by Pakistani nuclear official Abdul Qadeer Khan, as well as possible connections between Pakistani nuclear scientists and Al Qaeda, Islamabad has made additional efforts to improve export controls and monitor nuclear personnel. The main security challenges for Pakistan's nuclear arsenal are keeping the integrity of the command structure, ensuring physical security, and preventing illicit proliferation from insiders.

Pakistan continues to produce fissile material for weapons and appears to be augmenting its weapons production facilities, as well as deploying additional delivery vehicles—steps that will enable both quantitative and qualitative improvements in Islamabad's nuclear arsenal.

## NUCLEAR WEAPONS

Pakistan's nuclear energy program dates back to the 1950s, but it was the loss of East Pakistan (now Bangladesh) in a war with India that probably triggered a January 1972 political decision (just one month later) to begin a secret nuclear weapons program. Deterring India's nuclear weapons and augmenting Pakistan's inferior conventional forces are widely believed to be the primary missions for Islamabad's nuclear arsenal. Observers point to India's 1974 "peaceful" nuclear explosion as the pivotal moment that gave additional urgency to the program. Pakistan produced fissile material for its nuclear weapons using gas-centrifuge-based uranium enrichment technology, which it mastered by the mid-1980s. Highly-enriched uranium (HEU) is one of two types of fissile material used in nuclear weapons; the other is plutonium. The country's main enrichment facility is a centrifuge plant located at Kahuta; Pakistan may have other enrichment sites. Islamabad gained enrichment-related technology from many sources. This extensive assistance is reported to have included uranium enrichment technology from Europe, blueprints for a small nuclear weapon from China, and missile technology from China.

The United States had information during the 1970s that Pakistan was constructing a uranium enrichment facility. A. Q. Khan has stated that Pakistan began enriching uranium in 1978 and produced HEU in 1983. Although Pakistan subsequently told the United States that it would produce only low-enriched uranium (which is not used as fissile material in nuclear weapons),

U.S. and Pakistani officials who were in government in 1990 indicated during a 1994 meeting that Islamabad decided sometime after October 1989 to resume producing HEU. However, another Pakistani official suggested during the same meeting that the decision may have happened sooner. The United States had information during the 1970s and early 1980s that Pakistan was pursuing nuclear weapons designs, but exactly when Pakistan produced a workable nuclear explosive device is unclear. A 1985 National Intelligence Council report stated that Pakistan "probably has a workable design for a nuclear explosive device" and was "probably... a year or two away from a capacity to produce enough" highly enriched uranium for such a device. A 1987 National Security Council (NSC) memorandum described Pakistan's "continued pursuit... of its nuclear weapons option." A 1993 report to Congress, apparently from the NSC, stated that Islamabad's nuclear weapons efforts "culminated with the capability to rapidly assemble a nuclear device if necessary by the end of the 1980s." A. Q. Khan stated in an interview published in May 1998 that Islamabad "attained" the capability to detonate such a device "at the end of 1984." Similarly, Khan reportedly stated in a January 2010 speech that Pakistan "had become a nuclear power" in 1984 or 1985. Moreover, "senior Pakistani politicians" told a Canadian parliamentary committee in June 1998 that Pakistan had "reached the nuclear 'threshold' by 1984-85," according to a 1998 report. In any case, President Bush's failure to certify in 1990 that Pakistan did not "possess a nuclear explosive device" led to a cut-off in military and financial aid under the Pressler Amendment.

After India conducted nuclear weapon tests on May 11 and May 13, 1998, Pakistan's government responded on May 28 and May 30 with six tests in western Pakistan. Test yields were about 10 kilotons and 5 kilotons, according to seismic analysis. The United States imposed additional sanctions after the tests, but these were lifted after the September 11, 2001, terrorist attacks on the United States. According to public estimates, Pakistan has about 90-110 nuclear weapons, though it could have more. Pakistan's HEU-based nuclear warheads use an implosion design with a solid core of approximately 15-20 kilograms of HEU. Islamabad reportedly continues to produce HEU for weapons at a rate of at least 100 kilograms per year.

Pakistan has also pursued plutonium-based warheads and continues to produce plutonium for weapons. Islamabad has received Chinese and European assistance for at least some of its plutonium program. The 40-50 megawatt heavy-water Khushab plutonium production reactor has been operating since 1998. It appears that Islamabad is constructing three additional heavy-water reactors, which will expand considerably Pakistan's plutonium production capacity, at the same site. Whether one of those reactors is already operating is unclear.

Additionally, Pakistan has a reprocessing facility at the Pakistan Institute of Science and Technology (PINSTECH) and is apparently constructing other such facilities. Nuclear Fuel reported in 2000 that, according to "senior U.S. government officials," Islamabad had begun operating a "pilot-scale" reprocessing facility at the New Laboratories facility at PINSTECH. Pakistan also appears to be constructing a second reprocessing facility at the site and may be completing a reprocessing facility located at Chasma. Pakistani plutonium-based nuclear warheads likely contain approximately 4-6 kilograms of plutonium, according to one expert estimate.

Islamabad's construction of additional nuclear reactors and expansion of its reprocessing capabilities could indicate plans to increase and improve Pakistan's nuclear weapons arsenal in the near future.

Indeed, then DIA Director Michael Maples told the Senate Armed Services Committee on March 10, 2009, that "Pakistan continues to develop its nuclear infrastructure, expand nuclear weapon stockpiles and seek more advanced warheads and delivery systems." Similarly, Admiral Mullen confirmed during the May 14, 2009, hearing that the United States has "evidence" that Pakistan is expanding its nuclear arsenal. DIA Director Burgess's assessment during a March 10, 2011, hearing before the Senate Armed Services Committee was the same as his predecessor's.

### *Responding to India?*

The United Kingdom's Foreign and Commonwealth Office has argued that "Pakistan's strategic posture, including nuclear, is clearly framed around its perception of the threat from India." Similarly, DIA Director Burgess told the Senate Armed Services Committee March 10, 2011, that the "persistent India-Pakistan rivalry drives Islamabad to develop its nuclear infrastructure, expand nuclear weapon stockpiles which are based primarily on highly enriched uranium, and seek more advanced nuclear warheads and delivery systems, including cruise missiles."

Pakistan's Foreign Ministry stated February 2, 2011, that "Pakistan is mindful of the need to avoid arms race with India." Nevertheless, Pakistan appears to be increasing its fissile production capability and improving its delivery vehicles in order to hedge against possible increases in India's nuclear arsenal. Islamabad may also accelerate its current nuclear weapons efforts. Air Commodore Khalid Banuri, Director of Arms Control and Disarmament Affairs in the SPD, asserted in December 2011 that Pakistan's "deterrence requirement remains dynamic" and a precise number of nuclear weapons to satisfy this requirement "cannot be quantified." The government's National Command Authority (NCA) "expressed satisfaction" regarding "the pace of development and effectiveness of Pakistan's strategic deterrence," according to a December 14, 2010, statement. Despite its increasing nuclear arsenal, Pakistan's Foreign Secretary stated in October 2007 that Pakistan "will not be the first to test [a nuclear explosive device] in our region."

India has stated that it needs only a "credible minimum deterrent," but New Delhi has never defined what it means by such a deterrent and has refused to sign the Comprehensive Test Ban Treaty. Furthermore, both the 2008 U.S.-India nuclear cooperation agreement and associated 2008 decision by the Nuclear Suppliers Group (NSG) to exempt India from some of its export guidelines renewed New Delhi's access to the international uranium market. This access will result in more indigenous Indian uranium available for weapons because it will not be consumed by India's newly safeguarded reactors. Pakistani officials have offered estimates for the number of additional nuclear weapons that New Delhi could build. For example, Wajid Shamsul Hasan, Pakistan's High Commissioner to the United Kingdom, argued in an October 2010 letter to a British newspaper that eight Indian nuclear reactors that will not be subject to International Atomic Energy Agency (IAEA) safeguards have the potential to produce 280 nuclear weapons annually. India currently has approximately 60-80 nuclear weapons, according to one public estimate.

Pakistani officials have stated that the government may need to increase significantly its nuclear arsenal in response to possible Indian plans to do the same. According to an April 2006 television broadcast, Pakistani officials from the government's NCA expressed "concern" that the 2008 U.S.-India nuclear cooperation agreement could tilt the strategic balance between India and Pakistan in favour of the former. The officials suggested that Islamabad may need to increase or improve its nuclear arsenal in order to "to meet all requirements of minimum credible defence deterrence." Similarly, Pakistan's Permanent Representative to the IAEA wrote in July 2008 that the agreement could cause a nuclear arms race between Pakistan and India. Moreover, a Foreign Ministry spokesperson indicated during a May 21, 2009, press briefing that, despite the government's continued opposition to a "nuclear or conventional arms race in South Asia," Pakistan may need to increase its nuclear arsenal in response to Indian conventional and nuclear arms expansion. Dr. Syed Rifaat Hussain of Quad-i-Azam University in Islamabad argued in 2011 that "Pakistan would need three to four years to gain enough plutonium stocks to maintain a credible posture of nuclear deterrence" versus India.

Illustrating this point, a Pakistani Foreign Office spokesperson reacted to India's July 26, 2009, launch of its first indigenously built nuclear-powered submarine by asserting that "continued induction of new lethal weapon systems by India is detrimental to regional peace and stability," adding that "[w]ithout entering into an arms race with India, Pakistan will take all appropriate steps to safeguard its security and maintain strategic balance in South Asia." The Indian submarine, which is not yet deployed, will reportedly be capable of carrying nuclear-armed ballistic missiles. Admiral Mohammad Asif Sandila, the Chief of Pakistan's Naval Staff, announced "the formal establishment of the Naval Strategic Force Command of Pakistan" on May 19, 2012. Describing the Strategic Force as "the custodian of the nation's 2 strike capability," Sandila argued that it "will strengthen Pakistan's policy of Credible Minimum Deterrence and ensure regional stability," but he did not elaborate.

Similarly, according to the January 2010 statement, the NCA identified "developments detrimental to the objectives of strategic stability in the region," including India's acquisition of "advanced weapons systems" and missile defence systems. The NCA also noted that the 2008 NSG decision described above, as well as subsequent nuclear fuel supply agreements that New Delhi has concluded with several governments, "would enable India to produce substantial quantities of fissile material for nuclear weapons by freeing up its domestic resources." The statement suggests that Pakistan could increase or improve its nuclear weapons in response to these developments, but does not explicitly say so. Shahzad Chaudhry, a retired Pakistani Air Vice Marshall, argued during a July 18, 2011, U.S. Institute of Peace event that India's stockpile of reactor-grade plutonium is an additional concern for Pakistan.

Whether and to what extent Pakistan's current expansion of its nuclear weapons-related facilities is a response to the U.S.-India agreement is unclear, partly because descriptions of the government's decisions regarding those facilities are not publicly available. However, Air Commodore Banuri argued in December 2011 that "India's massive conventional military build up, the India-U.S. nuclear deal," and India's pursuit of missile defence systems, forced Pakistan "to make qualitative and quantitative adjustments." Banuri also cited Indian military doctrines that Islamabad describes as prescribing rapid conventional military action against Pakistan.

In addition to making qualitative and quantitative improvements to its nuclear arsenal, Pakistan could increase the number of circumstances under which it would be willing to use nuclear weapons. For example, Peter Lavoy has argued that India's efforts to improve its conventional military capabilities could enable New Delhi to achieve "technical superiority" in intelligence, surveillance, and reconnaissance, as well as precision targeting, providing India with "the capability to effectively locate and efficiently destroy strategically important targets in Pakistan." Islamabad could respond by lowering the threshold for using nuclear weapons, according to Lavoy. Indeed, a Pakistan Foreign Ministry spokesperson warned in May 2009 that Islamabad could take this step. The Pakistani government may also consider fielding non-strategic nuclear weapons in order to increase the credibility of its nuclear deterrent versus Indian conventional military operations. On April 19, 2011, Lieutenant General (Retired) Khalid Ahmed Kidwai, Director General of Pakistan's Strategic Plans Division, described the first test of a new nuclear-capable ballistic missile as "a very important milestone in consolidating Pakistan's strategic deterrence capability at all levels of the threat spectrum.

## THE A. Q. KHAN NETWORK

Proliferation networks stemming from Pakistan have their roots in the effort to develop a Pakistani nuclear bomb. Beginning in the 1970s, Pakistan used extensive clandestine procurement networks to obtain technology for its own nuclear weapons program. A report from Pakistan's Inter-Services Intelligence published September 15, 2011, stated that Pakistan, as an under-developed country with no industrial infra-structure, had to buy each and every bit of material and piece of equipment surreptitiously from abroad in the open market and had to establish a network of cover companies within the country and outside to by-pass embargoes and import all the necessary items.

Former Pakistani nuclear scientist A. Q. Khan directed this procurement and subsequently used a similar network to supply Libya, North Korea, and Iran with designs and materials related to uranium enrichment for profit.

The current status of Pakistan's nuclear export network is unclear, although most official U.S. reports indicate that, at the least, it has been damaged considerably. Then-Director of National Intelligence John D. Negroponte implied that the network had been dismantled when he asserted in a January 11, 2007, statement to the Senate Select Committee on Intelligence that "Pakistan had been a major source of nuclear proliferation until the disruption of the A. Q. Khan network." When asked about the network's current status during a July 25, 2007, Senate Foreign Relations Committee hearing, then-Under Secretary for Political Affairs Nicholas Burns replied that I cannot assert that no part of that network exists, but it's my understanding based on our conversations with the Pakistanis that the network has been fundamentally dismantled. But to say that there are no elements in Pakistan, I'm not sure I could say that.

Similarly, the London-based International Institute for Strategic Studies found in a May 2007 report that "at least some of Khan's associates appear to have escaped law enforcement attention and could... resume their black-market business." More recently, a January 12, 2009, State Department press release said that the network "is no longer operating." For its part, Pakistan's Foreign Office stated February 7, 2009, that Pakistan "has dismantled the nuclear black market network." Asked during a July 20, 2009, interview whether Pakistan was transferring "nuclear weapons" or related advice to North Korea, Secretary of State Hillary Clinton replied that there is "no evidence" that Pakistan is doing so. Furthermore, Acting Assistant Secretary of State Vann Van Diepen described the network as "basically defunct" during a July 22, 2010, congressional hearing, adding that "we're on the lookout for sort of the next A.Q. Khan network, so to speak." Similarly, State Department spokesperson P.J. Crowley told reporters during an August 3, 2010, press briefing that the United States monitors the Khan network "very closely for signs that others within his realm are still in business." A March 2012 State Department report described the network as "defunct."

Asked during the 2007 hearing about Pakistan's cooperation in investigating the network, Burns acknowledged that the United States has not had "personal, consistent access" to Khan, but added that he did not "have all the details of everything we've done." Similarly, the IAEA has not yet been able to interview Khan directly, according to an agency official. However, sources report that Islamabad has responded to written questions from the IAEA and has been cooperative with the agency's investigation of Iran's nuclear program. Former IAEA official Olli Heinonen, who investigated the Khan network during his time at the agency, stated in an interview published in October 2011 that Khan "answer[ed] some of my questions in writing through secret channels." Khan himself told Dawn News TV May 29, 2008, that he would not cooperate with U.S. or IAEA investigators. A Pakistani Foreign Office spokesperson told reporters in May 2006 that the government considered the Khan investigation "closed"—a position an office spokesperson reiterated February 6, 2009. The State Department announced January 12, 2009, that it was imposing sanctions on 13 individuals and three companies for their involvement in the Khan network. The sanctions were imposed under the Export-Import Bank Act, the Nuclear Proliferation Prevention Act, and Executive Orders 12938 and 13382. Pursuant to a requirement in the Enhanced Partnership with Pakistan Act of 2009 (P.L. 111-73), Secretary of State Hillary Clinton issued a certification on March 18, 2011, that Pakistan "is continuing to cooperate with the United States in efforts to dismantle supplier networks relating to the acquisition of nuclear weapons-related materials."

### *Interactions with Al-Qaeda*

According to reports, Al-Qaeda unsuccessfully sought nuclear weapons assistance from the Khan network but did receive limited help from at least one other group in Pakistan. Scientists who may have provided some help to al-Qaeda representatives were retired Pakistan Atomic Energy Commission scientists, long-time rivals of A. Q. Khan, and Islamic fundamentalists—Sultan Bashiruddin Mahmood and Chaudiri Abdul Majeed. The assistance under the umbrella of the UTN humanitarian organization was reportedly related to weapons of mass destruction, but details are scarce on the extent of the transfers, and the events following the September 11, 2001, attacks on the United States may have cut off this interaction.

Mahmood and Majeed met with Osama bin Laden and Ayman al-Zawahiri in August 2001 in Afghanistan to discuss, among other topics, what would be needed to develop a nuclear weapons infrastructure, details of nuclear bomb design, and how to construct radiological dispersal devices. Mahmood was a public figure well-known for his eccentric and extreme views about science and Islam, and he was demoted in 1999 to a lower rank in part because of his radicalism.

Mahmood then sought early retirement and started the UTN organization. After the United States briefed the Pakistani government about this activity at the highest levels in the fall of 2001, the Pakistani authorities detained the UTN scientists for multiple rounds of questioning. Through these interrogations and searches in Afghanistan, UTN's work with al-Qaeda on biological weapons and rudimentary nuclear weapons technology came to light. The Pakistani government did not press criminal charges against Mahmood and Majeed, but put the scientists under house arrest in 2002. This extreme case raised awareness of the "insider threat" and subsequently led to changes in Pakistani personnel security policy. Accounts raise the possibility of other groups or individuals also providing al Qaeda with nuclear expertise, but less information is publicly available.

## U.S. ASSISTANCE AND PAKISTANI NUCLEAR SECURITY

U.S. plans to secure Pakistani nuclear weapons in case of a loss of control by the Pakistani government were famously addressed during former Secretary of State Condoleezza Rice's confirmation hearing in January 2005. In response to a question from Senator John Kerry asking what would happen to Pakistan's nuclear weapons in the event of a radical Islamic coup in Islamabad, Secretary Rice answered, "[w]e have noted this problem, and we are prepared to try to deal with it." On November 12, 2007, responding to press reports about this contingency, a Pakistan Foreign Office spokesperson said, "Pakistan possesses adequate retaliatory capacity to defend its strategic assets and sovereignty," emphasizing that Islamabad's nuclear weapons have been under "strong multi-layered, institutionalized decision-making, organizational, administrative and command and control structures since 1998." The issue of U.S. contingency plans to take over

Pakistani strategic assets was raised again in the press following Benazir Bhutto's assassination, and was met with similar assurances by Pakistan's government.

More recently, a Pakistan Foreign Office spokesperson, responding to a report detailing alleged U.S.-Pakistani discussions regarding contingency plans for U.S. forces to help secure Islamabad's nuclear weapons, stated November 8, 2009, that Pakistan "does not require any foreign assistance in this regard." Pakistan will never "allow any country to have direct or indirect access to its nuclear and strategic facilities," the spokesperson said, adding that "no talks have ever taken place on the issue of the security of Pakistan's nuclear arsenal with US officials." U.S. Ambassador to Pakistan Anne Patterson stated the same day that the United States "has no intention to seize Pakistani nuclear weapons or material." Gates stated during the January 2010 television interview that the United States has "no intention or desire to take over any of Pakistan's nuclear weapons."

The United States reportedly offered nuclear security assistance to Pakistan soon after September 11, 2001. U.S. assistance to Islamabad, which must comply with nonproliferation guidelines, has reportedly included the sharing of best practices and technical measures to prevent unauthorized or accidental use of nuclear weapons, as well as contribute to physical security of storage facilities and personnel reliability. As noted above, Islamabad employs a system requiring that at least two, and perhaps three, people authenticate launch codes for nuclear weapons. Security at nuclear sites in Islamabad is the responsibility of a 10,000-member security force, commanded by a two-star general. Former Pakistani military officials have said Pakistan has developed Permissive Action Links (PALs) for its warheads without U.S. assistance. PALs require a code to be entered before a weapon can be detonated.

Former Deputy Secretary of State Richard Armitage confirmed in a November 2007 interview that there has been U.S. assistance in this area, explaining that the United States was unlikely to intervene militarily in a crisis in Pakistan because "we have spent considerable time with the Pakistani military, talking with them and working with them on the security of their nuclear weapons. I think most observers would say that they are fairly secure. They have pretty sophisticated mechanisms to guard the security of those." Rolf Mowatt-Larssen, former Director of the Office of Intelligence and Counterintelligence at the U.S. Department of Energy, pointed out in May 2009 that "there's not a lot of transparency into" how Islamabad spends the

U.S. funds, but he nevertheless characterized them as "money well spent." A Pakistani official said in November 2009 that Pakistan reserves the right to "pick and choose" the nuclear security measures it will undertake, adding that Islamabad will only accept such measures that are "nonintrusive."

The extent to which Pakistan has shared information about its nuclear arsenal with the United States is unclear. Although, as noted, former President Musharraf has acknowledged Islamabad's sharing of some information, General Tariq Majid, chair of Pakistan's Joint Chiefs of Staff Committee, stated November 9, 2009, that "there is absolutely no question of sharing or allowing any foreign individual, entity or a state, any access to sensitive information about our nuclear assets." Air Commodore Khalid Banuri, Director of Arms Control and Disarmament Affairs in the SPD, indicated in a 2008 interview that Islamabad accepts U.S. "education and awareness, but in a completely non-intrusive way," adding that Pakistan has "some rudimentary equipment and some training" from the United States. Banuri described giving U.S. officials access to Pakistan's nuclear weapons facilities as a "red line" that Islamabad will not cross.

The U.S. government has also reportedly offered assistance to secure or destroy radioactive materials that could be used to make a radioactive dispersal device, and to ship highly enriched uranium used in the Pakistani civilian nuclear sector out of the country. Pakistan's response to these proposals is unclear, and downturns in the bilateral relationship overall may have complicated efforts to make progress in this area.

It is worth noting that, according to some observers, spent fuel from Pakistan's Karachi and Chasma nuclear power plants could be vulnerable to theft or attack. However, Pakistani officials have expressed confidence in the security of its facilities and have said that Islamabad has no plans to transport spent fuel from either reactor. Moreover, the Pakistan Nuclear Regulatory Authority (PNRA) has a Nuclear Security Action Plan, which includes a description of regulations for handling spent nuclear fuel. The PNRA states that Pakistan follows IAEA physical protection standards.

### *Proliferation*

A fundamental aspect of nuclear security is ensuring that personnel with sensitive knowledge do not proliferate that expertise, but this aspect of nuclear security in Pakistan was recognized only in the past 10 years and resulted in significant reforms of its personnel security system. Many observers continue to be concerned that other states or terrorist organizations could obtain material or expertise related to nuclear weapons from elements in Pakistan. This view is only encouraged by recent instability and governance problems.

## COMPARING INDIA AND PAKISTAN'S NUCLEAR PROLIFERATION POLICIES DURING THE COLD WAR

The dawn of the Cold War, and the spread of its subsequent nuclear logic of deterrence, dramatically reconceptualised a series of classic principal notions in the field of international relations theory. The theoretical framework of concepts such as the balance of power, national security, deterrence and power status were fundamentally modified by the structural significance of nuclear weapons in the international system. The dynamics of Cold War rivalry provided a global infrastructure for nuclear weapons research, production, testing and deployment. While the two superpowers were heavily engaged in vertical nuclear proliferation, strategically-significant regional security complexes (i.e. the Middle East, the South Asia) witnessed the centrality of the quest for horizontal nuclear proliferation in their major states' perception of national security, independence and prestige. In spite of the apparent similarities in general objectives, factors directing the orientation of nuclear policies of states in conflictual geopolitical settings for horizontal proliferation varied greatly.

In the South Asian context, a conflictual bipolar security complex, India and Pakistan's transformational process of emerging as opaque nuclear powers was an example of different motivations, aspirations and ambitions for obtaining nuclear status. While the dominance of *realpolitik* trends over states' nuclear decision-making process is not an entirely surprising phenomena, the evolution of India's approach to the nuclear option is interesting from philosophical and strategic viewpoints. The genesis of the Indian nuclear policy from a categorical opposition to nuclear weapons in the Nehru era to Pokhran I, India's first so-called Peaceful Nuclear Explosion (PNE) in 1974, signified a discontinuity in New Delhi's post-1947 strategic thinking. What caused this discontinuity? What factor(s) led the country of Mohandas Gandhi, who once labelled nuclear weapons as 'diabolic', to obtaining potential nuclear power status under Indira Gandhi? Do the same factors suffice in explaining Pakistan's motives for developing its own nuclear capabilities in the mid-1980s? While some political scientists emphasised national security considerations in locating the roots of India and Pakistan proliferation policy, others have used an alternative theoretical approach with a greater level of structural balance between domestic, military security and symbolic motives. The latter multi-causal approach, summarised by Scott D. Sagan, is particularly useful in providing an inclusive analysis of nuclear proliferation causes. In this context and through the application of Sagan's explanatory models, the essay attempts to analyse the layers in India and Pakistan's 'nuclear thinking' leading to the development of military nuclear technology.

The alternative multi-causal explanation constitutes a practically efficient theoretical framework for the comprehensive understanding of states' hybrid logic for nuclear proliferation. Opposing the neorealist mono-causal security-oriented analysis (i.e. "the security model"), Sagan's approach considers the domestic and norms aspects as effective factors in triggering military nuclear proliferation, thus offering two additional explanations: "the domestic politics model" and "the norms model." According to Sagan, security model states (either weak or strong) perceive nuclear weapons as an enormously powerful means of deterrence to secure their national security in an anarchic international system, if their regional or trans-regional rival(s) acquire nuclear capability. Strong resourceful states develop their own bomb, while weak states, incapable of proliferation, are obliged to join a balancing alliance with a nuclear power to maintain their security and sovereignty with the promise of nuclear retaliation. In contrast, the domestic politics model reflects the influence of three main domestic actors on governments' nuclear proliferation policies: first, states' nuclear energy establishments (consisting of scientific institutions and civil companies); second, the military elites (especially in the Air Force branch) as domestic bureaucratic actors; and third, politicians who tend to profit from the nuclear weapons discourse for political parties or individual standing regarding pro-proliferation public opinion. Therefore, these pro-proliferation actors gain additional influence if nuclear weapons are a positive symbol in states' domestic debates – thus the states proliferate in accordance with the influence of one or more of the aforementioned actors. Finally, in the norms model, states' nuclear policies are pro-proliferation due to 'nuclear symbolism' and the 'nuclear myth': states observe military organisation and advanced weaponry as essential elements in their image as modern and sovereign states. The 'nuclear myth', or symbolic implications of nuclear proliferation (e.g. technological advancement, military might, projection of grandeur, etc), are perceived as a means of forming states' modern identity and enhancing their international prestige. While there seems to be an analytical overlap and theoretical interference between the domestic and symbolic models, Sagan's three models offer an efficient toolbox for examining the deciding factors in India and Pakistan's nuclear policies.

The security-model analysis of Indian nuclear policy prior to Pokhran I can be conducted by analysing India's threat perception at the regional and trans-regional levels. The trans-regional level analysis confirms the gravity of Sino-centrism in India's trans-regional threat perception sphere, and the validity of Sagan's security-model explanation. The dynamics of post-1962 Sino-Indian bilateral relations is the fundamental factor in India's horizontal proliferation policy in the security model. While the Sino-Indian protracted conflict began in 1953 over territorial claims, the 1962 Sino-Indian war and its disastrous consequences for the non-aligned India moved the Chinese threat factor from the periphery of New Delhi's threat perception circle to its centre, triggering incremental yet significant changes in Indian defence policy and military strategy. The subsequent Indian military reorientation towards re-equipment and operational reinforcement (e.g. the creation of ten mountain divisions designed for warfare in the Himalayas and increasing the Army's manpower ceiling to 825,000) confirms the demise of Nehru's *moralpolitik*-type policies regarding China. However, the fundamental shift in India's nuclear weapons position occurred when Beijing shocked New Delhi with the detonation of its first nuclear device in October 1964. New Delhi's subsequent reaction to China's nuclear capability demonstrated a paradigm shift in India's previously Nehruvian anti-proliferation policy towards what then Prime Minister Lal Bahadur Shastri reluctantly phrased as India considering "nuclear explosion for peaceful purposes". Compatible with the security-model's two policy scenarios, India's inability to develop its own nuclear weapons forced New Delhi to secure nuclear deterrence by joining a balancing alliance with a nuclear power. Accordingly, when India's request to the United States, the Soviet Union and the United Kingdom for nuclear guarantee was refused, India's only option for deterring a nuclear China and maintaining its national security was to obtain horizontal proliferation on its own, leading to the 1974 PNE.

Similarly, the regional-level analysis indicates the significance of nuclear weapons in India's quest for regional hegemony and security in the South Asian region, although against the much less significant threat of Pakistan. A quick glance at pro-Indian political scientists' analysis of the motivation of India's quest for regional security through nuclear weapons reveals New Delhi's mindset regarding Pakistani conventional threat as well as India's strategic policy manoeuvre to achieve several objectives at once. In the bipolar South Asian security complex, Pakistan was (and is) India's major regional security and strategic concern. In spite of its conventional inferiority to India, Pakistan attacked its greater and more militarily powerful neighbour in 1948, 1965 and 1971. While India's decisive military victory in the 1971 war, and the subsequent disintegration of Pakistan through the independence of Bangladesh, considerably weakened Pakistan, it managed to retain most of its military infrastructures. The series of Indo-Pakistani military conflicts convinced Indian strategists that Pakistan could use the period of Indian domestic political instability to launch other military attacks on India. In the light of alarming Sino-Pakistani cordial relations, and the presumption of Pakistani will to attack India, India's nuclear proliferation became instrumental in maintaining Indian regional security as well as establishing Indian regional hegemony through deterring Pakistan from future attacks. As Saira Khan formulates, the most efficient war-avoidance strategy for India in such conflictual regional settings was 'deterrence by possession of nuclear weapons.'

Similar to the Indian behavioural pattern for proliferation, but in contrast to India's multi-layered threat perception, the application of the security-model framework on Pakistan's nuclear policy produces a mono-causal explanation: Pakistan's nuclear proliferation was a linear reactionary policy to India's 1974 nuclear detonation. In addition to Indo-Pakistani territorial, ideological and ethnic elements of conflict that have formed the essentials of the South Asian security complex since 1947, the 1971 war and dismemberment of Pakistan reinforced Indo-centrism in Pakistan's threat perception. The war crippled Pakistan's economy and displayed the perceived unreliability of Pakistan's allies (i.e. the United States and China) in the time of crisis. Realising its conventional military inferiority to India, in 1972 President Zulfiquar Ali Bhutto initiated a nuclear policy in pursuit of nuclear weapons. Islamabad's nuclear program, however, gained a critical boost by India's 1974 PNE. Closely resembling the pattern of India's reaction to the 1964 Chinese nuclear test, Pakistan's nuclear policy was decisively directed towards inevitable nuclear proliferation after India's 1974 PNE. Against India's combined conventional military superiority and nuclear weapons capability, Pakistan had to obtain its own nuclear weapons as soon as possible to provide deterrence against the gravest threat to its national security. In this context, with Islamabad's failure to obtain security guarantees from the nuclear powers against a nuclear India, Pakistan had no other option other than to embark on its own nuclear proliferation program.

Applying the domestic-model of analysis on the Indian case clearly exhibits the decisive influence of two of the three domestic actors outlined by the model on India's nuclear decision for horizontal proliferation: nuclear energy establishments (consisting of pro-proliferation scientists and defence laboratories) and politicians eager to enhance their respective parties or/and individual standing in public opinion.

Due to the pattern of the civil-military relationship in India where the former utterly dominates the latter, military elites as bureaucratic domestic actors had practically no influence over New Delhi's process of nuclear decision-making. After the Chinese 1964 nuclear test, Homi Bhabba, the head of India's Atomic Energy Commission (AEC), tenaciously lobbied for the allocation of required resources for developing nuclear weapons. Eventually, the AEC leadership's lobbying for proliferation along with pro-nuclear Congress party pressure on the government forced the reluctant Shastri to order the initiation of a classified project to develop technical ability to design and detonate a PNE within a certain timeframe. In spite of Bhabba's successor, Vikram Sarabhai's fierce opposition to any form of nuclear proliferation, the AEC developed an alliance with defence laboratories for lobbying the new Prime Minister Indira Gandhi. In a meaningful coincidence, the dynamics of Indian domestic politics in the early 1970s were defined in terms of economic recession, large-scale riots in various regions and the internal conflict in the ruling Congress party, thus an all-time low domestic support for Gandhi's government. In such dire circumstances, with the Prime Minister acknowledging that a theatrical nuclear explosion could have been a decisive 'political ace' for increasing her standing in public opinion, Gandhi's approval of 1974 PNE is hardly surprising. In a later interview, in spite of her initial denial, Gandhi admitted that the PNE "would have been useful for election". As the result, immediately after the detonation, public support for Gandhi's government and the ruling Congress party increased by one-third, both being "restored to the nation's confidence." Considering the pre-PNE Indian domestic politics dynamics, the influence of AEC, the Prime Minister and the ruling party on nuclear proliferation is evident.

In contrast, the application of the domestic-model framework on the Pakistani case constitutes the presence of non-political domestic dynamics and a higher level of military influence on the process of Pakistan's pursuit of nuclear weapons. As mentioned earlier, a year after the 1971 war and two years before Pokhran I, Pakistan's former leader Bhutto instructed the country's top scientists to concentrate on the development of nuclear weapons. Yet, such policies could not be pursued without the involvement of the military institution in the process. Decades of military rule has promoted the Pakistani military as the strongest bureaucratic institution in the country, setting the pattern of the country's civil-military relationship in favour of military control. However, in spite of the military's vast influence in Pakistan's polity, nuclear decisions were made within a coordinated policy framework consisting of Prime Minister Bhutto, the chiefs of the armed forces, the Foreign Minister and the chief of joint services headquarters. The pro-bomb direction of Pakistani organic nuclear decision-making machinery was maintained even after the fall of Bhutto in 1977. The policy momentum and continuity in the country's pursuit for nuclear weapons in the post-Bhutto era confirms the absence of a domestic politics perspective in favour of the strong presence of a national security perspective: all Pakistani political leaders with different attitudes and policy perspectives maintained the essentials of Bhutto's nuclear policy. As for the nuclear establishment agency's influence, however, a division in the scholarly literature is detectable: while Kapur introduces I. H. Usmani, chairman of Pakistan Atomic Energy Commission (PAEC) as the most important figure in Pakistan's nuclear decision-making during 1970s, Khan maintains that the scientific institutions' influence was largely barred by the institutionalised military, limiting their range of influence to the lobbying of politicians and military elites in favour of proliferation. Yet, in spite of Kapur's exaggerated emphasis on Usmani's influence, the dominance of the security discourse over Pakistan's nuclear policy process is to such a degree that the domestic model's dynamics echoes the trends of the security model.

Finally, analysis of India's Cold War period nuclear proliferation policy signifies the link between India's quest for obtaining international prestige as a mean of gaining 'great power' status and its pursuit of the absolute weapon. From India's perspective, a direct link between nuclear proliferation and international prestige existed: countries in possession of nuclear weapons enhanced their standing in the international system's power pyramid. Nuclear states, developed or underdeveloped, were (and continue to do so) taken seriously by other members of the international community because of the practical implications of possessing the ultimate weapon. India's perspective regarding nuclear symbolism was formed by observing the impact of China's 1964 nuclear explosion on Beijing's power status and international recognition of Chinese power which followed. In addition, China obtained its seat in the United Nations which had previously been denied. The United States' recognition of China's power demonstrated to India the symbolic importance of nuclear weapons in establishing a state's prestige. Remembering the existence of rivalry between the two states, the Chinese model of enhancing prestige propelled India to embark on a quest for horizontal nuclear proliferation to enhance its prestige, not only in the international context, but in regard to its territorial quarrel with China.

In contrast to India, and in spite of the 'Islamic bomb' rhetoric, Pakistan's nuclear proliferation program did not focus on enhancing the country's international prestige nor did it perceive nuclear weapons as a means of promoting a sense of Islamic nationalism. Reviewing the views of Pakistani scholars, strategists and officials regarding the country's motivations for nuclear proliferation clarifies the symbolic-model inefficiency for explaining the rubric of Pakistani proliferation policy. In an interview with Khan, former Pakistani Foreign Minister Agha Shahi rejected the existence of any considerations of symbolic type in Pakistan's military nuclear program. Similarly, the strategist Ross Masud, the Chairman and Director General of the Islamabad's Institute of Strategic Studies confirmed Shahi's view that the projection of Pakistani grandeur by nuclear weapons "has never been a factor in Pakistan's decision-makers' minds", contributing any enhancement in Pakistani prestige to an unintended "spillover effect". In this context, Pakistan's nuclear policy was fundamentally less concerned about the notion of prestige enhancement than national security. However, as mentioned by Masud, while the Pakistani horizontal nuclear proliferation could produce the prestige dimension, such an outcome could not be regarded as the cause of proliferation but as its secondary consequence. In addition, the much referred notion of the 'Islamic bomb' was in fact more of a rhetorical strategy to attract financial support from wealthy Arab states than a symbol of the Muslim states' international prestige. Therefore, the application of a symbolic-model framework on Pakistan's proliferation policy does not demonstrate the symbolic motive as a primary factor in the country's nuclear weapons development.

In conclusion, this essay has attempted to examine the factors in the evolution of nuclear proliferation policies of India and Pakistan through applying Sagan's three models of proliferation on the two case studies. After outlining the general theoretical frameworks and their policy implication, the essay discussed India and Pakistan's motivations for horizontal nuclear proliferation according to the security model, the domestic politics model and the symbolic model, respectively. Analysing India's motivations through the security-model framework introduces nuclear China as primary incentive for India's nuclear proliferation and India's thrive for regional hegemony in the South Asia through deterring Pakistan as the secondary motivation. In contrast, the same model shows that Pakistan's sole concern for deterring India as its primary motivation for nuclear proliferation. In the domestic level, while India's nuclear policy was heavily influenced by leaders' political motivations and nuclear energy establishments lobbying – Pakistan's proliferation policy, witnessing a high level of military influence, lacked a domestic politics perspective and was mostly concerned with security perspective. Finally, while the application of symbolic model on India's nuclear policy confirms the significance of nuclear symbolism in India's quest for international prestige through nuclear proliferation, it demonstrates prestige angle as secondary to security-centric Pakistani proliferation policy.

## U.S. POLICY AND PAKISTAN'S NUCLEAR WEAPONS

The potential for the intersection of terrorism and nuclear weapons is arguably the greatest threat to American national, even global, security. As the U.S. seeks to deter the possibility of terrorists gaining access to nuclear weapons, it must consider carefully its policies toward Pakistan. The results of investigations into Pakistani nuclear scientist A.Q. Khan's nuclear black market and proliferation network demonstrate in stark terms the devastating consequences of nuclear proliferation by individuals with access to state-controlled nuclear programs.

Some observers have incorrectly characterized the threat of nuclear terrorism in Pakistan as stemming from the danger of radical Islamists overrunning the country and gaining control of the country's nuclear assets. However, given that the religious parties lack wide popular support and that President Musharraf and his senior Army commanders largely oppose the Islamist agenda, the probability of this scenario occurring is relatively low. When it comes to preventing terrorists from acquiring nuclear bombs, the more worrisome trend in Pakistan is the links between some retired military and intelligence officials and nuclear scientists to Taliban and al-Qaeda terrorists.

U.S. policy should therefore centre on helping to prevent the penetration of the nuclear establishment over time by individuals sympathetic to al-Qaeda goals. Despite Pakistan's arguments that its nuclear weapons are safely guarded, the U.S. must construct and implement policies that proactively thwart the unwelcome possibility of Pakistan's nuclear weapons falling into the wrong hands. Given the tangled history of U.S.-Pakistan relations, especially with regard to Pakistan's nuclear weapons program, the development of workable solutions to address the nuclear terrorism threat will be challenging and complicated. The best chance for success will lie within a framework premised on a robust U.S.-Pakistan partnership based on trust and mutual understanding.

## *U.S.-Pakistan Ties and Islamabad's Quest for Nuclear Weapons*

Pakistan's regional security concerns have led it to acquire nuclear weapons in the face of persistent and often severe international penalties. After the 1964 Chinese nuclear test, then-Foreign Minister Zulfiqar Ali Bhutto concluded India would also go nuclear and that Pakistan would have to follow in its footsteps.

Pakistan's humiliating defeat in the 1971 war with India that resulted in the dismemberment of the country further convinced Zulfiqar Ali Bhutto (by then President of the country) of Pakistan's need for a nuclear deterrent against India's conventional superiority. It was at this point that Bhutto decided Pakistan would secretly pursue a nuclear weapon. India's 1974 nuclear test accelerated the Pakistani efforts to acquire nuclear weapons and by late 1975, Bhutto had placed metallurgist Abdul Qadeer Khan in charge of a clandestine effort to produce enriched uranium for nuclear weapons.

Another India-Pakistan military crisis in 1987 sparked by a large-scale Indian military exercise called "Operation Brass Tacks" only strengthened Pakistani resolve on its decision to develop a credible nuclear weapons program. The Pakistanis believed "Operation Brass Tacks" was cover for a planned Indian invasion and so began amassing their own troops near the border. At the peak of the crisis, A.Q. Khan announced to an Indian journalist that Pakistan had a nuclear weapons capability.

Two years prior to "Operation Brass Tacks" in 1985, the U.S. Congress passed legislation referred to as the Pressler Amendment, requiring the U.S. President to certify that Pakistan did not possess a nuclear weapon as a pre-condition for further U.S. assistance. When President George Bush Senior decided he could no longer certify that Pakistan did not possess a nuclear weapon on October 1, 1990, the U.S. suspended its $564 million aid program to Pakistan for Fiscal Year 1991. The loss of $300 million annually of arms and other military supplies was a heavy blow to Pakistan's defence establishment, while the cut-off of economic assistance added to problems that were already severely weakening the Pakistani economy.

Pakistan conducted its first nuclear tests in May 1998 in response to a round of testing by India after it broke a 24-year self-imposed moratorium on nuclear testing. The Clinton Administration imposed fresh sanctions on Pakistan (and India) following the 1998 tests but gradually lifted the restrictions. Following the 9/11 attacks, the Bush Administration lifted all remaining nuclear sanctions against both Pakistan and India. After the 1998 nuclear tests, A.Q. Khan boasted that he made Pakistan's program more advanced and reliable than the Indian program, citing Pakistan's mastery of the uranium enrichment process.

## PAKISTAN'S STRATEGIC NEIGHBORHOOD

### *Pakistan-India Relations*

Pakistan's nuclear program is driven primarily by Islamabad's perception that it needs to counter the Indian threat and, to a lesser extent, by its desire to establish itself as a major Islamic power. There is genuine concern in Pakistan that India will take advantage of the U.S. civil nuclear deal to expand its weapons program. Reports over the last year about Pakistan's construction of a major heavy water nuclear reactor at the Khushab facility have raised concern that Islamabad will significantly boost its plutonium production capabilities, thereby fueling a regional arms race that could involve China.

The six-month-long India-Pakistan military crisis sparked by a terrorist attack on India's parliament in December 2001 was defused after Deputy Secretary Armitage secured a commitment from President Musharraf to end the infiltration of Kashmiri militants into Indian-held Kashmir. Shortly before the standoff ended, the U.S. Embassy in New Delhi evacuated the families of diplomats on the grounds that a military conflict between the two adversaries could escalate into a nuclear exchange. Although India says nuclear war was never a possibility, the Pakistani security establishment appears to believe that the crisis proved the effectiveness of its nuclear deterrent against India.

Pakistan and India formally launched a composite dialogue process in January 2004 that includes talks on nuclear confidence building. In June 2004, New Delhi and Islamabad agreed to continue a bilateral moratorium on further nuclear tests; to provide each other advance notice of nuclear-capable missile tests; and to establish a hotline between each other's foreign ministries. These talks marked the first follow-up discussions to the 1999 Lahore Memorandum of Understanding, designed to reduce the risks of a nuclear exchange due to accident or misunderstanding. Earlier this year, India and Pakistan furthered these talks by inking an agreement to notify each other immediately via their hotline links in the event of any accident relating to nuclear weapons.

### Pakistan-China

Pakistan and China have had long-standing, strategic ties. China is Pakistan's largest defence supplier, and the Chinese view Pakistan as a useful counterweight to Indian power in the region. In the run-up to Chinese President Hu Jintao's visit to Pakistan last November, media reports speculated that Beijing would sign a major nuclear energy cooperation agreement with Pakistan. In the end, however, the Chinese leader provided a general pledge of support to Pakistan's nuclear energy program but refrained from announcing plans to supply new nuclear reactors. China has helped Pakistan build two nuclear reactors at the Chasma site in the Punjab Province and provided Pakistan with nuclear technology as far back as the 1970s. China also is helping Pakistan develop a deep sea port at Gwadar in the Pakistani province of Baluchistan, near the mouth of the Persian Gulf.

One source of tension between Beijing and Islamabad that has surfaced in the past is over the issue of rising Islamic extremism in Pakistan and the ability of Chinese Uighur separatists to receive sanctuary and training among other radical Islamist groups on Pakistani territory. To mollify China's concerns, Pakistan in recent years has begun to clamp down on Uighur settlements and on religious schools used as training grounds for militant Islamists. Their tensions over Islamic extremism surfaced this past weekend when Islamic vigilantes kidnapped several Chinese citizens they accused of running a brothel in Islamabad. The extremists released the kidnap victims shortly after they were captured, saying they did so in the interest of maintaining Pakistan's good relations with China.

### Pakistan-Iran

Pakistan's relations with Iran have been far from smooth over the last three decades. Relations soured following the 1979 Iranian Revolution due to Pakistani President Zia's previous support to the Shah's regime and his encouragement to Sunni militant organizations that pushed a strict Sunni interpretation of Islam and targeted the minority Shiia population in Pakistan. Iran, in turn, began to export to Pakistan Shiia militants to counter the Sunni extremists. Sectarian violence has ebbed and flowed over the last 15 years in Pakistan and continues to have a chilling impact on Iranian-Pakistani relations.

Pakistan's support to the Sunni Taliban in the mid-1990s significantly raised tensions between Tehran and Islamabad. These tensions climaxed in August 1998 when the Taliban killed several Iranian diplomats in the northern Afghan city of Mazar-e-Sharif. Iran responded by amassing its military along the border with Afghanistan. If fighting had broken out between Iranian forces and the Taliban, Pakistan would have likely been drawn into the conflict in support of the Taliban. It is difficult to imagine Pakistan would have officially sanctioned nuclear cooperation with such an unsteady neighbor, although some analysts believe the bulk of the nuclear cooperation occurred in the early 1990s before the Taliban had emerged and shortly after the U.S. had cut off assistance to Pakistan.

Pakistan;s halt to official support to the Taliban following 9/11 has helped to improve Pakistani-Iranian ties, and they are actively engaged in talks on developing an Iran-Pakistan-India oil and gas pipeline.

## TERRORISM AND NUCLEAR WEAPONS

Former Director of Central Intelligence George Tenet reports in his memoirs that A.Q. Khan rebuffed several approaches by Osama bin Laden for access to nuclear know-how, although it was not clear why. Perhaps Khan understood that cooperating with the renowned terrorist leader was a bridge too far as it risked contributing to a scenario of nuclear Armageddon that could cause mass destruction and loss of life in his own country.

Although A.Q. Khan avoided engaging al-Qaeda on nuclear issues, earlier revelations about a group of former Pakistani military officials and nuclear scientists who met with Osama bin Laden around the time of 9/11 remind us of the continuing threat of the intersection of terrorism and nuclear weapons in Pakistan. On October 23, 2001, acting on an American request, Pakistani authorities detained Bashiruddin Mahmood and Abdul Majeed, two retired Pakistan Atomic Energy Commission (PAEC) officials. They had been involved in relief work in Afghanistan since their retirement from the PAEC in 1999 through a non-governmental organization (NGO) they established called Ummah Tameer-e-Nau (UTN). In November 2001, the coalition forces found documents in Afghanistan relating to the UTN's interest in biological weapons. This prompted Pakistani security forces to arrest seven members of the UTN's board, most of whom were retired Pakistani Army officials and nuclear scientists.

George Tenet speculates in his memoirs that UTN's contacts with the Taliban and al-Qaeda may have been supported by some elements within the Pakistani military and intelligence establishment. Tenet says Pakistani interrogations of the seven board members were initially insufficient. He further notes that despite CIA warnings to Pakistani officials about UTN's activities before 9/11, it was only when President Bush dispatched him to Pakistan in November 2001 following revelations of a meeting between Bin laden, al-Zawahiri, and UTN leaders that Musharraf took serious action.

## Outcome of Khan Investigations

Similar foot-dragging by the Pakistani authorities was evident in the case of the A.Q. Khan proliferation network. U.S. officials had repeatedly raised their concern about A.Q. Khan's activities with President Musharraf, but it was not until Washington provided indisputable proof of its knowledge of Khan's activities and threatened to go public with the information in late 2003 that Musharraf took direct action to halt Khan's activities.

Even after details emerged on the tremendous damage done by the A.Q. Khan proliferation network, there was no formal prosecution of the Pakistani associates of Khan, and Khan himself is merely under house arrest.

President Musharraf claims he cannot formally prosecute Khan or allow him to be questioned by U.S. or international authorities because of the hero status Khan enjoys for contributing to the development of Pakistan's nuclear weapons program.

## U.S. POLICY RECOMMENDATIONS

There are steps the U.S. can pursue to help ensure nuclear weapons do not fall into the wrong hands in Pakistan and to prevent a dangerous nuclear arms race between Pakistan and India. Washington has already begun to pursue such initiatives but will need to increase its attention and resources on expanding and strengthening such measures.

### *Leveraging, not Conditioning, U.S. Assistance*

Based on the negative consequences brought by the U.S. cut-off of assistance to Pakistan in 1990, it is unlikely that a narrow policy of cutting or even conditioning assistance to Pakistan through U.S. legislation now would help meet the above goals. The 1990 aid suspension cost the U.S. valuable leverage with Islamabad, damaged military-to-military relationships, and stoked strong anti-U.S. sentiment that still exists in the country.

Efforts to publicly condition assistance to Pakistan could actually weaken Musharraf's hand in convincing his military commanders that the U.S. is a reliable partner. President Musharraf already contends with public opposition to his support for U.S. counterterrorism goals in the region, and conditioning aid through legislation would awaken memories of 1990 and weaken Pakistani public support for pursuing relations with the U.S.

Instead of conditioning aid on specific actions by Islamabad, Washington should target its assistance programs more effectively to accomplish specific goals.

On the nuclear issue, the U.S. should seek to implement programs that help improve safety and security at nuclear facilities. Press reports indicate that the U.S. may already be cooperating with the Pakistanis on this front, but given Pakistani sensitivities on the issue of maintaining sovereign control of its nuclear assets, such cooperation will remain largely out of the public eye.

Perhaps over time, as the U.S-Pakistan partnership solidifies, it will be possible to develop a Nunn-Lugar Cooperative Threat Reduction (CTR) program with Pakistan similar to what the U.S. has established with Russia. Potential areas for cooperation with

Pakistan include nuclear reactor safety, safeguarding nuclear material, rapid response to nuclear-related emergencies, and expanded export control cooperation. The Pakistan parliament adopted export control legislation in September 2004 for nuclear and biological weapons and their delivery systems.

Tailoring a CTR program of assistance for Pakistan would be challenging since Pakistan is not a signatory to the Nonproliferation Treaty. The U.S. is prohibited both by legal and treaty obligations from assisting the nuclear programs of states outside the nonproliferation regime.

Another obstacle is the basic premise of the Nunn-Lugar legislation that requires recipients of CTR assistance to make "substantial investment of its resources for dismantling or destroying such weapons." It would be impossible to develop a CTR program with Pakistan along these lines without addressing the fact that Indo-Pakistani rivalry is what drives Pakistan's nuclear program.

### *Encourage India-Pakistan Nuclear Confidence Building*

India and Pakistanhave made significant strides in their dialogue over the last three years, including the maintenance of a ceasefire along the Line of Control that divides Kashmir since November 2003; the opening of rail and bus links across their borders; and increased people-to-people exchanges.

Efforts to build confidence on nuclear-related issues have been slow, however. Addressing the Indo-Pakistani nuclear issue also relies, to some extent, on perceived progress in resolving the Kashmir dispute as well as the status of China's nuclear programs.

Talks over the vexed Kashmir issue were expected to make progress this year, following President Musharraf's announcement of forward-leaning proposals to resolve the dispute last December. However, the judicial crisis in Pakistan sparked by the Government's March 9 dismissal of the country's chief justice and ensuing street demonstrations have sidetracked the Musharraf government and raised concern in New Delhi about negotiating with Islamabad during the political uncertainty.

## CONCLUSION

Preventing Pakistan's nuclear weapons and technology from falling into the hands of terrorists should be a top priority for the U.S. Revelations about the devastating impact of the A.Q. Khan proliferation network and nuclear black market will prevent Washington from considering a civil nuclear cooperation agreement with Pakistan similar to that being pursued with India. U.S. policy toward Pakistan's nuclear program should instead focus specifically on nuclear safety and security cooperation and encouraging India-Pakistan dialogue that will improve Pakistan's regional security perceptions.

Washington needs to maintain a robust partnership with Islamabad based on mutual trust and understanding. U.S. policymakers should refrain from compartmentalizing our myriad interests in Pakistan but instead integrate the various components of U.S. policy toward Pakistan. In other words, pursuing nuclear safety and security and nonproliferation in Pakistan should not be viewed as "competing" with other U.S. goals such as denying Taliban and al-Qaeda safe haven on Pakistani territory; shutting down madrassahs that feed terrorist groups; encouraging peace talks with India; as well as pressing for steps toward democracy. These goals are interrelated and mutually reinforcing and will eventually encourage the country toward a stable and moderate path.

# 3

# Pakistan's Nuclear Posture

Pakistan is considered to have as many as 50 nuclear weapons and enough highly enriched uranium (HEU) stock for 50 more, including the additional capacity to produce five to ten bombs a year. According to a more recent estimate, Pakistan is said to possess 55-90 weapons of highly enriched uranium and 20-60 plutonium bombs. No definitive information at official levels is available on such speculative assessments. The possible delivery systems for weapons are aircraft and missiles.

Pakistan President Pervez Musharraf has gone on record to say that the weapons are in a "disassembled state." Few other terms have also been used to project the deployment status of Pakistan's nuclear weapons such as "operationally deployed" or "in the component form." While the term component form has not been spelt out, it seems that "the situation in Pakistan may be murky and may in fact best be described as partial deployment."

Replying to the question of an interviewer, "Can you say, are the nuclear weapons ready to go as they are, or are they, as I have heard, in different parts, have to be assembled first?" Musharraf said: "Yes, you are right. They are not mated (inaudible). And there is geographical-they are geographically apart. They cannot be-they are not ready to be fired. So really, it's not the concept that NATO has been having (inaudible) United States system, where your finger has to be on a button and then finally can be pushed. That's not the condition there." As far as the doctrinal aspect is concerned, Pakistan has not announced any comprehensive doctrine document. However, two basic elements that emerge from statements by the country's leaders are: "a rejection of the NFU policy, and the role of nuclear weapons as minimum credible deterrent."

Realising the gap between the military strength in conventional terms, there is a view prevalent in Pakistan that an NFU posture of Pakistan could provide India the leverage of conventional attack. In the backdrop of such military planning, by asking for a 'no-aggression-pact' Pakistan seems to preclude even an Indian reprisal for its misadventures like the one in Kargil in 1999 and support to cross-border terrorism against India. Also, another factor of security complications for India vis-à-vis Pakistan is that "country's chief patrons, principally the US and China, are bound to try and [set] right the inherent imbalance in power by assisting it in ways inimical to Indian interests."

The implication for Pakistan being designated a 'major non-NATO ally' of the United States is being seen in India as more American military assistance to Pakistan. Pakistan's Ambassador to United Nations has argued: "We have to rely on our own means to deter Indian aggression. Wehave that means and we will not neutralize it by any doctrine of no first use." Pakistan's doctrinal declaratory policy is kept deliberately ambiguous. And, in terms of ability to ensure survival, Pakistan wants to have sufficient number and types of assets to create 'reasonable doubt'.

Relevant to the current discussion is the bottom line for use of nuclear weapons by Pakistan. This has been spelt out by Gen. Khalid Kidwai, Head of Strategic Planning Division (SPD) under the National Command Authority (NCA), to a delegation of Italian Scientists.

Toquote him: "Nuclear weapons are aimed solely at India. In case that deterrence fails, they will be used if India attacks Pakistan and conquers a large part of its territory (space threshold); India destroys a large part either of its land or air force (military threshold); India proceeds to the economic strangling of Pakistan (economic strangling); or India pushes Pakistan into political destabilization or creates a large scale internal subversion in Pakistan (domestic destabilization)."

In other words, without defining any limits Pakistan intends to use its nuclear weapons to counter even a primarily conventional conflict situation if it feels threatened with military, political or economic defeat.

However, there is a feeling in Pakistan that a nuclear response cannot be involved to deal with local contingencies and the nuclear threshold should be maintained at a high level.

Aformer foreign minister of Pakistan has opined that the destruction of even a single city would be an unacceptable risk for another country that contemplates a pre-emptive strike.

In an interview to CNN on June 1, 2002, Pakistani President Pervez Musharraf tried to allay the growing international fear of any nuclear war in the subcontinent by saying that, "I would even go to the extent of saying one shouldn't even be discussing these (nuclear war) things, because any sane individual cannot even think of going into this unconventional war, whatever the pressure."

A few months earlier, while chairing the meeting of the NCAin October 2001, Pervez Musharraf reaffirmed the Pakistani strategic assets as the cornerstone of country's national security and that there will be no compromise on the nuclear programme.

The statement had come in the light of increasing international concern about improving security and installing new safeguards on Pakistan's nuclear weapons after 9/11.

Musharraf assured the world that the country's strategic capability was fully safeguarded. Such assertions need further examination, especially when Pakistan is considered as a potential source for terrorists to get access to technology and materials.

A. Q. Khan's televised confessional statement in February 2004 of being involved in international nuclear black-marketing drew unprecedented media attention. However, "A.Q. Khan got off lightly, sending disturbing messages about US and Pakistani attitudes toward proliferation."

And, "the most troubling question of all remains how and to what extent Pakistan's free-market approach to proliferation has allowed terrorist groups like Al Qaida to acquire nuclear materials and technology."

## PAKISTAN'S OBJECTIVES IN CENTRAL ASIA

Pakistan's objectives in Central Asia are determined by its political and security imperatives; its economic and commercial gains; countering India's influence and its desire to be an energy transit-corridor in South Asia and the Asia-Pacific region. Pakistan has always desired to expand its influence in Afghanistan and beyond. Central Asia is seen as an area of natural expansion for Pakistan. Hafeez Malik believes that Central Asia presents Pakistan with a new security environment "...freed from the nutcracker squeeze the Soviet Union had created through an alliance between Afghanistan and India."

Related to Pakistan's ambition to expand its influence is the desire to be the leader of the Islamic bloc. Albeit this idea has not crystallised, but it has always dominated the thinking of the Pakistani leadership, including Prime Minister Bhutto in the 1970s and Gen. Zia in the 1980s. The debate still remains pertinent to Pakistan's geo-strategic formulations. The Islamic groups and parties viewed Central Asia as paving the way for an Islamic bloc thus providing an opportunity to unite Muslims in the CARs, Iran, Turkey, Pakistan and Afghanistan. It was felt that such a strategic bloc would acquire a central role in securing strategic interests vis-a-vis India or even the Christian-Jewish threat. The emergence of the CARs were perceived as an opportunity to form a large regional grouping stretching from the Arabian Sea in the south to the Black Sea in the west based on the common religious identity of Islam. Importantly, it was seen to offer a huge political and economic benefit to Pakistan. In fact, Central Asia does provide Pakistan with numerous opportunities in terms of trade in raw material and manufactured goods, contracting for regular power supply and opening up communications. The resource rich Central Asia is seen as a future source of energy for Pakistan.

## PAKISTAN'S STRATEGIES

### *Geo-Political*

After the emergence of the CARs, Pakistan moved actively into Central Asia, but policy makers were clearly divided as to what Pakistan would gain out of Central Asia. While some wanted an Islamic revolution in Central Asia, others wanted open trade links through Afghanistan. The dichotomy of views revealed the limits of Pakistan's Central Asia Policy. Moreover, during this period, the Central Asian leaders were extremely wary of Pakistan because of its involvement in the Afghan war and its support to the mujahideen. During the Pakistan-backed Taliban era in Afghanistan, bilateral relations between Pakistan and the Central Asian states touched rock bottom.

After Pakistan joined the global war against terrorism as a frontline state, bilateral relations began to be revisited. During the past few years, frequent visits by Central Asian and Pakistani officials to each other's states reflect the changing nature of their bilateral relations. A number of agreements have been signed covering such areas as trade and tourism, cultural and economic cooperation during these visits. Pakistan has developed institutionalised arrangements for this purpose. Joint Economic Commissions (JECs) have been established with all the Central Asian states. Under a Special Technical Assistance Programme (STAP) initiated in 1992-93, Pakistan provides training facilities, which are fully funded by Islamabad. The programme includes courses ranging from English language, banking and accountancy to diplomacy.

In this context President General Pervez Musharraf's visit to Uzbekistan and Kyrgyzstan in March 2005 was significant. Earlier, the two-day official visit of President Nursultan Nazarbayev of Kazakhstan in December 2003 to Islamabad was a step towards strengthening bilateral ties between the two countries. During this visit, both the leaders decided to hold annual foreign ministerial consultations. While speaking at the Pakistan-Kazakhstan Business Forum, President Nazarbayev identified three zones of technological parks of information and biotechnology where Pakistani companies could invest significantly.

It is important to note that during the Tajik Foreign Minister's visit to Islamabad in January 2004, he assured President Musharraf that Tajikistan would not allow Indian military bases on its soil. This was followed by the visit of Tajik President Emomali

Rahmanov to Islamabad in May 2004. During this visit, eight agreements were inked covering abolition of visas for holders of diplomatic passports, avoidance of double taxation, cooperation between the education ministers and justice ministers, combating drug trafficking, and cooperation between official news agencies and promotion and protection of investment.

Pakistan-Uzbekistan relations have also been improving over the past few years given the changed security paradigm. During Uzbek President Karimov's recent visit to Islamabad in May 2006, both sides agreed to expand trade and economic ties and coordinate anti-terrorism activities. It was also planned to extend road and rail links that would enable the CARs, particularly Uzbekistan, to make use of Pakistan's seaports to develop commerce with other regions. A joint fight against extremism and terrorism has, of late, been on top of the list for both the countries. During his March 2005 visit President Musharraf assured the Uzbek leader of his determination to wipe out terrorists, including a substantial number of Uzbek nationals, from the tribal areas. How far these promises will be fulfilled is yet to be seen.

In an attempt to build strong ties with Central Asia, Pakistan has sought to use its cultural links with this region. It is perceived that Pakistan is the cultural extension of the Central Asian region that in turn is seen to be in fusion with the South Asian social milieu. In this context, a Pakistani scholar opined, "Pakistan's political existence and emergence on the world map would not have materialised but for the primordial relationship that glues us together. The roots of our faith, undoubtedly, lie in the Arabian soil but our cultural linkages are with Central Asian civilisation, which in itself is an amalgam of diverse influence and cross-cultural fertilisation"

Cooperation in the fields of education and culture is an important aspect of Pakistan-Central Asia relations. There are number of Central Asian students studying in Pakistan and similarly Pakistani students in the CARs. The lack of information makes it difficult to provide the total number of Pakistani students studying in all CARs. However, the example of Kyrgyzstan can be cited. Kyrgyz students have been pursuing studies in Pakistani educational institutions in various fields such as engineering, business administration, information technology and the English language. Kyrgyz civil servants also attend training programmes in Pakistan. Conversely, over 350 Pakistani students are currently pursuing studies, mainly in medical colleges, in Kyrgyzstan.

## Quest for "Strategic Depth"

The emergence of Central Asia was viewed as an opportunity for Pakistan to spread its sphere of influence beyond Afghanistan thus providing "strategic depth" against India. As mentioned earlier, Pakistan's desire to expand its influence in Afghanistan has been very central to Islamabad's strategic thinking. In the view of Gen. Mirza Aslam Beg, "...Afghanistan will be a great source of strength to Pakistan to face any crisis and danger that it may encounter. In fact, the security of Pakistan, Iran and Afghanistan is interlinked and is indivisible..."

While examining Pakistan's Afghan policy, it has been argued that its defence planning has been handicapped by the lack of territorial depth to absorb an attack by India and then to retaliate. This elusive quest for strategic depth has guided Pakistan in its ambitious involvement in Afghanistan in spite of the multiple implications for its social fabric and political culture. Thus, Pakistan's Afghan policy was constructed with an objective to create a subservient government in Afghanistan that would be friendly to Pakistan, militarily too weak to question the Durand line and unstable to raise the Pushtunistan issue. In addition to this, the military strategists argued that a friendly Afghanistan would give Kashmiri militants a base from where they could be trained, funded and armed. The Central Asian region was seen as an extension of Pakistan's strategic space.

The end of the Taliban regime in Afghanistan has not brought any fundamental change in Pakistan's Afghan policy. Afghanistan is still very central to Pakistan's strategic thinking, and is akin to being Pakistan's backwaters. Wary about how the current situation would unfold in Afghanistan, Islamabad is trying to cement its ties with the current regime in Kabul while supporting Taliban elements and has not given up its grand strategy of establishing a friendly government in Kabul. It is believed that Pakistan's new proxy war in Afghanistan is slowly unravelling itself. There is the resurgence of Taliban in Afghanistan. The Taliban are supported by the Pakistani establishment itself – from low-level military officers and some ministers to religious parties and their jihadi infrastructure. The ISI too has been proactively working to bring the Taliban back to its life. There has been constant accusation by Afghanistan of Pakistan's interference and its support to the Taliban and Al Qaida elements to create trouble for Kabul. Afghan President Hamid Karzai during his visit in February 2006 provided evidence to President Musharraf implicating Pakistan in the recruitment, training and equipping of Islamic radical suicide bombers. The senior Afghan official who accompanied President Karzai said, "In places like Karachi, Pakistani extremist groups working on behalf of the Taliban for a fee, carry out the recruitment and then bring them to safe houses in Balochistan for training and equipping with vests." In a recent visit to Islamabad, Gen. Johan Abizaid, the head of the US Central Command reportedly showed the Pakistanis, intelligence photographs of Taliban training camps at an undisclosed location and asked for them to be shut down.

Three years ago, Dr. Timothy D. Hoyt, Associate Professor of Strategy and policy at the US Naval War College, in a hearing before the House Committee on International relations in October 2003 accused Pakistan of providing sanctuary to terrorist groups, that enjoy strong support among active and retired Army officers and intelligence officials. He said: "So long as Pakistan relies on terrorism to achieve its political objectives, it will be impossible to eliminate terrorism and the Al Qaeda presence in the region."

## *Islam as a Tool*

Religion is seen as an important factor in developing relations between Pakistan and the Central Asian states. It is felt that since the majority of the Muslim people living in most of the CARs were Sunnis, they would naturally gravitate towards Pakistan. Sardar Assef Ali, Minister of State for Economic Affairs, who led the Pakistani delegation to Central Asia in December 1991 said: "They (Central Asians) have problems with Iran. Besides bitter legacies of the past, a majority of people living in Central Asia are Turks. Also 95 per cent of them are Sunni Muslim of Naqashbandi order. So they are uneasy with Iran because of these factors". Leaders of the Jamaat-e-Islami expressed similar views. In a press statement on September 2, 1991, Jamaate-Islami Chief Senator Qazi Hussain Ahmed stated: "Independence of the three Muslim states of the Soviet Union–Azerbaijan, Uzbekistan and Kyrgyzstan–is the realisation of the dream of the Muslim Ummah at a critical juncture of history". He also said that the CARs were "looking up to Pakistan as their ideal owing to its ideological foundations. Besides, due to its role in Jehad-e-Afghanistan, these states also regard Pakistan as their benefactor and have pinned many hopes on it."

The Jamaat-e-Islami supported the Tajik fundamentalists in 1992 and 1993. According to Gen Liaskhovskii, one attempt to intervene in the civil war in Tajikistan was undertaken at the end of January 1993. In Peshawar, a conference of representatives of Muslim countries reviewed the measures to provide assistance to "Tajik brothers" in the "holy war" and resolved to place, at the head of the Tajik armed units, Afghans who had acquired combat experience in the war against the Soviet army. In addition, substantial material funds were allocated for Tajik Islamists. Pakistan supplied assistance to 60,000-80,000 Tajik refugees stranded in northern Afghanistan. When Tajik opposition leader Himatzadeh visited Pakistan in 1993, not only were his associates given access to the Foreign Office but also his criticism of the Tajik government was ignored. Meanwhile, the ex-Director General of the ISI, General Hameed Gul, even issued a statement in favour of the Tajik opposition.

The Uzbek government has referred to the activities of the Jamaat-e-Islami as a part of the grand Islamic alliance against the Tajik government and its support to the Islamic Movement of Uzbekistan (IMU) at various intervals. It is believed that the ISI's discreet support to IMU has remained fairly consistent. It also reportedly gave refuge to IMU leader Yuldeshev in 1990s and arranged Namangani's frequent clandestine visits to Pakistan. It is also believed that unlike the Taliban, ISI does not trust the IMU but at the same time it wants to keep the IMU on its payroll for tactical reasons. It wishes to use the IMU as leverage within Central Asia. The post-Taliban period has not seen any major reversal in Pakistan's support to these jihadi elements. As mentioned earlier, there are still strong elements within the Pakistani establishment wanting to install a weak and friendly government in Afghanistan. Such a government will also provide Islamabad easy access and influence in the CARs.

After 9/11, Pakistan followed a dual policy towards the Central Asian states. On the one hand, it adhered to a state policy of friendly relations with the CARs but on the other, it continued to back dissident groups to get more leverage over the régimes. In March 2004, Uzbek President Islam Karimov asked Pakistan to extradite a number of Al Qaida fighters of Uzbek origin captured during operations in Wana.

In addition to ISI's support, one also sees the involvement of other non-state actors such as extremist Islamic parties; Al Qaida; the truck and transport smuggling mafias; and drug traffickers who have close links with IMU and Taliban. This has resulted in an explosion of self-interest groups in Pakistan who have benefited from the Afghan civil war and the Islamic insurgency in the CARs. Therefore, these groups are interested in weakening the state authority, which in turn enables their business interests and Islamic agenda to flourish.

Pakistan's desire to use Islam as a tool to win over these states however received a major setback because of its support to extremist groups in the Tajik civil war. After this, a wave of extremist activities engulfed the region especially Tajikistan, Uzbekistan and Kyrgyzstan and these states began to view Pakistan with great suspicion.

Therefore, the much desired goal of the Pakistani policy makers to have a security belt stretching from Turkey to Pakistan with Central Asia as the 'Islamic heartland', providing it "strategic depth" and much-needed allies, in its policy struggle over Afghanistan and Kashmir, did not materialise. On the contrary, the secular Central Asian regimes looked towards Russia, China and the West for their security cooperation rather than Pakistan. The CARs signed the Commonwealth of Independent States (CIS)

Security Treaty in May 1992 and in 1996 joined Shanghai Five Forum, which later became the Shanghai Cooperation Organisation (SCO) in 2001. They also joined NATO's partnership of peace programme.

### Regional Organisations

Apart from using its Islamic card to tie the CARs in its strategic fold against India, Islamabad also sought to use multilateral bodies in the region. Its desire to balance India through regional organisations got manifested in their wooing neighbouring Iran, Turkey, Afghanistan, and the CARs into the Economic Co-operation Organisation (ECO). Under this forum, states are expected to develop closer economic interaction.

In November 1992, Pakistan, Iran, Turkey, Afghanistan and the five former Soviet republics of Kazakhstan, Azerbaijan, Kyrgyzstan, Turkmenistan, and Uzbekistan created an extended Muslim economic bloc linking Asia and Europe. Former Prime Minister Nawaz Sharif noted in a speech marking the occasion that the ECO "now corresponds to the boundaries of the ancient area, which brought prosperity and civilisation through fruitful exchanges along the historic silk route. The people of these lands have a shared history and common spiritual and cultural values." Nawaz Sharif added his belief that extensive investment in infrastructure and encouragement of the private sector were the most important immediate objectives. He noted that Pakistan was building a major highway network to link Central Asia to the Arabian Sea and that its railroads were "poised to link not only member-states but also ECO with Europe, Russia, and South Asia." He added: "peace in Afghanistan is essential for political harmony and fruitful cooperation in our entire region."

Speaking about the achievements of ECO, Pakistani foreign minister Khursheed Mahmood Kasuri stated that it had made considerable progress in the trade, transport and energy sectors. The second ECO Commerce Ministers' Meeting held in Islamabad in July 2003 approved the ECO Trade Agreement (ECOTA). The agreement envisages reduction of tariffs up to 15 per cent over a period of eight years (15 years in case of Afghanistan) on at least

80 per cent of goods on tariff lines. Para-tariff and non-tariff barriers would be eliminated within a period of two years. He further stated that the implementation of ECOTA would pave the way for economic integration of the region. New strategies and plans are expected to be adopted to make the organisation more effective.

Despite claims made by Pakistan's ministers about ECO's progress, it has so far been a non-starter. The establishment of a free trade zone is difficult when basic infrastructure necessary in this regard is lacking. Moreover, the competing interests of Iran, Pakistan and Turkey limit the role ECO can play in the region. Instability in Afghanistan remains a major obstruction for expanding the area of cooperation.

Islamabad also sponsored the membership of the newly independent Central Asian countries in the Organisation of Islamic Countries (OIC). This was yet another drive to bring the CARs into the Ummah. Pakistan has also been keen to join the SCO. In early 2001, Pakistan applied for observer status but the Central Asian members of the organisation blocked its entry. A major stumbling block was Pakistan's support for the Taliban government in Afghanistan. Though China supported Pakistan's membership, Russia wanted India to simultaneously join SCO. It was only in June 2005 that the applications of Pakistan, Iran and India were simultaneously considered and approved with consensus for granting observer status in the SCO at the Council of Heads of States Meeting in Astana on July 5, 2005. Pakistan is also a member of Conference on Interaction and Confidence-Building Measures in Asia (CICA). Much to the chagrin of Pakistan, India is included in both these organisations.

### Geo-Economic

Transport Corridors and Access to Warm Waters: Many Pakistani leaders refer to their country as the gateway to Central Asia and strongly believe that good relations with the region would not only enhance its security but also provide enormous economic opportunities. In the post-Cold War period, Islamabad tried to revive its fortunes with the West by selling its new geo-strategic importance. This brings us to the question, is Pakistan the gateway to Central Asia? Geographically, Pakistan provides a gateway to Central Asia from south/southeast; but it is not the only gateway to the seas of the south. This is the impression that Pakistani leaders have tried to create in an attempt to identify themselves with Central Asia, further their co-operation with the region and make Pakistan more relevant not only to the CARs and its neighbouring states but also to the West. In fact, Iran provides another gateway to Central Asia and has done a great deal to develop good communication systems with the region. Yet another gateway is via Turkey in the southwest.

Pakistan has been trying to make itself more relevant to Central Asia by offering the states several proposals for creating trade and transport corridors and access to ports. President General Pervez Musharraf has emphasised this time and again. He said, "...our geo-strategic significance can't be reduced. We need to realise that we have understood that and therefore we have constructed a new port at Gwadar which is at the mouth of the Gulf almost." In March 2005, he stated again: "we are fully focused on making use of our central location and constructing ports and putting in place a network of infrastructure." Recently, he has approved a railways reconstruction programme, which would link Gwadar with the other countries via rail. It is believed that this could make Pakistan the economic and trade hub for the CARs, Gulf, Western China and South Asia.

Pakistan's geo-strategic location admittedly makes it difficult for Central Asia to ignore it. For Turkmenistan and southern Uzbekistan, the shortest route to the sea lies through Iran, but for all other states, the shortest route is through Afghanistan and Pakistan. Karachi is the nearest port city for Central Asia and by air Islamabad is closer to Tashkent than it is to Karachi. Dushanbe is only an hour's flight from Islamabad, and by road through Afghanistan the distance from Dushanbe to Karachi is 2,720 km. In contrast, the port of Bandar Abbas is 3,400 km, Vladivostok 9,500 km and Rostov on the Don 4,200 km away. This makes Pakistan important for the CARs. Despite little success so far, Pakistan is trying to improve its connectivity to the CARs through Afghanistan and China.

The ADB has offered $2 billion to the Pakistan railway network, which will enable Pakistan to become one of the most attractive international trade routes to the CARs, Iran and China. Pakistan and Afghanistan have already agreed to lay a 103-km railway track between Chaman and Kandahar, which would be extended to Turkmenistan and other CARs. The feasibility study of the Quetta-Kandahar railway track has been completed and Pakistan would construct the 10-12 km railway track to the Afghan border. The track from the Afghan border to Kandahar would be the responsibility of the Afghan government. The World Bank has agreed to provide $1.8 billion to Pakistan for its $6 billion National Trade Corridor (NTC) improvement programme to meet domestic transportation requirements and provide transit facilities to Central Asia, Western China, Afghanistan and Iran.

Pakistan has also proposed to construct a $90-million road through the Boroghil Pass in the Yarkhun valley to link it with the CARs. Of the 13 passes, which lead to Afghanistan from Chitral district, the Boroghil Pass is the easiest and lowest in altitude. This pass remains closed for a very short period late in winter. The road will extend to Wakhan, 13-65 km wide strategic strip in northeast Afghanistan. The area links Afghanistan with Pakistan in the south, Tajikistan in the north and China in the east. The Wakhan-Boroghil route has been preferred against the one passing through the central parts of Afghanistan due to the security situation. This road will connect the 12,484-foot-high Boroghil pass at the northwest of the Yarkhum valley in Chitral with Sarhad-i-Langar in Wakhan at a distance of about 95 km and move on to Iskashim in Tajikistan leading to the Tajik capital Dushanbe via the Korung-Kalai Chumb and Kulob areas. From the Boroghil Pass, the road will traverse over 300 km long valley and reach Peshawar. The distance from Tajikistan to Peshawar via the Wakhan-Chitral route is estimated to be 700 km. This road will also branch off to the northern areas via the 10,500-foot-high Shandur Pass and merge into the Karakoram Highway. The Pakistan government has already sanctioned a number of road projects to interlink the northern areas and Chitral. The quadrilateral agreement signed by Pakistan, China, Kyrgyzstan, and Kazakhstan is expected to give a boost to trading activities among member-nations through the Karakoram

Highway. On October 10, 2006 a road connection along the Karakorum route, Islamabad-Kashgar-Bishkek-Almaty, was opened by Pakistan. Pakistan has also offered use of the Gwadar deep-sea port to the CARs. This port would serve as a mother port at the strategic location opposite to the Strait of Hormuz and at the mouth of the Persian Gulf. The first phase of this project is already over. The completion of the Gwadar Port would be a milestone for Pakistan in this context. When it comes online alongside Karachi, it will provide the shortest access to the Arabian Sea for large parts of Central Asia. On December 31, 2005, a meeting of Pakistan-Uzbekistan Joint Ministerial Commission was held in Tashkent, where the two sides agreed to enter into a trilateral transit trade agreement with Afghanistan to benefit from land routes and the Gwadar port facility.

During Kyrgyz President Askar Akaev's two-day visit to Pakistan on January 17-18, 2005, it was agreed that Pakistan would import electricity from Kyrgyzstan and both countries would build roads to improve trade. It was decided to strengthen links through Kashgar in China and on to Bishkek and also through the Karakoram Highway. The road being constructed on the Karakoram Highway to link the two countries completed by 2006, promoting Pak-Kyrgzy trade. Establishment of a railway link from Gwadar to Taftan in Iran via Saindak is also being planned. A road from Gwadar to Sandak, running parallel to the Iran-Pakistan border, will make it the shortest route to reach Central Asia from the warm waters of the Arabian Sea. Another 515-km long highway connecting Gwadar via Pangur, Khaan, Chaghi and Rabat up to the heart of Western Afghanistan is being planned. This would link Pakistan by road directly with the CARs.

Pakistan is also giving priority to road and rail links and related facilities for more effective and mutually beneficial access to Central Asia. Air services to Tashkent and Almaty have already been resumed. Similar services to other parts of the region are under active consideration. The laying of railway tracks from Turkmenistan to Pakistan via Afghanistan is an important part of this programme. Pakistan's Ministry of Railways has completed a feasibility study for a Chaman-Kandahar rail project.

The quadrilateral agreement is also gradually being implemented. The completion of the Murghab-Kulma road from Tajikistan to China linking the Karakoram Highway to Pakistan is also a significant development. Once operational, it will boost transit trade between Pakistan and Central Asia.

Energy and Pipeline Politics: Pakistan is also looking at the huge energy resources of Central Asia. It wants to make Pakistan the energy-transit corridor in South Asia and the Asia-Pacific region, which will bring huge economic gains for the country. Pakistan is most likely to face a energy crisis in natural gas, power and oil in the next 3-4 that could choke its economic growth for many years to come. It is estimated that Pakistan's total energy requirement would increase by about 48 per cent to 80 million tonnes of oil equivalent (MTOE) in 2010 from about 54 MTOE currently.

According to official energy demand forecast, the demand for natural gas, having about 50 per cent share in the country's energy consumption would increase by 44 per cent to the 39 MTOE currently. The power shortage is expected to be little over 5,250 MW by 2010. Oil demand would also increase by over 23 per cent to about 21 million tonnes in 2010 from the current demand of 16.8 million tonnes. Therefore, Central Asia could be a future source of energy for Pakistan.

Pakistan's importance for Central Asian countries needs to be viewed in the context of the entire pipeline politics in the region. As a transit country, Pakistan provides these states with an outlet of their energy resources. In view of the instability in Afghanistan and Balochistan, the success of these pipelines from Central Asia however remains a big question mark. Despite these uncertainties Pakistan wants to keep the Central Asian states engaged with the hope of providing a transit route for their energy resources. In pursuit of its strategy to control the pipelines and gain greater influence, it is trying to sign various agreements with these Republics. Pakistan has signed 21 agreements and MoUs in oil, gas, energy, trade, science and culture with Turkmenistan. In the energy sector, Turkmenistan, Afghanistan and Pakistan (TAP) signed an agreement in December 2002 for a gas pipeline from

Turkmenistan via Afghanistan to Pakistan, whose estimated cost is $2.5 billion. The ADB is the lead coordinating partner. It has, in addition to financial and technical assistance, played an important role in integrating efforts to realise the project. Several sessions of the Steering Committee on the TAP Gas Pipeline Project have been held so far. During a ministerial level TAP meeting on February 16, 2006, in Ashkabad, Turkmenistan agreed to provide sovereign guarantees to Pakistan to supply 3.2 billion cubic feet gas per day for 30 years. This assurance was restated during Pakistan Foreign Minister Khursheed Kasuri's visit to Turkmenistan in May 2006. However, a major hurdle to the project remains the volatile situation in Afghanistan.

While Turkmenistan can provide gas to Pakistan, Tajikistan and Kyrgyzstan have the potential to be substantial producers of hydroelectric power. Being geographically closest to Tajikistan, Pakistan stands to benefit from its hydroelectric potential. An inter-governmental agreement to that effect has already been signed. Pakistan's Water and Power Minister Liaquat Ali Jatoi has recently said, "the government is considering importing electricity from CARs via Afghanistan as an option to meet its demand and has signed an MoU with Tajikstan to import 1000 MW as well as initiated transmission routing assessment to bring such power to Pakistan." An advisor to Kyrgyz Prime Minister Omarov said that his government was also considering a transmission line from China to Pakistan with an estimated cost of $1.4 billion. Pakistan has also signed an agreement to import electricity from Kyrgyzstan through Tajikistan and Afghanistan. Indubitably, terrain and weather conditions are clear impediments to this project, yet both states appear determined to pursue it.

## *Trade*

With the emergence of the newly independent Central Asian States, the business elite group in Pakistan viewed this region as offering immense economic opportunities. Central Asia was seen not only as a source of needed raw materials but also as a potential export market. Some estimates even suggested that the region had a potential market of $80 billion and if Pakistan secures even 5 per cent of this market, it could earn up to $4 billion a year. In December

1991, a 23-member delegation was send to Central Asia headed by the then Minister of Commerce Sardar Asif Ahmed Ali. A $30-million credit facility was given to Uzbekistan and $10 million to all other Central Asian Republics. These credit lines were not utilised by the Central Asian countries and Pakistan was unable to keep its commitment to provide the credit lines in future. The effort to open a fullfledged National Bank of Pakistan (NBP) met with complete failure. The NBP representative office was set up in 1995 in Tashkent but it could not facilitate the opening of a branch till 2002.

Despite high hopes, the trade between Pakistan and Central Asia remains limited. During 1992-93 Pakistani exports to the region amounted to $5.6 m and imports were $0.51 m. The figures for 1993-1995 indicate an increase as compared to 1992-93. During 1997-98 Pakistan's total trade with Kazakhstan accounted for $19.9 m.; for Kyrgyzstan 07.91m; Tajikistan $10.29m; Turkmenistan $07.75m; and Uzbekistan $35.34m. However, in subsequent years the trade figures do not indicate any major increase.

Pakistan's recent initiatives in Central Asia involve strengthening economic ties with the CARs. As mentioned earlier, Pakistan has established JECs with all the CARs. In its trade policy for 2006-07, Pakistan seeked to focus on export growth in regional Muslim countries, particularly Iran, Afghanistan and the CARs. It has been decided to establish export centres and warehouses at Peshawar and Quetta and an export centre in Islamabad. In this context the visit of Kyrgyzstan President Askar Akaev on January 17, 2005 is of significance. Both countries signed a MoU on cooperation between the foreign ministries of the two countries on different regional and international issues. Two agreements were signed on cooperation and mutual assistance in customs related matters and avoidance of double taxation. President Akaev also offered to provide electricity to Pakistan. This was his third visit, earlier ones being in 1994 and 1995. Kyrgyzstan and Pakistan are signatories to the Quadrilateral Agreement along with China and Kazakhstan, effective since May 2004, which aims at promoting regional trade through Pakistan's Karakoram Highway. During the first meeting of the Pakistan-Kyrgyz Joint Ministerial

Commission (JMC) in Islamabad, both sides negotiated on issues of taxation, culture, and visa restrictions for enhancing the volume of bilateral ties. Pakistan is also exploring the possibility of investing in the pharmaceutical sector in Turkmenistan.

As mentioned earlier the ECO provides another common platform to generate economic activity in the region. Within the framework of the ECO the volume of trade has not increased significantly. In fact, the ECO has failed to bring about great economic or commercial results. Competition among the member-states has been the major limitation for the success of this organisation. As Pakistan's Prime Minister Shaukat Aziz recently emphasised, the organisation needs to be used for making result-oriented policies instead of offering mere lip service. ECO can be an effective organisation if the ECO Trade Agreement, Transit Transport Agreement and the Trade and Development Bank become operational. So far, Pakistan has not been able to achieve much in terms of building economic and trade ties with the CARs. Their efforts to set up banks and hotels have received severe setbacks in Central Asia.

## NUCLEAR THREAT REDUCTION IN INDIA AND PAKISTAN

The Carnegie Endowment for International Peace (CEIP) published a draft report, 'Universal Compliance: A Strategy for Nuclear Security', in June 2004. The report proposes a strategic blueprint for US leadership to rethink international nuclear nonproliferation and global nuclear security. In this report, the recommended measures for nuclear risk reduction between India and Pakistan include:

- o Establishment of national risk reduction centres in both countries to administer agreed upon confidence-building measures.
- o Acommitment not to develop, produce, and use 'tactical' nuclear weapons.
- o Agreement not to flight-test missiles in the direction of the other country.
- o Agreement to flight-test missiles only from designated test ranges.

- o Provision of advance notification of the movement of missiles for training purposes.

The Henry L. Stimson Centre's report, 'Reducing Nuclear Dangers in South Asia', argues that: "The stability-instability paradox that was formulated in the West to characterise the dangers of nuclear deterrence is alive and well in South Asia. This paradox holds that, while offsetting nuclear capabilities might indeed prevent a full-blown conventional or nuclear war, the presence of these fearsome weapons could also encourage the use of violence at lower levels in the expectation that escalation would be contained by a mutual desire to avoid the nuclear threshold." And that, "Kashmir has been inflamed since the advent of covert nuclear capabilities on the subcontinent, and tensions have grown even more pronounced with the demonstration of overt nuclear capabilities in 1998. The region is now experiencing crises with greater frequency and severity."

The deliberations during two workshops, November 14-18, 2002, and May 20-23, 2003, with participants from the US, India and Pakistan, convened by the Stimson Centre to discuss escalation control and scenarios that could lead to crossing of the nuclear threshold. It provides the following 'doable' steps in the near term:

- o Establishment of national risk reduction centresto serve as focal points for the administration of confidence-building measures.
- o Missile-related measures to formalise and properly implement the agreement concerning prior notification of missile launches; to formalise and extend the time-line for such notifications; to forego missile flight tests in the direction of the other country; to flight test missiles only from designated test ranges; and to provide advance notification of the movement of missiles for training purposes.
- o Clarifying terminology or developing common terminology on nuclear-related programmes, deployment, and doctrine could reduce misunderstanding and increase crisis stability.

- o Leadership declarations affirming responsible nuclear stewardshipcould help defuse nuclear dangers and facilitate an improvement in bilateral relations.
- o Increased awareness of nuclear dangers, particularly with regard to the possible acquisition of nuclear materials by terrorist groups, would be advisable.

In the Stimson Centre's report, the proposals collected in the workshops on escalation control are grouped in five categories: improving bilateral relations; nuclear risk reduction and strategic restraint; safety and security measures; and, improving intelligence through communication.

Both the reports, by CEIP and the Stimson Centre, have this presumption that 'deterrence' may not work between India and Pakistan as similar to the Cold War experience. Such assumptions are not completely invalid for the two countries did resort to nuclear rhetoric during the 1999 Kargil conflict and indulged in 'nuclear signalling' during the period of crisis in 2001-2. In addition, the absence of a doctrine without no-first-use policy and repeated calls from the Pakistani side to lower the threshold could have a certain bearing on the thinking of Western analysts. Already, the strategic debate had reached a slightly higher level than was normally prevalent in the subcontinent when the Indian Army Chief stated that a limited war with Pakistan is possible.

For any future war in the subcontinent, the two most likely scenarios discussed in the Cooperative Monitoring Centre Occasional Paper of Sandia National Laboratories, are: a breakdown along the common border in Kashmir, and failure of nuclear policy. The authors propose an alternative approach through which India and Pakistan can begin to cooperate in managing their common border to prevent a breakdown. The ultimate concern in the report about the existence of nuclear weapons is the possibility of their use in a time of conflict. The following are the enumerations in the Cooperative Monitoring Centre Occasional Paper that focuses on the monitoring of nuclear safety, security, and stability:

- o The ability to assess the current operational and deployment status of nuclear weapons is perhaps the most critical factor in near-term crisis prevention.

- o Developing measures to prevent escalation.
- o National decisions to include both technical and procedural mechanisms to restrict use of weapons and delivery systems will permit more time to attempt diplomatic solutions to conflict before initiating weapons use.
- o Another element of nuclear stability is determining the readiness of launch systems. There may be a number of indicators associated with launcher alert status. These include: Flight parameters loaded, other software updates (if appropriate); Vehicle fuelled (missile or aircraft); Crews readied; Delivery vehicle in launch location (moved to launch point); Transporter system in ready position (e.g., transporter erector launcher [TEL] in raised launch position); Weapon armed. While most of these indicators of launch preparation are difficult to monitor, some, such as missile fuelling and launcher movements, might be monitored through electronic sensors.
- o There is the possibility of use through miscalculation or misinterpretation.
- o Sharing information on any of the concerns for safety, security or accident will require an infrastructure of capabilities and procedures. These include methods for providing timely, reliable, secure, accurate, and authenticated communications.
- o Ensuring safety of nuclear weapons and materials will primarily be a state responsibility because of the highly classified nature of most safety issues. These issues involve detailed design, as well as material and handling details. An expanded mission for hotlines between the Directors-General of Military Operations and between the Heads of State might be established to address this critical issue.

Acknowledging the fact that only the Indian and Pakistani governments can decide whether and on what basis, to establish new risk reduction measures, the 'Working Group Report of the Centre for Strategic and International Studies (CSIS)' recommends the following steps for nuclear risk reduction:

- o A new communications mechanism-nuclear risk reduction centres (NRRCs) in India and Pakistan-should be established to complement existing bilateral channels.
- o The main functions of the NRRCs would be to provide each party a dedicated, secure means of: (a) notifying the other side about activities or events on its territory that might be wrongly perceived or misinterpreted that could lead to conflict, (b) sharing information that the two countries are obliged to exchange under existing security agreements, and (c) seeking and receiving clarifications about ambiguous events on the other' sterritory. Other functions could include the conduct of joint exercises of certain NRRC notification procedures, technical back-up during crises, and support for consultations on the implementation of existing confidence-building measures (CBMs).
- o Adequate infrastructure already exists in South Asia to support a wide range of secure communication options, including data, voice, video, or a combination of these.

  The approximate cost for a dedicated cable permitting teletype and voice communication would be US$10,000-50,000 annually. For a dedicated satellite channel permitting teletype, voice, and video, the annual cost would be roughly US$560,000.
- o The centres would operate on a continuous, round-thè-clock basis. Written messages using agreed formats would be the norm, although voice and video capability would also be desirable. It would be the prerogative of each government to decide where it would institutionally house its NRRC and to determine how its NRRC would relate to other government organisations. The Indian and Pakistani solutions to these questions need not be symmetrical.

The Working Group Report concluded, that "the circumstances in South Asia today are very different from the circumstances surrounding the current US-Russian relationship and the relationship that existed when the US-Soviet Centres were brought into being. To tailor a new communications mechanism to the needs of South Asia, the mechanism could appropriately take on a wider range of functions than the US and Russian Centres."

Rodney W.Jones assumes that there lies intense political conflict over Kashmir and that the escalation in South Asia has the potential of becoming a nuclear war. In one of the papers presented during the fourth nuclear stability roundtable during March 12-13, 2002, in Washington on 'Military Asymmetry and Instability in Emerging Nuclear States: India and Pakistan,' he suggests the following conditions of nuclear stability in the region:

- o High nuclear threshold (strong conventional defence)
- o Secure second strike capabilities (robust C4I)
- o Rough parity in size and defence space
- o Neither falling behind the other's first strike edge (good early warning?) Supposing that "nuclear deterrence might provide the security that allows a general improvement in security relations" in South Asia, the UNIDR (United Nations Institute for Disarmament Research) research paper depicts various aspects of nuclear confidence-building measures between India and Pakistan. Commenting on the current conflict situation between the two countries, the authors of the paper subscribe to developing CBMs in connection with the 'central issue-Kashmir'. An interim suggestion is made to work on the possibilities of addressing the 'central sore-cross-border terror raids' from Pakistan.

With regard to nuclear CBMs, according to the UNIDR paper, India and Pakistan should share the development of respective nuclear doctrines and security concepts to have clarity over 'red lines'; develop mechanisms on notification of ballistic and cruise missile tests; create nuclear risk reduction centres with robust safety systems to deal with the issues of accidental or unauthorised use; and install a secure and dedicated line of communication including safe command and control systems between the national authorities (the nature or constitution of national authority remains undefined). The paper categorically puts the 'Kashmir issue' to be discussed as in the final stages of CBMs between the two countries.

The UNIDR study concludes that the two countries should seize the ripe moment (that has begun since the two countries agreed to peace talks during the sidelines of the SAARC summit in January 2004) in the context of possibility of conflict.

"Any future terrorist incident might provoke India into punitive action, which in the worst case might lead to uncontrolled or accidental responses, all the way to a nuclear exchange.

This suggests that, although the nuclear aspects will have to be part of the general discussions on security, it might also be worth considering whether they can be made separable, in case the moment passes too quickly."

The aspect of geographical proximity of the two countries is also discussed in one of the reports dealing with nuclear threat reduction measures. Based on some hypothetical South Asian launch point-target combinations, the missile travel time between India and Pakistan is estimated between 8 to 13 minutes.

Taking account of the danger of false alarms and miscalculations, the Pugwash Discussion Paper of 2002 suggests that a posture of De-alert (most basic measures would be to keep the weapons de-mated from delivery systems; use of locking devices), and installation of best available safety measures into the weapons, like use of Insensitive High Explosive (IHE) and fire-resistant pits would significantly reduce the risk of inadvertent or unauthorised use of weapons.

From the above discussed strategic policy recommendations, there emerge two sets of proposals that could draw attention of the diplomats and strategic planners of India and Pakistan. In the first set, one can identify mechanisms for escalation control and nuclear force management within each state. The second set includes possible measures of nuclear CBMs by the two countries to work towards long lasting stability in the region.

## *Issues Related to Escalation Control and Nuclear Force Management*

- o Leadership declarations affirming responsible nuclear stewardship (avoidance of shrill rhetoric).

- o Developing strategies to avoid escalation of conventional confrontation to nuclear exchange level.
- o Avoiding sensitive targets in the event of a conventional war.
- o Raising the level of nuclear threshold (strong conventional defences).
- o Securing second strike capabilities.
- o Review of decision-making to develop, produce, and use 'tactical' nuclear weapons.
- o Regular assessment of each other's current operational and deployment status of nuclear weapons (missile fuelling and launcher movements might be monitored through electronic sensors).
- o Determining the readiness of launch systems.
- o Improvements in intelligence to avoid miscalculation or misinterpretation.
- o Acquisition of technology to help provide prompt and accurate information concerning missile launches and nuclear detonations.
- o Advancement in respective command and control mechanisms including establishment of effective early warning systems.
- o Refraining from giving pre-delegation of authority to use nuclear weapons.
- o Effective physical safety of nuclear materials and installations.
- o Ensuring safety and security of nuclear weapons and materials.

### *Steps Required for Nuclear CBMs*

- o Improving bilateral relationship.
- o Sharing knowledge of decision-making processes.
- o Agreement on advance notification of missile testing and movements.
- o Flight test missiles only from designated test ranges.

- o Provision of advance notification of the movement of missiles for training purposes.
- o Review of policy decisions related to tactical nuclear weapons (including development, production, or use).
- o Establishment of multi-layered, reliable, secure, accurate, and authenticated communication mechanisms.
- o Establishment of Nuclear Risk Reduction Centres (NRRCs).

Most of the above-mentioned studies on South Asia suggest that problems related to Kashmir may be the spark to trigger a nuclear exchange between India and Pakistan. Linking of the Kashmir issue with Indo-Pak nuclear strategy is quite complex. In fact, such an assumption indirectly endorses (and is born out of) Pakistan's nuclear blackmailing. In reality, it is the Pakistani military that has crossed the Line of Control (LoC) in the past to provoke Indian defence. Pakistan does not adhere to no-first-use (NFU) and keeps making frequent calls to lower the nuclear threshold in the apprehension of India taking reprisal measures to stop Pakistan-sponsored terrorism in Indian territory.

Pakistan insists on Kashmir being the 'core' issue of stability/ instability between India and Pakistan. India maintains that the scourge of 'terrorism' in South Asia has adverse implications for both regional and international security. In between the two exclusive views, remains a pertinent question unanswered-who is to guarantee that if the issues related to Kashmir remains resolved, towards which India has already been making significant efforts, Pakistan's military-ISI sponsored terrorist activities in other parts of India would end? In such a complex security environment, bilateral confidence-building measures alone would keep the escalation under manageable limits.

## NUCLEAR WEAPONS ARE NOT FOR WARFIGHTING

In the 1950s, the US made extensive efforts to develop, produce and deploy, tactical nuclear weapons in the European and the Pacific theatres. By the mid-1960s, approximately 7,000 warheads had been deployed in Europe and an undisclosed number in the Pacific. The Soviet and Warsaw Pact forces soon followed suit and are known to have deployed about 3,500 of these weapons.8

However, unlike the surfeit of intellectual debate and discussion on the strategic nuclear issue, tactical nuclear weapons generated only limited interest. Explicit doctrinal criteria for tactical nuclear forces were not formulated. Employment policies were initially hazy and for long training to fight in a nuclear environment was almost completely neglected.

Even the US Department of Defence, on whose insistence NATO's flexible response strategy centred around the first use of nuclear weapons despite the misgivings of some allies, by and large had a decided aversion to using tactical nuclear weapons and an ambivalent and muddled policy embracing their role. William R. Van Cleave and S. T. Cohen write that the 1977-78 doctrinal manual The Army in the Field stated:

"Unless the enemy uses them first, nuclear weapons will not be authorised before conventional defences have been severely tested and found inadequate. The situation facing corps at the time nuclear weapons are requested must therefore be grave – under sustained attack by superior forces, own forces becoming fully committed and not likely to hold, reinforcements not available, insufficient combat support and combat service support available to sustain the defence, and the survivability of the force in question."

Proponents of tactical nuclear weapons justified their requirement on the following grounds:

- They deter the use of tactical nuclear weapons by the enemy.
- They provide flexible response over the whole range of possible military threats.
- They offer nuclear military options below the strategic level.
- They help to defeat large-scale conventional attacks.
- And, they serve the political purpose of demonstrating to the European allies the US' commitment.

Throughout the 1970s and 1980s, the NATO allies of the US were never happy with the manner in which tactical nuclear weapons were stored in a limited number of storage sites where these were highly vulnerable to a pre-emptive attack and destruction. Exacerbating the problem were the vintage, lack of technological sophistication and, consequently, the questionable effectiveness of most of the warheads and some of the delivery systems. The only new warhead to be introduced into service was the so-called 'clean' enhanced radiation 'neutron' bomb, but its production was slow and not enough numbers reached the NATO theatre. Opponents of tactical nuclear weapons asserted that such 'more usable' weapons would lower the nuclear threshold and make nuclear war more likely. Before the INF treaty came into force in 1988, the Honest John rocket was over 30 years old, the Sergeant missile had mostly been retired and the F-4 aircraft which carried the bulk of NATO's tactical atomic bombs during the 1960s and 1970s was designed in the late 1950s. Fears of collateral damage in the extensively populated and developed NATO heartland also spurred European opposition to tactical nuclear weapons. Many European political and military leaders convincingly argued that NATO would be better off without tactical nuclear weapons. Alain Enthoven wrote: "Tactical nuclear weapons cannot defend Western Europe; they can only destroy it there is no such thing as tactical nuclear war in the sense of sustained purposive military operations"

In the US too there was a lack of unanimity about the usefulness of tactical nuclear weapons and lack of coherence in policy. The 1975 US Department of Defence annual report left considerable doubt about the possibility of the use of tactical nuclear weapons: "...as a practical matter, the initiation of a nuclear engagement would involve many uncertainties. Acceptable boundaries on such a conflict would be very difficult to establish. A nuclear engagement in the theatre could produce much higher military and civilian casualties and more widespread collateral damage than its non-nuclear counterpart:

"What is more, it is not clear under what conditions the United States and its allies would possess a comparative military advantage in a tactical nuclear exchange.

"...We must recognise in our planning that the decision to initiate the use of nuclear weapons—however small, clean, and precisely used they might be—would be the most agonising that could face any national leader."

While the West was debating the merits and demerits of tactical nuclear weapons, Soviet military doctrine was predicated on the selective use of nuclear weapons in consonance with well-defined political and military objectives. The Soviets emphasised the increased effectiveness of nuclear weapons for warfighting purposes and it was their expectation that large-scale military conflicts, such as a NATO-Warsaw pact confrontation, would involve the use of nuclear weapons. Marshal Grechko wrote:12

"The art of conducting military operations with the use of nuclear weapons and that of employing conventional forces have many fundamental differences. But they are not in opposition, are not mutually exclusive, and are not isolated one from the other; on the contrary, they are closely correlated and are developing as a single body "Nuclear missiles will be the decisive means of armed combat. Along with this, conventional weapons will also find use, and under certain conditions, the units and subunits can conduct actions solely with conventional means."

The use of tactical nuclear weapons can be a rational option only if it does not finally lead to irrational, more destructive levels of warfare. Gradually, but inexorably, it dawned on the military planners on both the sides of the Iron Curtain that the first use of tactical nuclear weapons was bound to lead to uncontrollable larger nuclear exchanges. After protracted negotiations, the Intermediate-range Nuclear Forces (INF) Treaty between the US and the Soviet Union, was signed in Washington on December 8, 1987 by President Reagan and General Secretary Gorbachev. The treaty proposed the elimination of all INF missiles and practically outlawed the use of tactical and theatre nuclear weapons in Europe.13 Since then, all tactical nuclear weapons have been removed from Europe. It is now universally accepted that nuclear weapons are political weapons and are no longer weapons of 'warfighting'. By extension, 'tactical' or battlefield nuclear weapons should now have no role to play in combat.

## *Tactical Targets and Yields*

Strategic nuclear targets are either counter-value or counter-force targets. Counter-value targets include major enemy cities and industrial centres and these are the ones that generate the 'terror' of the 'balance of terror' through the threat of causing millions of civilian casualties. Counter-force targets primarily comprise the nuclear assets of the adversary including delivery means, bases, nuclear warheads and missile storage sites, command and control elements and early warning and targeting infrastructure. While the aim of selecting counter-value targets has generally been to maximise deterrence, counter-force targets aim to degrade the enemy's capability to make optimum use of his nuclear forces. Military planning for the use of nuclear weapons, in the eventuality that deterrence fails, includes a judicious mix of both counter-value and counter-force targets in first use as well as retaliatory strikes.

Tactical or battlefield nuclear targets are normally those that are either located within the tactical battle area (TBA) or have a direct bearing on it. Besides the enemy's forces, tactical targets include his military infrastructure such as important bridges and choke points on the transportation systems, airbases and communications centres. Tactical military nuclear targets would include the following:

- Locations of headquarters and adjacent communications centres.
- Bridgeheads established by a 'break-in' force on a defensive obstacle system to facilitate a 'break out'.
- Leading 'combat groups' forming the spearheads of an 'operational manoeuvre group' (OMG) or an Indian or Pakistani Strike Corps.
- Defence fortifications and nodal/strong points, to facilitate a breakthrough.
- Mechanised forces—deployed for defence, assaulting, laying off in harbour or being transported to the TBA.
- Surface-to-surface missiles (SSMs) and rocket artillery positions.
- Self-propelled and towed medium artillery regimental gun areas.
- Logistics support areas (LSAs).

Some or all of the above mentioned targets may be close to areas having civilian population. As such, the aim would always be to minimise 'collateral' damage. This can be achieved by firing a low air burst nuclear weapon which, by definition, is designed to ensure that the fireball does not touch the ground surface and, hence, produces extremely little fallout. Troops on foot can normally transit through the 'ground zero' of a low air burst within 30 minutes to one hour of the explosion and troops in armoured fighting vehicles can do so almost immediately. On the other hand, ground burst nuclear explosions with fractional kiloton yields that are necessary to accurately hit point targets such as an individual missile launcher, would produce a fairly large amount of fallout and are best avoided altogether. Such targets should be attacked by 'smart' munitions fired from artillery weapons or by air force aircraft or attack helicopters.

Yields of 10 to 20 kilotons would be adequate to destroy all types of tactical nuclear targets. These yields can be delivered by SSMs like Prithvi-150 and Prithvi-250 or by nuclear bombs dropped by fighter-bomber aircraft. Multi-barrel rocket launchers (MBRLs) such as Smerch and perhaps Pinaka and 155 mm medium artillery gun/howitzers (atomic artillery) are capable of firing fractional kiloton yield nuclear warheads. Atomic Demolition Munitions (ADMs) that have the potential to deny ground to an aggressor, are also part of the family of tactical nuclear weapons. Such weapon systems are normally part of the army's battlefield inventory, as is the case in the United States (US) and the Russian armies. Indian proponents of the use of tactical nuclear weapons argue that these should form part of India's armoury, to be used when necessary. What needs to be critically analysed is whether it is the effect that is relevant or the means of delivery. Today, the distinction between strategic and tactical nuclear weapons has been blurred. General Sundarji had the following view:

" in the case of a super power one could say—yes, the five megaton warhead sitting on top of the intercontinental ballistic missile is a strategic weapon, distinct and separate; even if the strategic yields have shrunk to kilotons because of dramatically greater accuracies, and no longer require megaton monsters, these are still distinctly strategic; it is the fractional kiloton artillery shell which is a tactical weapon. But in the case of the third world countries, this distinction has little relevance as of today."

During the Pokhran II nuclear tests in May 1998, Indian scientists conclusively demonstrated the capability to design fractional kiloton weapons. The three smaller, 'experimental' devices had yields of 0.2, 0.3 and 0.5 kilotons, as reported in the May 1998 issue of the Bhabha Atomic Research Centre (BARC) Newsletter.15 Although a number of Western scientists expressed scepticism about the results claimed by India's nuclear establishment, they were not able to provide reliable data to prove their counter claims of lower yields. Hence, the capabilities declared by Indian scientists must be accepted. It follows that India is in a position to develop tactical nuclear weapons of fractional-kiloton yields although their manufacture and subsequent maintenance is extremely complex. This research and development capability must be nurtured and built upon so that the option to develop and produce tactical nuclear weapons if necessary can be kept open through laboratory testing, should India decide to become a party to the Comprehensive Test Ban Treaty (CTBT). While it may not be in the national interest to develop, produce and stockpile tactical nuclear weapons at this juncture, the capability to do so is a strategic capability and must be sustained.

## WEAPONS DEVELOPMENT AND THE NATIONAL DEFENCE ECONOMY

It is common knowledge that modern warfare is not only the competition of weapons on the battlefield but is also, at the same time, an all-out competition of the total strength of the opposing side's politics, economics, military, and science and technology. During the development of weaponry, the four aspects of politics, economics, military and science and technology are completely brought into play. In today's climate of rapid development of national defence science and technology and the daily emergence of new weapons, the material base of the actual national defence economy should be not only strong but also exceptional.

- With the upgrade in the tactical and technical performances of weapons, manufacturing costs would correspondingly be also more expensive. Since the end of WWII, science and technology development has flourished. There has been a multitude of achievements in science and technology that have continuously increased weapon precision, its powers to cause casualties, and its military effectiveness. The explosive power of a small atomic bomb has the same effectiveness as 100 bombers from WWII. The fire power of today's tank is tenfold greater than that of WWII. A mission to destroy 60 percent of the equipment of a tank division would today require only 1 percent of the aircraft used 40 years ago. During the Falklands War between England and Argentina, the EXOCET missile, which cost only $200,000, fired by the Argentinean Air Force was able to sink a British SHEPHARD missile destroyer that costs $200 million. The ratio of the two costs effectiveness is 1:1,000. The precision of precision-guided bombs and artillery shells is 2 to 3 times better than that of non-guided bombs and artillery shells. However, the upgrading of weapons performance has also brought with it the consequence of more expensive manufacturing costs. The cost of scientific research and technical components compared to the cost of a system with microcomputer technology, new materials, and new techniques imported in great quantities would appear to be prominently greater. Each of the U.S.'s HELLFIRE antitank missile costs about $28,100 to buy, but the scientific research to produce it costs $310 million. Each of the LEOPARD-II tanks of the Federal Republic of Germany costs $3.58 million to buy, yet the scientific research cost was $360 million. The research cost of Japan's MODEL 61 tanks cost •500 million to research and develop in the 1950s, its MODEL 74 tanks cost •2.5 billion to develop in the 1960s, and the MODEL 88 tanks that currently are under research and development have a budgeted cost that could reach •25 billion. The research and development expenditures of three generations of tanks seem to have increased geometrically. According to statistics, the costs of fighters and tanks increase about tenfold every 20 years and the costs of aircraft carriers increase by tenfold every 30 years. Weapons development has come to rely more and more on the national defence economy, causing great burdens for many countries.

- The increase in weapon power has also created battlefield situations where the consumption of battlefield material and economic losses are immense. It requires a huge quantity of material reserves. The 4th Middle East War lasted only 18 days and both sides, Egypt and Israel, suffered economic losses of over $5 billion. The loss of aircraft by both sides was comparable to the combined loss in aircraft in a year by all of the participant countries during WWII. In the first 3 days after the war started, the total number of tactical missiles launched by both sides was equivalent to the combined total of all the reserves of the countries in NATO. The loss of tanks was equal to one-third the number of those in the possession of NATO countries at that time. Both sides strategic reserves and materials were exhausted a week into the war. We can infer the amount of economic loss that could be created by modern warfare from this. In the Falklands War, the English spent a total of $2.16 billion, about $1.2 million every hour. This kind of consumption, to fight one mid-size modern war, is difficult for even an economically great power to support.

The research and production of weapons, ammunition, technical facilities and engineering equipment all consume large amounts of metal and various kinds of nonferrous metals. They also need the support of the chemical industry and energy resources, as well as military industrial products. According to the statistics from affiliated departments at the United Nations, 15 to 16 percent of the world's copper output and 10 percent of it tin, nickel, lead, and zinc outputs are used for weapons production and toward the building of other national defence installations. The consumption of energy resources is even greater. During WWI, the consumption of fuel by each soldier for each day averaged about 6 kg. During WWII, it was increased to 20 kg for each person each day. In the several local area wars fought in recent years, the fuel consumption of each man each day increased to 90 kg. The consumption level is shocking! This not only raises problems for logistics support, it also increases the economic and energy resources burden.

- The rapid increase and shorter intervals in the updating and replacement of weaponry have sharply increased military expenditures and expenses. The advancements of science and technology have caused new weapons to emerge in an endless stream and greatly accelerated replacement and updating of weaponry. Before and after WWI, the time period for a weapons system to go from research and design, through trial tests and production to its deployment within the service required about 20 to 30 years. At present, this procedure requires only 10 to 15 years or an even shorter period. According to the analysis of a Soviet economist, Maj. Gen. Guluofu, a new weapons system for the Soviet military from research to its deployment in the services requires 10-15 years. Since the 1960s, Soviet missiles have already been updated three generations. The majority of its aircraft, submarines, and surface ships underwent updating long ago. Its anti-air defence missiles, radar, command equipment, communications equipment, and other equipment have also been through several generations of updating. The research of new weapons and the updating of existing weapons have greatly increased the military expenditures and expenses of every country. According to an analysis by western observers, "The world economy is already shouldering a burden of massive destructive weapons, poverty, and debt. Militarization will further sap its strength." Since the 1960s, the global expenditure for weapons has been about $14 trillion. In 1985 it was about $800 billion, in 1986 about $900 billion. Every second of every year about $1.7 million are spent. Immense military expenditures have become serious economic problems for each of the world's countries.

- The research and production of modern weapons have made even greater demands on the national defence economy and national defence industries. Since WWII, especially during the 1960s and 1970s, the unceasing discovery of new technology has led to a great revolution in weapons and military-use equipment.

In 1945, the atomic bomb appeared. The research of computers for weapons use came in 1946. In 1952, the first transistorized computer was developed. In 1953, the world's first hydrogen bomb was exploded. In 1955, the first nuclear-powered submarine was launched. In August 1957, the first intercontinental ballistic missile was fired, and in October of that same year, the first manmade satellite was orbited. In 1960, mankind recovered its first satellite. In 1961, the world's first manned satellite did an orbit around the earth and returned to the surface. In 1967, the first integrated circuit was successfully developed. In 1969, man had his first landing on the moon. In 1977, the neutron bomb was researched and developed. In April 1981, the world's first spacecraft flew. The research and production of all these new weapons and equipment and a large portion of the new technology that entered into the sphere of the national defence economy not only greatly changed the production and industrial structure of the national defence economy, it also added a series of new production and industrial sectors. These changes helped to restructure the traditional national defence industries, moving them in the direction of technological improvement, and development of a technological reserve. The diffusion of a large quantity of high technology made it possible to turn a consuming national defence economy into a propagating field of national defence economy.

Weapons development is reliant on the development of the national economy. It also encourages the growth of national defence science and technology. Military high-technology also gave impetus to the development of the economy. Looking at this from two-dimensional space, this big "O" cycle could possibly expand further. Analysing it from a three-dimensional space, this kind of spiraling trend is perfectly suited to the objective laws of material development.

## *Weapons and Equipment Development and Military Scientific Theory*

"Technology determines the tactics." The appearance of large quantities of technical equipment inevitably brings about great transformations in military theory and tactics; this in turn leads to great changes in strategic thinking, patterns of combat, combat style, and military structures:

- Weapons development enhances man's strategic consciousness, deepens his strategic reflections, and increases the emphasis on strategic projections. In today's world, strategic research is extremely dynamic. With the development of strategic rockets and various spacecrafts, as well as the gradual development of energy beam weapons, kinetic energy weapons, and other space weapons systems, war has extended from the surface, air, and sea toward outer space. The areas of man's activities have already extended beyond the earth and moved into space. This has opened up man's field of vision and expanded his modes of thinking. In the wideness of space, the earth is no longer "boundless and limitless," but has become one of the "global villages" in the universe. In the eyes of the strategist, the earth has become small and man's strategic reflection is becoming more profound and his strategic consciousness has been greatly enhanced. Man's heart embraces the whole of the universe. The development of strategic research is even more important than at any time in history and has become an especially important issue for all countries globally. What is coming will be conflicts in space. One of the conflicts will be the military struggle for "control of the high ground in space." The other will be exploitation and use of space, the struggle for the resources of space. For this reason, every country in the world is busily formulating and developing strategic plans. In March 1983, the United States became the first to formulate a "Star Wars Plan." This caused global commotion in strategy research. The Soviet Union responded with "defensive measures" to the "Star Wars

Plan." Western Europe came up with the "Eureka Plan." Each of the COMECON countries announced a "Plan for the integrated advancement of science and technology by the year 2000." Japan had its "Policy outline for science and technology;" China had a "Policy for a new technological revolution;" India came out with "Policy statements for new technology;" South Korea had its "Conceptions for long range national growth;" and Yugoslavia had its "National science and technology development strategy." To rank within the world's family of nations, to live and survive in the "global village" in this universe, each nation must come up with ideas for a "grand strategy." "To stand shoulder to shoulder with the giants" one must intensely fix one's eye on the growth of national defence construction and weapons in the next century.

- Modern weapons are not only direct combat strengths between opposing combat opponents, they are also strategic deterrents and tools for international political struggles. The appearance of offensive strategic weapons like missiles, atomic bombs, nuclear-powered submarines, and long-range bombers has caused great changes in military strategy. The research, production, and large stockpiles of strategic weapons are already more than needed to seek out and kill an enemy. It has turned into a tool for political and diplomatic struggle. The large-scale arms race have caused the United States to stockpile over 9,400 nuclear warheads with a total nuclear weight equivalent of over 4 billion tons. The Soviet Union's stockpile of over 8,000 nuclear warheads has a total nuclear weight equivalent of over 5 billion tons. The quantity of nuclear warheads possessed by these two nuclear powers comprises above 97 percent of the global total. Both have the capacity to destroy the other several times over. Living under these conditions, the military strategy of both sides has gone through many changes; strategic ideologies have been revised about every 10 years. However, pressure from the threat that "destroying the enemy doesn't necessarily mean one's own survival" has kept them from crossing the "nuclear threshold" and taking the next step of pressing the button to launch those nuclear missiles. England, France, and China have independently and on their own developed into national nuclear powers. The limited power of these countries is not enough to compete with the capabilities of the United States and the Soviet Union, but they do play a role in the even development of political, economical, and military affairs within the world. This power is entirely a symbol of a country's independence and its existence within the world of politics, economics, military affairs, and science and technology. In addition to nuclear weapons, the emergence of strategic weapons has definitely caused reforms within the military, changing past combat theories that we must go through war and campaigns to achieve strategic objectives to the possibility that strategic weapons could directly attack the opponent's strategic targets and achieve the strategic objectives. The development of various space weapons has not only intensified military struggles in space, it has also increased ways in which strategic objectives could be directly achieved.

- Today's weapons systems are very mobile. They also have long range, high accuracy, and great power, causing the time and spatial aspects as well as the intensity of war to change greatly. The development of these weapons and the great number of these weapons being deployed within the services have caused the arenas of war to be extended into deep sea and space, the length of war to shorten, and the suddenness, destructiveness, savageness, and mutation to increase unprecedentedly. In the "blitzkrieg" of the German armoured troops during WWII, they could advance only about 30 km daily. Today, under normal circumstances, the Soviets could do 50 km and under nuclear conditions it could reach above 100 km. When the Soviet Union invaded Afghanistan, its push towards Kabul, a distance of 900 km took only 6 days. The time it takes for an

> intercontinental ballistic missile to travel its whole distance is only slightly more than 30 minutes and there is no more than 20 minutes of early warning for its defence.

During the Falklands War, England's SHEFFIELD class missile destroyer did not even have the opportunity to react before it was hit by Argentina's EXOCET missile. With this short span of time, it is very difficult to react. This has made even greater demands on command and control. The largeness of the battlefield and the number of troops involved have given rise to immense increases in technical weaponry and specialized technology and have caused even greater problems in the coordination of operations and commands. According to reports, there were only 20 different military specialties during Word War I. It grew to 160 during World War II, and at present, the number of military technologies and specializations exceed 2,000. During combat, the army, navy, air force, and the other different service branches are all involved at the same time. The types of weapons used are never less than a dozen and usually are in the hundreds. This alone would demand that the commander prepare detailed plans and coordinate his commands well. There must be no mistakes in differentiating missions, allotting time, and coordinating activities. Any small error could lead to major mistakes and even greater disasters.

First strike has always been the combat phase that militarists attach greatest importance to. The success or failure of the first strike impacts the whole battle. In modern combat, because of the short time needed for combat, the phases of combat are no longer clearly delineated. The long range surprise attack or the counterattack during the preliminary period of the combat has become the main combat model for first strike. Thus, every nation has given special attention to studying the first strike phase of a war. The United States emphasizes that "every preparation must be made to win with the first strike." The Soviet Union also believes that "surprise attacks are the most effective combat opening moves to implement in future wars.... Victory can basically be determined in the first phase of a war." This will demand that commanders make complete preparations for first strikes. Intelligence, reconnaissance, personal observations with automatic and rapid analysis, processing and judgment, decisionmaking, formulating careful plans, and even reactions must be quick and accurate because only then could the "first strike win" objective be achieved.

- The extensive use of modern weapons has caused great changes in military structures. Before WWI, the military was basically composed of land forces that included the infantry, artillery, calvary, and navy. Before WWII, there was a great deal of aircraft and tanks in the military, thus the air force, armoured troops and motorized troops came into existence. The air force itself was divided into bomber, fighter, and attack aircraft forces. There were surface vessels, submarines, naval aviation forces and marines in the navy. After WWII, strategic rocket forces, army airborne forces and other service branches were formed. With the development of space technology and the successful development of various spaceflight vehicles as well as the development of various space weapons, the militarization of space will possibly strengthen the military deployment of a new independent military service branch "Space Forces." In 1982, the United States established the Air Force Spaceflight Command (a command comparable to the Strategic Air Force and Tactical Air Force Commands combined), and in 1983, the United States established the Naval Spaceflight Command. In 1985, the two commands and affiliated army commands were combined to form the U.S. Spaceflight Command. Not long after the United States had established the Air Force Spaceflight Command (1982), the Soviet Union appointed Lt. Gen. Sadaluofu as the "Aeronavigation Forces Commander." Some reports have said that "it is possible that the Soviet Union had already established a military spaceflight command like the U.S. Air Force Spaceflight Command and that the aeronavigation force was nothing but a subforce of that command." Various evidence has shown that the growth of the militarization of space has brought about the birth of the "Space Forces." With the advancements made in

> microelectronics, computers, and artificial intelligence technology, multipurpose robots could soon be used more and more in military applications and in those work areas where the labour is heavy and environmentally dangerous; thus a "robot force" would have to be deployed. The influence of weapons development on military administrative systems and deployment and on the overall structure can be easily seen. At present, the strategic course for overall military development is: a reduction in the overall personnel strength, a rise in the proportion of technical military personnel in the overall structure, a decrease in the proportion of personnel directly involved in combat, and a different scale for the increase in the proportion of logistic personnel (including technical support personnel).

The impact of modern weapons on military theory has been profound and extensive. The various sophisticated tools, means and methods of modern policy decision studies, projection studies, and futures studies have scientifically given impetus to and provided directions for military theories and strategic growth. It has allowed the military to grow scientifically so that it can completely anticipate conflicts and play a better leadership role.

# 4

# Pakistan's Nuclear Diplomacy

Although it is a client state of the US and dependent upon it in many critical ways, Pakistan has resolutely rejected US efforts to move it away from nuclear weapons. It is currently under criticism for having blocked talks between 64 countries to limit fissile materials under the Conference on Disarmament (CD) in Geneva. The current posture reflects Pakistani anger at the US-India nuclear deal and the subsequent enhancement in India's capacity to generate fissile materials. It also assumes – perhaps correctly – that the Afghanistan situation makes Pakistan too essential to the US for it to take a hard stance.

Indian and Pakistani diplomacy has reflected the desire within their military-civil establishments to ward off criticism, particularly that which followed periods of high tension. It has been particularly important to project the image of a state that is fully aware and in control of itself.

In fact, nuclear respectability is implicitly and jointly sought by Indian and Pakistan elites, both military and civilian. Their goal is to show that their nukes are in responsible hands, that they can handle nuclear weapons just as well as anyone else, are sternly opposed to proliferation, and they are victims rather than supporters of terrorism. Officials and experts from both countries meet at arms control workshops and seminars, behave civilly (if not cordially) towards each other, and appear to be rational actors. CBMs, nuclear risk reduction measures, etc. have become their standard vocabulary items. The underlying mistrust and hostility is thereby effectively concealed. Indian establishment intellectuals had grasped the value of creating the responsible actors image much before their Pakistani counterparts. The clinching of the US-India nuclear deal in 2007 owes much to this. Indeed, the Indian strategic analyst C. Raja Mohan had observed years earlier that,

*"New Delhi and Islamabad should know that the willingness of the rest of the world to accept them as part of the official nuclear club depends on the ability of India and Pakistan to responsibly manage their own nuclear relationship.....If India and Pakistan want to be taken seriously, they must show results from their nuclear talks."*

Musharaf's predecessor as chief of army staff, General Jehangir Karamat, while he was ambassador of Pakistan to the United States, was also keen to show that Pakistan and India are not trigger-happy,

*"For those who observe South Asia from the outside it is considered a most dangerous place and a region in which a nuclear exchange could be a reality. It is thought that the India-Pakistan confrontations in 1987, 1990 and 2002, as well as the Kargil conflict in 1999, all had a nuclear dimension of some sort. This is not what most South Asians think".*

Nevertheless, Gen. Karamat did admit that during the Kargil crisis, as well as in the crisis that followed the attack by Islamic militants upon the Indian Parliament in December 2001, that statements and signaling through missile tests could have had unintended consequences xlvi.

As argued in the earlier part of this essay, the velvet gloves are rapidly discarded once the going gets rough. The politeness of diplomats, while welcome, merely hides the visceral feelings beneath.

The success of diplomacy speaks for itself. Giving primacy to its geo-political interests, the US fundamentally changed its posture on India: sanctions imposed in 1998 were gradually withdrawn, criticism became inaudible, a grudging acceptance of nuclear status followed, and then – in a dramatic blow to the Nuclear Non-proliferation Treaty – the US ended up making a special deal that now makes it a supplier of nuclear equipment and materials to India. Pakistan, while faring not quite so well and not being privileged by a similar deal, was de-facto accepted as a nuclear power with the safety and security of its nuclear arsenal reduced to the level of a nagging, low-level worry.

## PREDICTING PAKISTAN'S NUCLEAR DIRECTION

Looking at the next 5-10 years, one can make reasonable guesses for where Pakistani nuclear forces are likely to be, and the direction of its nuclear policy.

Unless a global fissile material cutoff is somehow agreed upon and implemented, Pakistani production of fissile materials and bombs, as well as intermediate-range ballistic missiles, will continue at the maximum possible rate permitted by technological and resource limitations. A shift towards smaller plutonium weapons, or composite warheads, will accelerate as the Khushab military reactors come on line.

The increasing number of warheads will demand increasing number of delivery vehicles. In spite of the substantial induction of JF-17 aircraft, as well as newly purchased F-16's, missiles will steadily replace aircraft as delivery vehicles for nuclear weapons.

Flight tests and command post exercises will continue to be periodically conducted. Although Pakistan will make efforts to match India's efforts in using outer space for reconnaissance and early-warning systems, it will not be able to do so.

If India is successful in acquiring and installing an anti-ballistic missile system, MIRVing, or in deploying submarine launched nuclear-tipped missiles, Pakistan will counter by lowering the strike-threshold and wider dispersion of its mobile launchers, as well as employing decoys and moving towards SLBMs.

In the past, Pakistan had securely hitched its nuclear policy to India's. It had assumed that India's nuclearization would be allowed to justify its own.

But the de-hyphenation of Pakistan from India – a word that gained particular currency after the visit to India and Pakistan by President George W. Bush in 2006 – has now forced its nuclear policy to be more than a mirror image of India's. New challenges are now appearing because of the Obama administrations initiatives to reduce nuclear weapons held by the US and Russia. US ratification of CTBT, which was rejected by the Senate in the Bush years, will put pressure on India and Pakistan to sign. Would Pakistan go along? The answer is: probably yes. Unless India resumes nuclear testing, Pakistan will not test further.

It is also certain that the US will go forward with talks on a verifiable Fissile Material Cut-off Treaty [the Bush administration had not supported verification].

Pakistan is already seen as being obstructive. Would Pakistan be ready to negotiate? Sign the FMCT? What about on-site inspections? The future does not look promising in the absence of a move that is widely accepted as genuinely proceeding towards global nuclear disarmament.

## EFFECTS OF PAKISTAN'S ROLE IN THE WAR

### *On the International Stage*

Pakistan's role in war against terrorism significantly improved her international status. Scholars argue that, US would leave Pakistan after gaining her objectives in war against terrorism. After joining the war on terror Pakistan gained billions of dollars of economic and military aid and also made some gains diplomatically but has lost its control over Afghan affairs.

### *Within Pakistan*

After September 11 and US invasion in Afghanistan there has been a dramatic rise in domestic terrorism, extremism and sectarianism in Pakistan. Pakistan is in the grip of regular suicide bombings, and has suffered high levels of civilian and military casualties as a result. Baluchistan and Tribal area issues are other implications for Pakistan, with US drones attacks in tribal areas being a real source of concern for Pakistani citizens. The US so far has carried out number of attacks in Pakistani territory. These attacks have led to deterioration of the security situation in tribal areas and the rest of the North-West Frontier Province. In Pakistan there is a growing resentment among people against these attacks on Pakistani soil.

## Western Involvement in Terrorism Inside Pakistan

On July 8, 2010, Pasha categorically stated that foreign powers are involved in terrorist activities inside Pakistan. He said, ""The foreign powers are involved in terrorism and destabilization of the country." During a briefing in the National Security Committee session headed by Senator Raza Rabbani, DG ISI Ahmed Shuja Pasha said that the western powers are involved in the terror activities inside the country.

"The US policy against terrorism is under consideration and the changes will be brought with time in accordance with the national interest," he said. This is not new claim inside Pakistan, many Pakistani political commentators have been speaking publicly about this phenomenon. It is alleged that terrorist activities inside Pakistan were actively carried out by the CIA, the RAW and the MOSSAD for different purposes. Chief among those, is changing the public perception of the War on Terror in the favour of the United States. There are confirmed reports that to achieve its objectives the CIA hired the services of at least a dozen Afghan warlords inside Afghanistan and provided through them arms and finances to militants in FATA and Swat to carry out murders and devastation in the country. It was like a double-edged sword not only to get the Army launch attacks against Taliban on Pakistani side of the border but also to give a message to the ISI that the CIA can use the Pakistani Taliban against their own security forces. Thousands of people have been killed in Pakistan due to terror attacks since the beginning of war on terror.

## Future Concerns

There is no doubt that a military campaign is necessary against extremists in the country but it must be supported by social, economic and political change with political reforms being at the top of agenda. The future of Pakistan's role in the war against terrorism is dependent on its political and economic ties with the US. Pakistan is a part of global war on terrorism and was not only defending itself, but also protecting the entire world form the catastrophe of terrorism and extremism, therefore, needs strategic partnership with the rest of the world to foster peace and stability in the region, promote economic stability and address energy needs.

## WAR IN NORTH-WEST PAKISTAN

The War in North-West Pakistan is an armed conflict between the Pakistan Armed Forces and armed religious groups such as the Tehrik-i-Taliban Pakistan (TTP), Lashkar-e-Islam, TSNM, Arab and Central Asian militants including Al-Qaeda, regional armed movements and elements of organized crime. The armed conflict began in 2004 when tensions, rooted in the Pakistan Army's search for Al Qaeda fighters in Pakistan's mountainous Waziristan area (in the Federally Administered Tribal Areas), escalated into armed resistance. Pakistan's actions were presented as Pakistan's role in the War on Terror in the international War on Terrorism. Clashes erupted between Pakistani army troops and Arab and Central Asian militia forces. The foreign militants were joined by Pakistani non-military veterans of the War in Afghanistan (2001–present) which subsequently established the Tehrik-i-Taliban Pakistan and other militia organizations such as Lashkar-e-Islam. The Tehreek-e-Nafaz-e-Shariat-e-Mohammadi (TSNM) established in 1992 allied with the Tehrik-i-Taliban Pakistan and Lashkar-e-Islam.

### *Background*

December 2003: Waziri attempts on President Musharraf's life. In December 2003, two assassination attempts against President Pervez Musharraf were traced to Waziristan. The government responded by intensifying military pressure on the area, however the fighting was costly and government forces would sustain heavy casualties throughout 2004 and into early 2005 when the government switched to a tactic of negotiation instead of direct conflict.

### *2004: Fighting Breaks Out*

On March 16, 2004, the bloody mountainous battle between Pakistan Army and the combined Taliban and Al-Qaeda fighters was insued. Both the International and National media speculated that Pakistan Armed Forces had surrounded the *"High Value Target"* in the mountainous region, possibly Al-Qaeda's Second-in-

Command Ayman al-Zawahiri. The battle was concluded as the Army had captured the entire mountainous region, and captured hundreds of Al-Qaeda fighters. However, the Army was failed to captured Ayman al-Zawahiri as he was either later escaped or he was never among the fighters.

## *Peace Deals*

In April 2004, the Government of Pakistan signed the first of three peace agreements with militants in South Waziristan. It was signed with militia commander Nek Muhammad Wazir, but was immediately abrogated once Nek Muhammad was killed by American Hellfire missile in June 2004. The second was signed in February 2005 with Nek's successor Baitullah Mehsud, which brought relative calm in the South Waziristan region. This deal will be later mimicked in the neighboring North Waziristan territory in September 2006 as the third and final truce between the government and the militants. However, all of these truces would not have a substantial effect in reducing bloodshed. The later two deals were officially broken in August 2007 with the Lal Masjid siege, which raised the suicide attacks on Pakistani forces tenfold throughout the country.

## *2005-2006*

On May 4, 2005, Pakistani commandos captured Abu Faraj al-Libbi after a raid outside the town of Mardan, 30 miles northeast of Peshawar. Abu Farraj al-Libbi was a high ranking al-Qaeda official, rumored to be third after Osama bin Laden and Ayman al-Zawahiri. Al-Libbi replaced Khalid Shaikh Mohammed after his arrest in March 2003 in connection with the September 11th attacks. The Pakistani government arrested al-Libbi and held him on charges in relation to being a chief planner in two assassination attempts on the life of President Pervez Musharraf in December 2003.

On January 13, 2006, the U.S. launched an airstrike on the village of Damadola. The attack occurred in the Bajaur tribal area, about 7 km (4.3 mi) from the Afghan border, and killed at least 18 people. The attack again targeted Ayman al-Zawahiri, but later evidence suggests he was not there.

### *June 2006: Ceasefire*

On June 21, 2006, pro-Tehrik-i-Taliban Pakistan militants in the Bannu region of North Waziristan stated they shot down a Bell military helicopter that was reported to have crashed. The government denied missile fire as the cause, stating it was due to technical faults. The helicopter had taken off from a base camp in Bannu at around 7am for Miramshah and crashed 15 minutes later into the Baran Dam in the Mohmandkhel area on Wednesday morning. Four soldiers were killed including Captain Shams (pilot), Captain Faisal (co-pilot), Lance Naik Ikram and sepoy Altaf, while three other, Sardar Ali, Waseem Abbas and Mohammad Arshad, were rescued.

On the same day militants killed an inspector and two constables on a road connecting Bannu and the main town of Miranshah.

On June 21, 2006, Afghan Taliban leader Sirajuddin Haqqani issued a decree that it was not (Afghan) Taliban policy to fight the Pakistan Army. However, the Tehrik-i-Taliban Pakistan intentionally did not circulate the decree in North Waziristan thereby keeping pressure on the government.

### *September 2006: Waziristan Peace Accord Signed*

On September 5, 2006, the Waziristan Accord, an agreement between tribal leaders and the Pakistani government was signed in Miranshah, North Waziristan. to end all fighting. The agreement includes the following provisions:

- The Pakistani Army will help reconstruct infrastructure in tribal areas of North and South Waziristan.
- The Pakistani Military will not tolerate any assistance to intruders in North Waziristan, and will monitor actions in the region.
- The Pakistan government is to compensate tribal leaders for the loss of life and property of innocent tribesmen.
- "Foreigners" (informally understood to be foreign jihadists) are not allowed to use Pakistani territory for any terrorist activity anywhere in the world.

- 2,500 foreigners who were originally held on suspicion of having links to the Taliban were to be detained for necessary action against them.

The agreement, dubbed the Waziristan accord, has been viewed by some political commentators as a success for Pakistan. Further details of the agreement, as well as comments on the agreement made by US, Pakistani, and Taliban spokesmen is available in the Waziristan accord article.

### *October 2006: The Madrassa Air Strike*

On October 30, 2006, the Pakistani army conducted an air strike against a madrassa in the Bajaur region bordering Afghanistan. The madrassa was destroyed killing 70 to 80 people. In retaliation for the attack the militants conducted a suicide bombing on an army camp on November 8, 2006, killing 42 Pakistani soldiers and wounding 20.

### *2007*

In March, Pakistan signed a peace treaty with Faqir Mohammed, the main militant leader in Bajaur. Militant groups now held three districts in the Federally Administered Tribal Areas: South Waziristan, North Waziristan and Bajaur Agency.

### *Waziri-Uzbek Tensions*

Reportedly, the fighting sparked by the killing of Saiful Adil, an al-Qaeda-linked Arab, blamed on the Uzbeks by Maulavi Nazir, described as a top pro-Taliban militant commander in the region. According to the other version, fighting started after Mullah Nazir, whom the government says has come over to its side, ordered the Uzbek followers of Tohir Yo'ldosh, formerly a close confidant of Osama bin Laden, to disarm. It was also preceded by the clashes between the IMU and a pro-government tribal leader in Azam Warsak, in which 17 to 19 people died before a ceasefire was announced.

### *Defeat of the Islamic Movement of Uzbekistan*

Local militants allied to the tribesmen were reported attacking and seizing the IMU's private jail in Azam Warsak. The Pakistan

Army said it did not intend to step in, but witnesses say government artillery fired on the Uzbek bunkers they set up to fight the tribesmen. Heavy fighting resumed on March 29, ending a week-long ceasefire between tribal fighters and foreign militants. According to initial reports, tribesmen attacked a checkpoint manned by Uzbek militants and captured two of them. The clashes also left one tribal fighter dead and three wounded. The following day, a senior Pakistani official announced that 52 people were killed during the past two days, 45 of them Uzbeks and the rest tribesmen.

One of Maulvi Nazir's aides put the death toll at 35 Uzbeks and 10 tribal fighters. However, residents in the area said that the death toll on both sides was inflated. The conflict further escalated on April 2 when a council of elders declared jihad against foreign militants and started to raise an army of tribesmen. According to Pakistani security officials, heavy fighting concentrated in the village of Doza Ghundai left more than 60 people dead, including 50 foreigners, 10 tribal fighters and one Pakistani soldier. He also said that "dozens" of Uzbeks had surrendered to tribal forces and that many bunkers used by militants were seized or destroyed. On April 12, 2007 the army general in charge of South Waziristan said that tribal fighters had cleared the Uzbeks out of the valleys surrounding Wana and the foreign militants had been pushed back into the mountains on the Afghan border. Four days later, the local tribesmen has urged Islamabad to resume control of law and order in the area.

### *Lal Masjid siege*

On July 3, 2007, the militant supporters of Lal Masjid and Pakistani security forces clashed in Islamabad after the students from the mosque attacked a nearby government ministry building with stones. Their resultant faceoff with the military escalated, despite the intervention of then-ruling Pakistan Muslim League (Q) leaders Chaudhry Shujaat Hussain and Muhammad Ijaz-ul-Haq. The Pakistani security forces immediately put up a siege around the mosque complex which lasted until July 11 and resulted in 108 deaths. This represented the main catalyst for the conflict and eventual breakdown of the truce that existed between Pakistan and the Pakistani Taliban groups. Already during the siege there were several attacks in Waziristan in retaliation for the siege.

## Truce in Waziristan Broken

As the siege in Islamabad ensued, several attacks on Pakistani troops in Waziristan were reported. On July 14, 2007, a suicide bomber attacked a Pakistani Army convoy killing 25 soldiers and wounding 54. On July 15, 2007, two suicide bombers attacked another Pakistani Army convoy killing 16 soldiers and 5 civilians and wounding another 47 people. And in a separate incident a fourth suicide bomber attacked a police headquarters killing 28 police officers and recruits and wounding 35 people. The assault on the Red Mosque prompted rebels along the border with Afghanistan to scrap the controversial Waziristan Accord with the government.

## The new war in Waziristan

The Army moved large concentration of troops into Waziristan and engaged in fierce clashes with militants in which at least 100 militants were killed including wanted terrorist and former Guantanamo Bay detainee, Abdullah Mehsud. The militants also struck back by attacking Army convoys, security check points and sending suicide bombers killing dozens of soldiers and police and over 100 civilians. In one month of fighting during the period from July 24 to August 24, 2007, 250 militants and 60 soldiers were killed. On September 2, 2007, just a few dozen militants led by Baitullah Mehsud managed to ambush a 17-vehicle army convoy and captured an estimated 247 soldiers without a shot being fired, an event that shocked the nation. Several officers were among the captured.

After the army returned to Waziristan, they garrisoned the areas and set up check-points, but the militants hit hard. In mid-September the Tehrik-i-Taliban Pakistan and other forces attacked a number of Pakistani army outposts all across North and South Waziristan. This resulted in some of the heaviest fighting of the war. Following the Lal Masjid Siege, On September 12, 2007, the first outpost was attacked and overrun by the militants resulting in the capture of 12 Pakistani soldiers.

The next day on September 13, 2007, a suicide bomber in Tarbela Ghazi attacked a Pakistani army base, destroying the main mess hall and killing 20 members of the Karrar commando group; Pakistan's most elite army unit. A series of attacks ensued and by September 20, 2007 a total of five Pakistani Army military outposts had been overrun and more than 25 soldiers captured. More than 65 soldiers were either killed or captured and almost 100 wounded. A little over two weeks later, the Army responded with helicopter gunships, jet fighters and ground troops. They hit militant positions near the town of Mir Ali. In heavy fighting over four days, 257 people were killed, including 175 militants, 47 soldiers and 35 civilians.

### Battle of Swat Valley

By the end of October fighting erupted in the Swat district of the Khyber Pakhtunkhwa province, with a large Tehreek-e-Nafaz-e-Shariat-e-Mohammadi force, under the command of Maulana Fazlullah, trying to impose Sharia law. Around 3,000 paramilitary soldiers were sent to confront them. After almost a week of heavy fighting the battle came to a standstill with both sides suffering heavy casualties. Then on November 1 and November 3, 220 paramilitary soldiers and policemen surrendered or deserted after a military position on a hill-top and two police stations were overrun.

This left the Tehreek-e-Nafaz-e-Shariat-e-Mohammadi (TNSM) in control of most of the Swat district. The fighting in Swat is the first serious insurgent threat from militia forces in what is known as a settled area of Pakistan. Forces loyal to Maulana Fazlullah, including some foreign fighters, after taking control of a series of small towns and villages, tried to implement strict Islamic law in November 2007. In mid-November the regular army was deployed with the help of helicopter gunships to crush the uprising. The Pakistan Army deployed over 2,500 men. By the beginning of December the fighting had ended and the Army recaptured Swat. Almost 400 of Maulana Fazlullah's fighters were dead along with 15 Pakistani soldiers and 20 civilians in the military offensive. Despite the victory by the Pakistani army, TNSM militants slowly re-entered Swat over the coming months and started engaging security forces in battles that lasted throughout 2008. By early February 2009, the whole district was in Pakistan Army Control.

### The Rawalpindi Attacks

On September 3, two suicide bombers targeted a military intelligence (ISI) bus and a line of cars carrying ISI officers. The bus attack killed a large number of Defence Ministry workers and the other attack killed an Army colonel. In all 31 people, 19 soldiers and 12 civilians, were killed. Over two months later on November 24, one of the targets was a military intelligence bus. Almost everyone on the bus was killed. The other bomber blew up at a military checkpoint. 35 people were killed, almost all military.

### State of Emergency

The 2007 Pakistani state of emergency was declared by Pervez Musharraf on 2007-11-03 and lasted until 2007-12-15. During this time the constitution of the country was suspended. This action and its responses are generally related to the controversies surrounding the re-election of Musharraf during the presidential election that had occurred on 2007-10-06, and also was claimed by the government to be the reaction to the actions by militants in Waziristan.

### Benazir Bhutto's Assassination

On December 27, 2007, Pakistani opposition leader Benazir Bhutto was killed upon leaving a political rally for the Pakistan Peoples Party (PPP) in Rawalpindi, Pakistan. A suicidal assassin reportedly fired shots in Bhutto's direction just prior to detonating an explosive pellet-laden vest, killing approximately 24 people and wounding many more. Musharraf and the army blamed the attack on Al-Qaida, but the following day a statement by Baitullah Mehsud was sent to the media saying that he and Al-Qaida had no involvement in the murder of the former Prime Minister, he briefed that these were the crimes of Musharraf and the army.

The killing was followed by a wave of violence across the country that left 58 people dead, including four police officers. Most of the violence was directed at Musharraf and the pro-Musharraf political party, Pakistan Muslim League (Q). The public chanted slogans against the army and Musharraf: "Musharraf Dog", "General is a murderer", "uniform (army) wearing murderers", etc. Bhutto had previously survived an assassination attempt made on her life during her homecoming which left 139 people dead and hundreds wounded.

### 2008: More fighting in South Waziristan

In January 2008, militants overran Sararogha Fort, and may have overrun a fort in Ladah as well. Both forts are in South Waziristan, and were held by the Pakistani army. On February 25, 2008, a suicide bomber struck in the garrison-town of Rawalpindi killing Pakistani Lt. Gen. Mushtaq Baig along with two more soldiers and five civilians. Baig was the highest-level military official to be assassinated since Pakistan joined the war on terror.

### Operation Zalzala

A full-fledged security operation called 'Zalzala' (*earthquake*) by Pakistan Army's 14th Infantry Division in January to flush out Baitullah Mehsud's Tehrik-i-Taliban Pakistan militants from the area. Until then the area was infested with militants, with some villagers providing them support and shelter. Many militants were killed during the operation, and within three days the security forces were in full control of the area. The army later captured a few other villages and small towns to put the squeeze on Baitullah Mehsud. However, the operation led to a huge displacement of local population. According to 14 Division GOC Maj Gen Tariq Khan, about 200,000 people, including men, women and children, were displaced. Khalid Aziz, former NWFP chief secretary and expert on tribal affairs, said the displacement was "one of the biggest in tribal history" adding that human cost of the conflict in Waziristan "has gone unrecorded."

### Peace agreement

On February 7, 2008, the Tehrik-i-Taliban Pakistan (TTP) led by Baitullah Mehsud offered a truce and peace negotiations resulting in a suspension of violence. On May 21, 2008 Pakistan signed a peace agreement with the Tehrik-i-Taliban Pakistan (TTP). Despite the agreement sporadic fighting continued until late June and escalated with the takeover of the town of Jandola on June 24, by the militants. 22 pro-government tribal fighters were captured and executed by the TTP at that time. On June 28, 2008, Pakistan's Army started an offensive against militia fighters in Khyber, codenamed *Operation Sirat-e-Mustaqeem*. The military took control of a key town and demolished an insurgent group's building. 1 militant was reportedly killed while 2 soldiers died in Swat valley. The operation was halted in early July.

On July 19, 2008, clashes erupted between the Tehrik-i-Taliban Pakistan and a faction of pro-government Taliban militants. 10-15 of the pro-government fighters were killed and another 120 were captured. Among the captured were two commanders who were tried under "Islamic" law by the Taliban and then executed. On July 21, 2008, heavy fighting in Baluchistan killed 32 militants, 9 soldiers and 2 civilians. More than two dozen militants were captured and a large weapons cache was found. Between July 28 and August 4, 2008, heavy fighting flared up in the northwestern Swat valley leaving 94 militants and 22 soldiers and policemen dead. Another 28 civilians were also killed.

### *Bajaur Offensive Starts*

Heavy fighting erupted on August 6, 2008, in the Loisam area of Bajaur district. Loisam lies on the strategically important road leading towards the main northwestern city of Peshawar. The fighting started when hundreds of militants poured into the area attacking government forces.

After four days of fighting on August 10 the military withdrew from the area. 100 militants and 9 soldiers were confirmed killed and another 55 soldiers were missing, at least three dozen of them captured by the militants. While the fighting was going on in Bajaur, in the Buner area of Khyber-Pakhtunkhwa militants killed at least nine policemen in an attack on a check post. The checkpoint was then abandoned, and the local Pakistani forces withdrew to Khar, the main town of Bajaur Agency. There were reports that the town of Khar was then besieged by tribal militants. On August 21, 2008, in response to the military offensive in Bajaur, two suicide bombers attacked the Pakistan Ordnance Factories in Wah while workers were changing shifts. The attack killed at least 70 people.

## *Tribesmen Declare War Against the Militants*

By the beginning of September 2008, Pakistani tribal elders began organising a private army of approximately 30,000 tribesmen to fight the militias. A lashkar, or private army, composed of Pakistani tribesmen, began torching the houses of militia commanders in Bajaur, near the Afghan border, vowing to fight them until they are expelled. This included the house of a local militant commander named Naimatullah, who had occupied several government schools and converted them into seminaries. A tribal elder named Malik Munsib Khan, who heads the lashkar, said that tribesmen would continue their struggle until the militants were expelled from the area, adding that anyone found sheltering militants would be fined one million rupees and their houses will be torched. The tribesmen also torched two important centres of the militants in the area and gained control of most of the tehsil.

The main reasons for this was that the operations that were taking place in the Federally Administered Tribal Areas had displaced some 300,000 people while dozens of citizens have been killed in clashes between the militants and military. Since the start of Pakistan's war against the militants some 150,000 tribesmen have sided with them.

## *US Support and Aid for Pakistani Tribesmen*

Recent American military proposals outlines an intensified effort to enlist tribal leaders in the frontier areas of Pakistan in the fight against Al Qaeda, the Afghan Taliban and Pakistani militia groups, as part of a broader effort to bolster Pakistani forces against militancy in the region. The proposal is modeled in part on a similar effort by American forces in Iraq that has been hailed as a great success in fighting foreign insurgents there. But it raises the question of whether such partnerships can be forged without a significant American military presence in Pakistan. And it is unclear whether enough support can be found among the tribes. Small numbers of United States military personnel have served as advisers to the Pakistani Army in the tribal areas, giving planning advice and helping to integrate American intelligence. Under this new approach, the number of advisers would increase. American officials said these security improvements complemented a package of assistance from the Agency for International Development and the State Department for the seven districts of the tribal areas that amounted to $750 million over five years, and would involve work in education, health and other sectors. The State Department's Bureau of International Narcotics and Law Enforcement Affairs is also assisting the Frontier Corps with financing for counternarcotics work.

### Islamabad Marriott Hotel Bombing

On September 23, 2008, the Pakistani Army, backed by helicopter gunships and artillery killed more than 60 insurgents in northwest Pakistan in offensives as the response to the Islamabad Marriott Hotel bombing over the weekend at the Marriott hotel in the capital Islamabad that killed 53 people. In the nearby Bajur tribal region, the Army killed at least 10 militants, according to government officials. The Bajur operations, which the army says has left more than 700 suspected militants dead, has won praise from U.S. officials.

### Renewed Bajaur Offensive

Pakistani President Asif Ali Zardari publicly vowed revenge in response to the Islamabad Marriott Hotel bombing. By September 26, 2008, Pakistani troops had successfully conducted and completed a major offensive in the Bajaur and the Tang Khata regions of the Federally Administered Tribal Areas, codenamed *Operation Sherdil*. Pakistani troops had killed over 1,000 militants in a huge offensive, a day after President Asif Ali Zardari lashed out at US forces over a clash on the Afghan border.

Tariq Khan, Inspector General of the Paramilitary Frontier Corps, mentioned to journalists that since the beginning of the Bajaur operations, there were up to 2,000 militant fighters including hundreds of foreigners who were fighting with the soldiers and the security forces. The overall death toll was over 1,000 militants and also adding that 27 Pakistani soldiers had also been killed with 111 soldiers seriously wounded. Five top Al-Qaeda and militia commanders were among those killed in a month-long operation in Bajaur. Of the five militant commanders killed, four appeared to be foreigners: Egyptian Abu Saeed Al-Masri; Abu Suleiman, an Arab; an Uzbek commander named Mullah Mansoor; and an Afghan commander called Manaras. The fifth was a Pakistani commander named only Abdullah, a son of ageing hardline leader Maulvi Faqir Mohammad who is based in Bajaur and has close ties to Al-Qaeda second-in-command Ayman al-Zawahiri.

Between October 22 and October 24, security forces engaged in another push against militants in the restive Bajaur and Khyber tribal regions. Air strikes were carried out in the Nawagai and Mamond sub-districts of Bajaur Agency. The troops destroyed several centres of militants at Charmang, Chinar and Zorbandar and had inflicted heavy losses on them. Gunship helicopters shelled in Charming, Cheenar, Kohiand Babarha areas of Nawagai and Mamund Tehsil of Bajaur agency, destroying various underground hideouts and bunkers of militants. The security forces had also taken control of different areas of Loisam, a militant headquarters, and advanced towards other areas for complete control.

## Intensified U.S. Strikes

Since the end of August 2008, the United States had stepped up its attacks in the Federally Administered Tribal Areas. On September 3 a commando attack took place in a village near the Afghan border in South Waziristan, and there have been 3 strikes from unmanned drones in North Waziristan, culminating on the morning of September 8, 2008, when a United States Air Force drone aircraft fired a number of missiles at a "guest house for militants arriving in North Waziristan", which unsuccessfully targeted Jalaluddin Haqqani, killed 23 people.

On September 25, 2008, following exchanges of gunfire between US and Pakistani forces on the frontier, President Zardari told the United Nations that Pakistan would not tolerate violations of its sovereignty, even by its allies. The incident happened after two US military helicopters came under fire from the Pakistani side, a US military spokesman said, insisting that they had been about a mile and a half inside Afghanistan.

President Zardari told the United Nations, "Just as we will not let Pakistani's territory to be used by terrorists for attacks against our people and our neighbours, we cannot allow our territory and our sovereignty to be violated by our friends," he said, without citing the United States or the border flareup.

### Militants Targeting of Tribesmen

On October 10, 2008, Islamic militants beheaded four kidnapped pro-government tribal elders in the Charmang area of Bajaur on Friday. The militants had killed them because the elders had been pro-government.

On October 11, 2008, a suicide bomber struck an anti-Militant gathering of tribal elders, just as they had decided to form a lashkar (tribal militia), killing at least 110 anti-Taliban tribesmen and wounding 125 others. The suicide bomber drove his car into the gathering itself and blew himself up. The attack on the tribal council took place in Orakzai, normally a relatively quiet corner of the nation's restive tribal areas.

### Fighting for the NATO Supply Lines

On October 19, 2008, the Pakistan Army was locked in a fierce battle with militants to keep open the fuel and arms supply routes to British and American forces in Afghanistan. For months, militants had been trying to either attack or seal off the supply routes. The army claimed that Mohammad Tariq Alfridi, the militant commander, had seized terrain around the mile-long Kohat tunnel, south of Peshawar, three times since January. He had coordinated suicide bomb attacks and rocket strikes against convoys emerging from it. Maulvi Omar, a Tehrik-i-Taliban Pakistan spokesman, said that his fighters would lay down their arms if the Pakistan Army ceased fighting. The Pakistan Army ignored his offer. The battle for the tunnel began at the start of the year when Tehrik-i-Taliban fighters seized five trucks carrying weapons and ammunition. They held the tunnel for a week before they were driven out in fierce fighting with the Army. Since then, Tariq and his men have returned several times to attack convoys. The army launched its latest onslaught after a suicide bomb attack at one of its bases near the tunnel six weeks ago. Five people were killed and 45 were injured, including 35 soldiers, when a pickup truck packed with explosives was driven into a checkpoint.

On November 11, 2008, militants attacked two convoys at the Khyber Pass capturing 13 trucks which were headed for Afghanistan. One convoy was from the United Nations World Food Programme and was carrying wheat. The second was intended for NATO troops and one of the captured trucks was carrying with it two U.S. military Humvees, which were also seized. On December 8, 2008, militants torched more than 160 vehicles destined for US-led troops in Afghanistan. The militants attacked the Portward Logistic Terminal in the northern city of Peshawar at around 02:30 AM, destroying its gate with a rocket-propelled grenade and shooting dead a guard. They then set fire to about 100 vehicles, including 70 Humvees, which shipping documents showed were being shipped to the US-led coalition forces and the Afghan National Army. At the same time, militants torched about 60 more vehicles at the nearby Faisal depot, which like Portward is on the ring road around Peshawar, where convoys typically stop before heading for the Khyber Pass.

### 2009

On February 3, 2009, militants blew up a bridge at the Khyber Pass, temporarily cutting a major supply line for Western troops in Afghanistan. After the attack supplies along the route had been halted "for the time being", according to NATO.

### Swat Ceasefire

Pakistan agreed to impose Sharia law and suspend military operations in the scenic Swat Valley. The decision is troubling for the United States, which believes that it will embolden militants who are fighting US-led troops in Afghanistan and want to impose Islamic law across nuclear-armed Pakistan. US officials believe that it will now provide another safe haven for the militants within 80 miles of Islamabad, the Pakistani capital, as well as a corridor between the Afghan border and the disputed region of Kashmir. Pakistani officials said that it was the only way to pacify a fierce Islamist insurgency and avoid more civilian casualties in Swat – whose ski resort and mountain scenery once made it a popular tourist destination. Amir Haider Khan Hoti, the chief minister for the Khyber Pakhtunkhwa province, announced the government's decision after a meeting with militant leaders in the provincial capital, Peshawar. He said that local authorities would impose Islamic law across Malakand region, which includes Swat. Officials said that Asif Ali Zardari, the Pakistani President, would sign off on the deal once peace had been restored. The agreement came the day after the militants in Swat said that it would observe a ten-day ceasefire in support of the peace process. Pakistani officials say that the laws allow Muslim clerics to advise judges, but do not outlaw female education, music or other activities once banned by the Afghan Taliban in Afghanistan.

## *Defeat of the Militants in Bajaur*

On March 1, 2009, the Pakistan Army finally defeated Bajaur militants and foreign militants in Bajaur, which is a strategically important region on the Afghan border. Major-General Tariq Khan, who was commanding the military operations in five of the seven agencies, said his Army and the Frontier Corps had killed most militants in Bajaur, the smallest of the agencies but a major infiltration route into Afghanistan, after a six-month offensive. By the time the six-month long battle in Bajaur was over, the Pakistan Army killed over 1,500 militants while losing 97 of their own soldiers and another 404 soldiers seriously injured.

## *Militant Counter-attack*

On March 30, militia commandos struck in Lahore. They attacked the Munawan Police Academy killing and taking hostage police cadets. A siege was under way for about eight hours after the militants had barricaded themselves in the academy. Eventually police forces managed to retake the compound. 18 people were killed in the attack: eight policemen, eight militants and two civilians. At least 95 policemen were wounded and 10 were taken hostage before being rescued. Four gunmen were captured by the police. On April 4, a suicide bomber attacked a military camp in Islamabad killing eight soldiers. Less than 24 hours later on April 5, two more suicide attacks occurred. One bomber targeted a market on the border with Afghanistan killing 17 people and the other attacked a mosque in Chakwal, in the eastern Pakistani province of Punjab, killing 26 more civilians. The next day, the leader of the Tehrik-i-Taliban Pakistan, Baitullah Mehsud, promised that there were to be two suicide attacks per week in the country until the Pakistani army withdraws from the border region and the United States stops its missile attacks by unmaned drones on militant bases.

### *Militants Violate Swat Deal*

In March 2009, many Pakistanis were horrified when a videotape surfaced that showed miliant enforcers publicly whipping a 17-year-old girl in Swat accused of having an affair. The girl had not committed fornication or adultery but was flogged simply because she refused her brother's demand to marry someone of his choosing. Protests broke out all over Pakistan to demonstrate against the flogging. Raja Zafar ul-Haq, a well-respected Pakistani Islamic scholar and political activist said this summary punishment of flogging simply for refusing a marriage proposal was totally un-Islamic and had nothing to do with Sharia. He went on to say that Prophet Muhammad had strictly forbidden the practice of forced marriages and in this case, the girl had not done anything wrong by refusing a marriage proposal.

A five-member team appointed by the Supreme Court investigated the video's origins, and concluded that it had been faked, raising questions at Pakistani intelligence agencies. In Buner, the Taliban continued their criminal activities when residents said Taliban fighters had been stealing cattle for meat, stealing other livestock, berating men without beards and recruiting teenagers into their ranks. The Taliban also began to steal vehicles belonging to government officials and ransacked the offices of some local non-government organisations for no apparent reason. 12 schoolchildren were killed by a bomb contained in a football.

### *Second Battle of Swat*

On April 26, 2009, the Pakistani Army started Operation Black Thunderstorm, with the aim of retaking Buner, Lower Dir, Swat and Shangla districts from the Pakistani Taliban after the militants took control of the area since the start of the year. The operation largely cleared the Lower Dir district of militia forces by April 28 and Buner by May 5. On May 5, operations started to retake Swat and later on Shangla. Fighting in Swat was particularly fierce since the Taliban threw away their insurgent tactics and the army their counter-insurgency tactics. Both sides favoured more conventional frontline warfare as a means of fighting each other. By May 14, the military was only six kilometres south of Mingora, the milita-held capital city of Swat, and preparations for all-out street fighting was under way.

On May 23, the battle for Mingora started and by May 27, 70 percent of the city was cleared of militants. On May 30, the Pakistani military had taken back the city of Mingora from the Pakistani Taliban, calling it a significant victory in its offensive against the militants. However, some sporadic fighting was still continuing on the city's outskirts. In all, according to the military, 128 soldiers and more than 1,475 militants were killed and 317 soldiers were wounded during operation Black Thunderstorm. 95 soldiers and policemen were captured by the militants, 18 of them were rescued while the fate of the others remained undetermined. 114 militants were captured, including some local commanders. At least 23 of the militants killed were foreigners.

Sporadic fighting throughout Swat continued up until mid-June. On June 14, the operation was declared over and the military had regained control of the region. Only small pockets of Taliban resistance remained and the military started mopping up operations.

This led to a refugee crisis, and by August 22, 1.6 million of 2.3 million have returned home according to UN estimates.

### *Blockade of South Waziristan*

On June 16, 2009, in the aftermath of the successful victory and recapture of the entire Swat valley, the Pakistan Army began a massive troop build-up along the southern and eastern borders of South Waziristan. Pakistan was now taking the fight to Mehsud's mountainous stronghold, ordering an expansion of its current offensive against Tehrik-i-Taliban Pakistan fighters in the Swat valley. On Sunday night, denouncing Mehsud as "the root cause of all evils," Owais Ghani, the governor of the Khyber Pakhtunkhwa, said the government has called on the army to launch a "full-fledged" military operation to eliminate Mehsud and his estimated 20,000 men. The crucial battle may prove to be the most difficult that Pakistan's military has faced on its soil in recent years. Islamabad's decision to launch the offensive against Mehsud signals a deepening of Pakistani resolve against the militants. The army has targeted the Tehrik-i-Taliban Pakistan leader on three separate occasions — in 2004, 2005 and 2008 — but walked away each time after signing ruinous "peace deals" that have only served to embolden Mehsud. But the military appears more determined this time. It also enjoys the backing of a government that has gained public support as the recent wave of terrorist attacks has heightened revulsion against the Taliban.

### *Killing of Baitullah Mehsud*

The leader of Tehrik-i-Taliban Pakistan, Baitullah Mehsud, was killed in a drone attack in early August 2009. This was later confirmed by captured chief spokesman Maulvi Umar. He was replaced by Hakimullah Mehsud.

### *Militant October–November 2009 Counter-offensive*

In early October 2009, the Tehrik-i-Taliban Pakistan started a string of attacks in cities across Pakistan. The goal of the attacks was to show that the militants were still a united fighting force following the death of their leader and to disrupt a planned military offensive into South Waziristan.

Places targeted include the U.N. World Food Program offices in Islamabad, Khyber bazaar in Peshawar, Army General Headquarters in Rawalpindi, a market in Shangla, security establishments in Lahore, police stations in Kohat and Peshawar, the International Islamic University in Islamabad, and Pakistan Air Force Complex in Kamra.

The month ended with a car bombing of Meena Bazaar, Peshawar killing 118 civilians. The army then began a ground offensive in South Waziristan. November saw suicide bombings of the Army's National Bank of Pakistan in Rawalpindi, a market in Charsadda and six bombings of Peshawar including the regional headquarters of the ISI and the Judicial Complex.

## South Waziristan Offensive

On October 17, the Pakistani Army launched a large-scale offensive in South Waziristan involving 28,000 troops advancing across South Waziristan from three directions.

On October 19, the first town to fall to the Army was Kotkai, the birthplace of the Pakistani Taliban leader Hakimullah Mehsud. However, the next day, the Tehrik-i-Taliban Pakistan re-took the town from the military.

Troops had thrust into Kotkai only to be hit by a determined counteroffensive that killed seven soldiers, including an army major, and wounded seven more. Still, the Army managed to take the town once again on October 24, after days of bombardments.

On October 29, the town of Kaniguram, which was under the control of Uzbek fighters from the Islamic Movement of Uzbekistan, was surrounded. And on November 2, Kaniguram was taken.

On November 1, the towns of Sararogha and Makin were surrounded, and fighting for Sararogha started on November 3. The fighting there lasted until November 17, when the town finally fell to the military. The same day, the town of Laddah was also captured by the Army and street fighting commenced in Makin. Both Sararogha and Laddah were devastated in the fighting. By November 21, more than 570 militants and 76 soldiers were killed in the offensive.

On December 12, 2009, the Pakistan army declared victory in South Waziristan.

## 2010

## Orakzai and Kurram Offensive

In an offensive in Bajaur by Frontier Corps, a militants' stronghold village Damadola was captured and cleared by February 6, 2010. Bajaur was declared conflict free zone by April 20. On March 23, 2010, the Pakistan army launched an offensive to clear Orakzai. Officials also announced a future offensive in North Waziristan. The week prior the Pakistan military killed approximately 150 militants in fighting in the region. It is expected that all tribal areas would be cleared by June 2010. June 3, Pakistani authorities announced a victory over the insurgents in Orakzai and Kurram.

### Casualties

2,637 security forces members and 12,847 militants were killed between January 2003, and November 12, 2009, according to government sources. On February 18, 2010, the Pakistani military confirmed that since September 11, 2001, 2,351 soldiers have been killed in the war and another 6,512 have been wounded. Also, there have been 21,672 civilian casualties (at least 7,598 of these were killed). The military stated that 17,742 militants have been killed or captured. Among these, by November 2007, were 488 foreign extremists killed, 24 others arrested and 324 injured. An additional 220 policemen were killed in fighting in 2007 and 2008. Before all-out fighting broke out in 2003, independent news sources reported only four incidents of deaths of Pakistani security forces members in 2001 and 2002, in which a total of 20 soldiers and policemen were killed. The independent South Asia Terrorism Portal website has estimated that at least 1,865 soldiers and policemen were killed between 2003 and 2008. The Pak Institute For Peace Studies has estimated that 1,185 soldiers and policemen were killed in 2009.

Also, at least 857 soldiers and policemen have been reported captured by the militants since the start of the war, with at least 558 of them being released. Mr. Naushad Ali Khan Superintendent of Research and Analysis, NWFP Police in his article *Suicide and terrorist attacks and police actions in NWFP, Pakistan* has provided details of different activities of the terrorists during 2008. Accordingly 483 cases were registered with 533 deaths and 1290 injured. Similarly 29 suicidal cases were registered that resulted in the death of 247 persons while 695 persons sustained injuries. During the same period 83 attempts of terrorism were foiled by the NWFP Police.

### United States Role

Until July 2009 the conflict, as well as terrorism in Pakistan, had cost Pakistan $35 billion. According to US Congress and the

Pakistani media, Pakistan has received about $18 billion from the United States for the logistical support it provided for the counter-terrorism operations from 2001 to 2010, and for its own military operation mainly in Waziristan and other tribal areas along the Durand line. The Bush administration also offered an additional $3 billion five-year aid package to Pakistan for becoming a frontline ally in its 'war on terror'. Annual instalments of $600 million each split evenly between military and economic aid, began in 2005.

In 2009, President Barack Obama pledged to continue supporting Pakistan and has said Pakistan would be provided economic aid of $1.5 billion dollars each year for the next five years. Unfolding a new US strategy to defeat Taliban and Al-Qaeda, Obama said Pakistan must be a 'stronger partner' in destroying Al-Qaeda safe havens. In addition, President Obama has also planned to propose an extra $2.8 billion dollars in aid for the Pakistani military to intensify the US-led war on terror along the Pakistan-Afghanistan border. The military aid would be in addition to the civilian aid of $1.5 billion dollars a year for the next five years from 2009 onwards.

In his autobiography, President Musharraf wrote that the United States had paid millions of dollars to the Pakistan government as bounty money for capturing al-Qaeda operators from tribal areas bordering Afghanistan. About 359 of them were handed over to the US for prosecution. Pakistan has bought 1,000 laser-guided bomb kits and 18 F-16 fighter jets from USA, to attack militants.

Amongst Pakistanis opinion about the role of the US is generally negative. Incidents of terrorism cause rage and anger against the terrorist organizations but they also cause frustration with the United States. According to Pew Global Polls only 17% of Pakistanis have a positive view of the US and only 11% it as a useful partner in the war on terror.

## SAFETY AND SECURITY PAKISTAN'S NUCLEAR ARSENAL

Determined to retain and expand its nuclear capabilities but shaken by the reaction to A.Q. Khan's global nuclear entrepreneurship, in 2004 Musharraf's government had sharply reversed its earlier policy of keeping all nuclear matters under the wrap. It hoped thereby to assure the world that Pakistan's nuclear weapons were in safe hands. A stream of highly placed official visitors made a beeline for Washington's think-tanks and military colleges across the United States. A few years earlier this would have been unthinkable. Visits from top officials of the Strategic Plans Division (SPD), which is charged with the possession, maintenance, and safety of Pakistan's nuclear weapons became routine, and still continue.

It is especially significant that the director general of the SPD, Lt. Gen. Khalid Kidwai, is a visitor to the US. He was, for example, invited to a special guest lecture to the faculty, students, and guests of the Naval Postgraduate School in Monterey where he sought to debunk the notion that Pakistani weapons could fall into the hands of religious extremists, were on hair-trigger alert, or be used irresponsibly. Other Pakistani military officers associated with the nation's nuclear program are paid by US funding sources for writing reports and papers for US think-tanks and research institutes. Still others are in the process of writing books that will reveal the true history of the Pakistani nuclear program xlviii.

To safeguard Pakistan's crown jewels is a relatively recent preoccupation that dates to the September 11, 2001 attack. Although Pakistan's military government insisted that there was no danger of any of its nuclear weapons being taking for a ride, it did not take chances. Several weapons were reportedly airlifted to various safer, isolated, locations within the country. This nervousness was not unjustified – two strongly Islamist generals of the Pakistan Army (the head of Pakistan's ISI intelligence agency, Lt. General Mehmood Ahmed, and Deputy Chief of Army Staff, General Muzaffar Hussain Usmani), close associates of General Musharraf, had just been removed. The seriousness of betraying the progeny of Pakistan's intelligence services was something that Musharraf feared – and for good reason.

Internationally, there are widespread fears that instability in Pakistan could make its nuclear weapons and stocks of nuclear explosive material dangerously vulnerable to theft. As could be expected, Pakistan's position has been one of emphatic denial: the

Foreign Ministry claims that our [nuclear] assets are 100 percent secure, under multiple custody.

Soothing words, however, have not taken away a general sense of worry. Pakistan is now in the grip of a full-fledged insurgency by Islamic groups. Some of these view Pakistan's nuclear weapons as belonging to the *Ummah*, rather than Pakistan alonel. This has enhanced the feeling internationally that Pakistan's nuclear weapons, fissile materials, and other nuclear components are unsafe.

The dangers to Pakistan's nuclear weapons are potentially four-fold:

- From India and the US, separately or together. Israel is a distant possibility but not to be ruled out.
- From outside: Islamic militants attacking a nuclear storage site or facility with the purpose of capturing a nuclear weapon.
- From inside: Islamic elements in the army who have responsibility for protecting and operating nuclear sites or facilities.
- From a collaboration between insiders and outsiders.

There is concern in Pakistan of the growing Israeli-Indian strategic alliance, underscored by the supply of four Phalcon AWAC-type systems. These have the capability of tracking Pakistani aircraft over the entire geographical area. India has already acquired two Israeli Green Pine radars, capable of tracking missiles at a distance of 400 km. These are normally used in conjunction with the Arrow II anti-missile system. These early-warning systems could be effectively used by Israel to launch a pre-emptive strike at Pakistan's nuclear facilities with India's direct assistance or by using India as a base.

Only an extreme crisis would result in India or the US, whether acting together or separately, to attack a nuclear armed state with all the obvious dangers this contains. Even a massive use of force is unlikely to net all of well-hidden and well-protected Pakistani nuclear weapons. Moreover, the job would be incomplete unless the major nuclear weapon facilities, reactors, and uranium enrichment plants were also destroyed completely. This would involve nothing short of total war.

On the other hand, Islamic extremists may seek a weapon for ultimate use against a US or European city. But, because it would be much easier to arrange, they may seek the destruction of an Indian or Pakistani city, with the hope of provoking total war between Pakistan and India. This would be consistent with the suicide bombing strategy followed by Al-Qaida elsewhere. In the extremist mindset, it is best if infidels are killed. But if Sunni Muslims are killed, they will simply make it to heaven a bit earlier.

Defending against other nations as well as internal enemies poses a difficult security dilemma: Pakistan would like to keep the location and details of its nuclear weapons secret in order to increase their chances of a strike by India, the US, or Israel. On the other hand army insiders are already, by definition, in the know. Perhaps in collusion with an external Islamic group they could be plotting a move unknown to the Nuclear Command Authority (NCA), the SPD, or the Chief of Army Staff. How could such an attempt be foiled?

Only partial safety is possible no matter what the technical fix. One obvious mechanism is to reduce the readiness level. Pakistan is widely believed to store the fissile core and bomb mechanisms separately in safely guarded vaults. As early as December 1999, it had requested senior US officials visiting Islamabad for Permissive Action Links (PALs) that are directly integrated into the firing mechanism and electronics of a nuclear weapon, as well as Environment Sensitive Devices (ESDs), in order to enhance protection against unauthorized use or accidental nuclear detonations.

At that time, the US had declined for obvious reasons: these devices make it possible for the weapons to be maintained at a higher state of alert for the same level of safety, thereby increasing the threat perceived by India. But subsequent to a reversal of Pakistan's relationship with the US after 911, it is possible that the US may have acceded to Pakistan's request without demanding that Pakistan reveal the location or details of its nuclear weapons.

According to an ISIS report, US Secretary of State Colin Powell had offered nuclear protection assistance to Pakistan after 911li. Pakistan found the offered technology to be quite rudimentary but nevertheless accepted it under the condition that the end point usage would remain opaque. Other aspects of the assistance included training courses for Pakistani nuclear weapons personnel in US labs where they were instructed on nuclear safety and security issues.

David Albright, a US nuclear security analyst, prescribed the following forms of additional assistance to Pakistan in the aftermath of 911:

*"Generic physical protection and material accounting practices; theoretical exercises; unclassified military handbooks on nuclear weapons safety and security; more sophisticated vaults and access doors; portal control equipment; better surveillance equipment; advanced equipment for materials accounting; personnel reliability programs; and programs to reduce the likelihood of leaking sensitive information. In addition, aid could focus on methods that improve the security of nuclear weapons against unauthorized use through devices not intrinsic to the design of the nuclear weapon or through special operational or administrative restrictions. Excluded assistance would include nuclear weapons design information aimed at making more secure, reliable or safer nuclear weapons or devices, PALs, coded launch control devices, and environmental sensing devices."*

While technical measures to reduce the chances of nuclear sabotage and accident must undoubtedly be implemented, there is a fundamental tension that cannot be avoided – a perfectly safe nuclear weapon is also one that cannot be used. Hence, by definition, it is useless. In times of crisis and war, when casualties and passions run high, there will be a strong urge to weaken the safety mechanisms in place.

## INDIA, PAKISTAN, AND AMERICAN NUCLEAR DIPLOMACY

India's nuclear tests at Pokhran on May 11, 1998, stunned the world—including American intelligence and policy officials. Pakistan's response, five nuclear weapons detonated in the

Baluchistan desert, confirmed officially that the two military rivals were now also nuclear powers. In one of the most populous regions of the world, bitter adversaries in the midst of along-standing and hot war over Kashmir each achieved proven destructive power reaching well beyond their contiguous territories or the region as a whole.... How do we account for the sobering reality that nuclear tests conducted on the Indian subcontinent in mid-May 1998 were neither predicted nor prevented by U.S. policy-makers or intelligence officials? The specifics of the tests aside, the India-Pakistan case is instructive as an example of the failure of the instruments of U.S. statecraft to dissuade states from acquiring active nuclear forces. It also is a microcosm of the growing complexity of U.S. regional relations which will require far more nuanced and sophisticated forms of diplomatic and intelligence operations reaching well beyond engagement only of governments or heads of state.

Unlike the other cases examined in the course of the Study Group's project (North Korea, Iran, and Libya), the United States was intricately involved in discussions with the governments of both India and Pakistan at the time of the nuclear tests and had for decades been seeking nuclear restraint from both parties, using a mixture of carrots and sticks. That such efforts failed to alter nuclear ambitions significantly, including reaching any agreement to postpone or certainly to abandon plans to conduct tests, speaks to possible misjudgments made by both the U.S. policy and intelligence communities about how the U.S. could best wield influence in the region. At the same time, the case puts into question whether the U.S. ever had the influence it thought it had to persuade states that had repeatedly expressed the conviction that nuclear capabilities were vital to their national interest and the willingness, at least rhetorically, to do so regardless of the costs. Does this mean that the various U.S. attempts to halt nuclearization in the region were largely quixotic? A key difficulty of assessing the impact of U.S. nonproliferation policy on South Asia is that the objectives sought by policymakers changed repeatedly over time. To understand whether U.S. nonproliferation policies succeeded or failed in South Asia, it is important to recognize that these policies have not been fixed and constant over the years.

In his introductory remarks to the Study Group, a lead speaker described four stages of U.S. nonproliferation efforts in South Asia, and each of these stages had different goals and different policies. In the first stage (1970s-1980s), U.S. policy was focused on persuading countries not to seek nuclear weapons and on getting them to sign onto the NPT. In many ways, the United States succeeded during this stage, despite the fact that India and Pakistan never signed the treaty. After India's initial test in 1974, it never publicly declared itself a nuclear weapons state: as an undeclared power, it achieved its desired security objective while preserving the global nuclear regime. Study Group participants noted that nonproliferation policies worked for 24 years thereafter—not a small achievement. These policies limited nuclear escalation on the Indian subcontinent, and they may have contributed to ensuring the credibility of the NPT. As one senior official put it, "In 1974 there were key countries like Japan, many advanced countries, that had really not yet decided whether to have nuclear weapons or to join the NPT. I think that if at that time India and Pakistan had pursued active, overt nuclear weapons programs, it would have been very, very difficult to persuade a lot of these countries to join the NPT." During the second stage (1990s–1998), according to this expert, "we had realized that it was simply unrealistic to expect to roll back these capabilities." The policy goal of this period was to try to convince the Indians and Pakistanis to be satisfied with untested, undeclared nuclear capability. Einhorn added that in private discussions, U.S. officials had stopped pressing India to join the NPT. Clearly, for many of the reasons described above, however, U.S. policies failed to prevent India and Pakistan from testing nuclear weapons. In the face of a perceived existential threat, both India and Pakistan defied world opinion, forming, along with Israel and now North Korea, a special category of non-NPT-sanctioned nuclear weapons states. Given the conditions that compelled India and Pakistan to test, many have suggested that nuclearization was inevitable or at least unpreventable. Regardless of whether it could have been prevented in theory, it seems clear that, with the policy tools and bureaucratic conditions available to the United States at the time, an outcome of failure was understandable. The third period of American policy began with the tests in May 1998 and lasted until 9/11. After the 1998 tests, the policy goal of the United States was to persuade India and Pakistan to accept limitations on their programs. While a concerted effort was launched under Strobe Talbott at the end of the Clinton administration to convince India to agree to limitations, the timing of these efforts was ill-fated. As one senior official in the Study Group noted, events—including the Kargil episode, the plane hijacking to Kandahar, the Musharraf coup, and the fall of the BJP government—made the prospect of nuclear limitations very unlikely.

In the final and most recent period (from 9/11 to the present), the U.S. agenda was refocused on preventing terrorists from acquiring access to nuclear weapons. This new focus allowed the United States to make a distinction between India, which had been a responsible caretaker of its nuclear capability, and Pakistan, which had been a major proliferator, not least as a result of the A.Q. Khan nuclear supply network, two of whose retired scientists reportedly met with Osama bin Laden. In addition, U.S. policy in South Asia emphasized avoiding regional conflict and on installing protections on nuclear facilities and materials. Aside from the 10-month conflict between India and Pakistan in late 2001 and early 2002, these two objectives have so far been successful.

### The Decision-Making Process

In any given period, certain incompatibilities, if not outright contradictions, have arisen among the goals the U.S. sought in South Asia. For example, during the Soviet occupation of Afghanistan and again after the Taliban seized power in the 1990s and began harboring Al Qaeda terrorists, the American preoccupation with Pakistan shifted squarely from nonproliferation to combating terrorism. During the Reagan administration, for example, State Department officials were called upon each year to testify in Congress that, against all evidence and available intelligence, Pakistan could be "certified" to not be engaged in certain proscribed nuclear weapons activities so as to avoid triggering congressionally-mandated sanctions.

Shifting preoccupations were accompanied by commensurate shifts in the level and type of policy and intelligence resources devoted to the region, elevating some officials and agencies while subordinating others at different times. On the whole, however, it was the consensus of the study group that nonproliferation objectives were repeatedly overtaken by other priorities, first in Pakistan and later in India. Combined with the freewheeling use of sanctions imposed by both the Executive and Legislative branches, such policies were often perceived by the respective regimes as ill-conceived and high handed. Sanctions, in particular, seem to have impinged on critical leverage the U.S. needed to sustain an effective strategy to stem regional nuclearization.

The insufficiency of high-level policy attention accorded the region or to the internal dynamics of each state compounded the likelihood that American diplomacy would fail. As one Study Group participant noted, South Asian proliferation issues typically garnered the attention of Principals only in conjunction with more pressing high-level events, such as a state visit to Washington or a major flashpoint like Kargil. This was not because concerns about proliferation in South Asia remained within the purview of a few policy or intelligence specialists, as might have been the case in other, more remote areas of the world. To the contrary, developments on the subcontinent involved key players across several government agencies, including the National Security Council, the State Department, and the intelligence community; only the Defence Department remained a second-tier player.

The tension in the U.S. government between regional bureaus and functional bureaus which had an interest in South Asian nuclearization was a common feature of policy deliberations, as is typically the case with issues that cut cross traditional bureaucratic alignments. South Asia was dubbed by one Study Group member as the "theme park for the functional bureaus." Two participants argued that regional experts who see themselves as responsible for maintaining the overall relationship of the U.S. with key states are likely to be better equipped to manage the inevitably competing priorities which can arise in diplomatic and security affairs. This is not so for functionalists, who, some argued, pursue singular agendas can prove costly to other urgent objectives and the larger relationship. Thus, it was argued, while regional bureaus can be informed by functional specialists, regional specialists are an inherently better choice to manage the complexities of diplomatic and security relationships.

This view invited strong opposition, especially from a veteran non-proliferation diplomat who countered that it is essential and indeed routine for functional specialists to work closely with and learn from regional experts. The idea that there is an inherent dichotomy between the two is not just patently false but a hindrance to effective policymaking. Several participants noted, in turn, that it is the skill and attention of senior officials— undersecretaries and above—that is essential in balancing vital interests while preventing unnecessary internecine domestic rivalries.

Participants identified additional institutional alignments in the decision-making process that affected the design and choice of U.S.-South Asia policy options. The realignment of military commands that led to splitting India into the Pacific Command while leaving Pakistan in Central Command, it was argued, complicated efforts to sustain an accurate strategic vision which could take the entire region and its complex interests into account. On the policy side, the decision to move Afghanistan and the rest of South Asia from its traditional Near East/South Asia office in the National Security Council into the East Asia office in 2001 also was said to prompt confusion over portfolios and bureaucratic alignments in a way that may have interfered with policy-formulation— especially with respect to Afghanistan, but also in the region as a whole. Study Group participants generally agreed that the team that was pulled together by Deputy Secretary of State Strobe Talbott to work toward nuclear limitations in South Asia after the 1998 tests serves as a good example of team work and trans-agency cooperation that is needed to tackle such inherently interdisciplinary challenges. Talbott's group included individuals from the intelligence community, State, Defence, Treasury, and other agencies. It was, remarked one former intelligence official, "an example of [an] informal mechanism that was not part of the national security apparatus that played a very important role." In addition, meetings convened by Assistant Secretary Inderfurth during the Kargil Crisis also were said to have brought the intelligence and policy communities together in a productive way. Study Group members noted that both of these instances were the result the thoughtful planning by certain individuals, however, and not standard or enduring organizational procedure.

The group also addressed the role of the ambassadors to Delhi and Islamabad in advancing American interests in the region, particularly after the 1998 tests. During the early Bush 2 Administration, for example, one participant remarked that "the tail of events was wagging the dog of the bureaucracy." Ambassador Wendy Chamberlin, while serving in Pakistan after 9/11, was perceived by one observer as having to spend too much time pitted in competition with her counterpart in India, Ambassador Robert Blackwill, to get the attention of senior decision-makers. Blackwill and his aide, Ashley Tellis, participants agreed, were strong advocates of an improved U.S.-India relationship and made a very strong case to this effect. Indeed, the decision to appoint such powerful bureaucratic players both signalled and in turn strengthened the growing bond between the United States and India in recent years. The competition of ambassadors for attention in Washington both reflects the relative scarcity of interest in these countries as well as a failure to engage in efforts based on a genuine strategic consensus.

## The Quality of Intelligence

What kind of intelligence or information did U.S. policymakers have available to them at different stages of the development of nuclear programs in each case? With some notable exceptions, the quality of technical intelligence on India and Pakistan in 1998 was considered to be above average. Some Members of the Study Group recalled the quality of technical intelligence in India and Pakistan at the time of testing in 1998 as "excellent" compared with the level of information on Iraq, Iran, and North Korea. One participant noted that the United States had "a much better handle...

on Indian and Pakistani nuclear and missile programs than each of the two had against each other." The conventional wisdom about South Asia posits the 1998 nuclear tests as the sine qua non of the overall failure of intelligence to track and predict nuclear events in the region accurately, notwithstanding intelligence reports which had been tracking nuclear advancements in India and Pakistan for decades. With respect to the tests specifically, participants variously acknowledged that:

1. Some US officials dismissed BJP statements about pursuing a nuclear deterrent as campaign rhetoric;
2. Most policy makers bought senior-level Indian assurances that testing would not occur;
3. The Intelligence Community gave little weight to a Sikh newsletter in Canada that claimed it had evidence of test preparations; and
4. Intelligence did not detect most of the physical preparations at the Indian test site at Pokhran.

U.S. intelligence clearly lacked information about the nuclear plans and intentions of the Indian government elected in early 1998. The lesson drawn from this observation was that "in democratic countries we should start making sure we have the human assets in the opposition party early on, long before they get to power." Most importantly, some participants noted that, while technical intelligence in the region was strong, there was insufficient attention to the domestic political drivers for India's proliferation behaviour. A final problem in the India case was the difficulty, absent reliable information about the intentions of the new leadership, of having to "infer intentions from observables," which was compared with difficulties faced in the North Korea case.

The group also addressed some apparent blind spots in the U.S. government when it came to India. In particular, one participant noted that "we have a low appreciation for the power of nationalism," and an intelligence official added that "we need to find ways of better dealing with the affective and emotional sides of... issues." Similarly, in Pakistan, American policymakers failed to grasp the significance on "the streets" in Pakistan of its decisions first to approve (and contract) the sale of F-16 fighters s only later to delay their transfer as part of a punitive policy. This issue, among others, highlighted the concern that the United States may be insufficiently attuned to the effects of demographic and generational change and to the impact of the information and communications revolutions on local public awareness.

One participant noted that while the 1998 Indian tests were clearly an intelligence failure, they were also a policy failure: "there were things out there if we would have been inclined to... dig a bit." At the same time, many members of the group felt that even if the United States had detected the upcoming test, it would not have been able to prevent it: "[T]hey were bound and determined they were going to [test]. They weren't going to get pushed around. They were going to conduct this test. [T]hey would defy the U.S. and the entire international community if necessary."

However, many aspects of the domestic context that required human intelligence— such as political dynamics in the new coalition government, public sentiment and the appeal of nationalism which emphasized the "status' accorded by nuclear weapons among the Indian and Pakistani populace, or the possibility that influential domestic interests might possibly have been encouraged to oppose nuclear programs on grounds of their political and economic costs—were given insufficient weight. Policymakers at times failed to challenge their own decisions and ideas, even when confronted with new intelligence information. Restrictions placed on intelligence may have limited the information available to policymakers and hindered their ability to consider alternative approaches, even if on the whole it appears that the range of issues that policy-makers thought important rarely exceeded the intelligence that was readily available.

What policy tools and options do policymakers have available and/or consider addressing the potential challenges posed by incipient nuclear programs? Which are selected or rejected? Why? The topic of policy tools was one of great interest among members of the Study Group. A common theme was that "the U.S. ability to use incentives and disincentives flexibly to encourage changes in behaviour in South Asia... was heavily constrained by certain pieces of legislation." Sanctions legislation was given particular attention, and participants noted that neither carrots nor sticks had any significant effect.

In terms of sticks, the United States by the late 1990s had become, as one participant put it, "obsessed with sanctions." Many participants were critical of so-called automatic sanctions—sanctions legislated by Congress that left the President with no option but to implement them. Not only did the sanctions—such as the Nuclear Nonproliferation Act of 1978, the Pressler Amendment of 1985, and the Glenn Amendment of 1994—fail to coerce India and Pakistan into behaving as the United States wished, but they may have actually been provocative. Strobe Talbott suggests this in his book Engaging India: "Not only were they [India and Pakistan] undeterred, they tested largely to demonstrate that they rejected American and international admonitions and that they were confident they could survive the consequences." As one participant summarized, "Automatic sanctions work as a threat, not as an actual tool." If the targeted states see through the threat, then the sanctions will be meaningless.

Not only are automatic sanctions difficult for a President who is bound by their limitations, but they also can make the job of the intelligence community harder, another participant noted. The sanctions "put the administration in the understandable position of trying to discredit the intelligence information." Another participant had a different perspective on the impact of automatic sanctions within the U.S. government: "Congress resorts to automatic sanctions legislation out of frustration with an executive branch that has already lied to it so many times that they just get desperate."

As it happens, one of the most prominent set of sanctions passed—under the Pressler amendment—came about in a very idiosyncratic, as a senior congressional staff member explained. A more stringent bill had been proposed in 1984 by Senator Cranston—a bill that would have cut off aid to Pakistan immediately—and the Pressler bill was offered as an alternative that would "buy time for the administration to address the

Pakistanis on the nonproliferation issue." Instead, the executive branch failed to act decisively in mounting new diplomatic operations. By 1990, nuclear activity in Pakistan could no longer be easily glossed over, leading to the charade of annual State Department testimony to "certify", against all available evidence, that Pakistan was not involved in proscribed nuclear activities.

Defenders of sanctions suggested that sanctions can slow down nuclear proliferation. Sanctions could be credited with the 24-year gap between India's initial testing in 1974 and its full-fledged test at Pokhran in 1997, for example, a reflection of the higher costs and greater difficulties which sanctions impose on states seeking technical advancement. Critics of sanctions, remarked one participant, are frequently members of the executive branch who have been "traumatized by what they see as their failures." Carrots also proved less than effective. Residual distrust, left over from the Cold War, has lingered in the relationship between India and the United States, and it seemed for years that there was little that the United States could credibly offer India. In the case of Pakistan, legislative restrictions left the United States with very few carrots, aside from rather ill-conceived effort such as offering the Pakistanis the F-16s that they had already purchased in 1990 that had not yet been delivered. A former official, discussing the negotiations on preventing the Pakistani test, recalled that when presented with this unappealing offer, Pakistani General Wahid snarled, "We choke on your carrots." In short, neither the carrots nor the sticks offered by the United States to elicit nuclear restraint proved particularly attractive, leaving Indian and Pakistani determination to develop nuclear forces largely intact.

For reasons of geopolitics and national pride, the Nuclear Non-Proliferation Treaty and associated such agreements represented a form of post-colonial discrimination that did not sit well with the polities of either state. As one participant noted, discussions of the PPT or the CTB were unproductive: "The Indians felt immediately [like] secondclass citizens." Why, India asked, should the door be slammed shut on their right to possess nuclear weapons based on the arbitrary cut-off date of 1967? "Why should India be in the doghouse and China a respected player at the table?" was a typical lament. As Jaswant Singh put it only slightly differently in a *Foreign Affairs* article published in September/ October 1997, "If the permanent five's possession of nuclear weapons increases security, why would India's possession of nuclear weapons be dangerous? If deterrence works in the west as it so obviously appears to since western nations insist on continuing to possess nuclear weapons, by what reasoning will it not work in India?" As a result of these basic incompatibilities, according to one expert, diplomatic exchanges with Delhi more often than not meant that "We (the U.S) were (always) lecturing; while the Indians were moralizing."

As a former senior official noted in the Study Group, "I'm of the view that the reason that we were not more successful over the years in actually finding a way to deal with India was because we never answered any of those questions." Neither the United States nor India went out of its way to allay fears harboured by the other. The Indians have long expressed the view that issues inherent to their national interest were being dictated to them by an upstart and perhaps even a lesser power. This response, in turn, left Americans with the notion that India was trampling on global regimes that are supported by a wide majority of nations without concern for the potential damage this could do to international stability.

## THE NATURE OF DISCOURSE

A problematic relationship between the intelligence and policymaking communities involved in South Asia was frequently addressed over the course of the meeting. There was broad consensus that while Deputy Secretary of State Strobe Talbott's frequent gathering of experts was a good example of how the policy and intelligence communities could be brought together, this mechanism was temporary and ad hoc. An important question, raised several times, was whether policymakers have ever been sufficiently attuned to strategic intelligence ("the big picture") in South Asia. One former intelligence official suggested that because "U.S. policymakers have resisted looking at alternative outcomes... [and] are not doing a mid-course reality check", the risk of continuing to misjudge the evolving motives and behaviour of the two states will continue to be high. Substantial frustration was expressed that the policy community was never "... asking the right questions... [and] not going beyond the sort of quotidian next step of its bureaucratic plan to do something that really embraces a long term vision of security." In addition, as another participant noted, the psychology of decision-making plays out when policymakers are confronted with information that directly contradicts their ideas or policies: "The literature says that very, very frequently, they set aside information that increases their level of discomfort with their own decision, and then they... cherry-pick... what they really want to hear."

A participant highlighted the frustration shared by many intelligence analysts that they seldom have a chance to hear what the policymakers actually do with the intelligence that is produced. During the Kargil Crisis, however, it was noted that intelligence officials were invited to meetings at the State Department, thereby allowing them to get immediate feedback about how the intelligence was received by the policymakers. On the other side, frustration was expressed by a congressional committee staff member that much intelligence was "so sensitive that it might not have gotten to the policymakers who really had to read it." Without exposure to this intelligence—not just the general conclusions but also the facts to back them up—it is difficult for policymakers or members of Congress to cultivate a larger strategic vision.

The Study Group cited the increasingly powerful Indian-American community as a substantial domestic (U.S.) factor affecting policy toward South Asia. One participant remarked that "Next to the Israelis now. Indian Americans are the most important ethnic lobby in the United States." In addition, "Indians per capita are the wealthiest minority group we have in this country." As a domestic political factor, the influence of the Indian-American community may be partially credited with President Clinton's swift turnaround on India after the tests: his visit to India in March 2000 (not even two years after the tests) signalled the beginning of a strong push by the United States—continuing to this day—to improve relations with an India that is rapidly gaining economic and geopolitical clout on the world stage.

## Regional Political Dynamics

In a part of the world as charged as South Asia, regional political dynamics inevitably affect the impact and efficacy of U.S. strategies. For one, the sheer differential in power and size between India and Pakistan ensured that India would be the "independent variable" in any strategic equation, leaving Pakistan as the dependent variable. U.S. strategy was designed around this dynamic, with the most effort being spent to woo Delhi. The group pointed out, however, that the United States largely failed to account for India's broader strategic horizon. As mentioned above. U.S. policymakers did not fully appreciate that China loomed very large in India's nuclear calculation. American officials typically failed to demonstrate that they understood India's legitimate concerns about Chinese nuclear assistance to Pakistan. Unable to acknowledge India's security concerns regarding China, one participant remarked, Washington made matters worse by issuing a statement with the Chinese in 2001 which essentially stated "We're going to work together to deal with the Indians."

Another participant added that divisions within the bureaucracy prevented the U.S. intelligence and policy communities from fully appreciating the implications of alternative strategic groupings—for example, groupings including China, Iran, or Southeast Asia. By defining South Asia by the India-Pakistan conflict, the United States may be missing other important relationships and developments in the region. Nonetheless, more recent revisions to this system intended to avoid such narrow regional analysis— such as the grouping of India thin PACOM and Pakistan within CENTCOM—may complicate the U.S. reaction in the event of further outbreaks of violence between India and Pakistan.

## Net Assessment: Success or Failure?

U.S. discourse with India and Pakistan, as well as domestic discourse about the region as it figured in the U.S. strategic calculus, traditionally has been sporadic and relatively shallow. The level of official attention paid to the region drops routinely absent an immediate crisis demanding a prompt U.S. response. The lack of sustained, high-level engagement has hindered the development of trust in bilateral relationships and undercut U.S. credibility as a broker for peace and military restraint in the region as a whole. For the Pakistani regime, in particular, U.S. engagement and aid is widely perceived as opportunistic and fleeting, not as building blocks for an enduring relationship or genuine alliance. Attention paid to Pakistan is far too often not about Pakistan's direct concerns but aimed instead at furthering other U.S. interests in the region, such as combating global terrorism. The decision by the U.S. to let the Pakistani government make its own decisions about how to deal with A.Q. Khan and thereby avoid penalizing him too severely for running a global proliferation network is one such bargain, Faustian or otherwise.

The official discourse between the United States and India before the 1998 tests also has been hindered by sporadic engagement, following years of outright isolation during the Cold War when India was perceived as little more than a Soviet puppet state. A number of Study Group participants judged that U.S. policy was in some measure fundamentally flawed, marked by the chronic failure to understand Indian perspectives on a host of topics, its domestic security perceptions in particular. "One of the things I think we tend to miss," remarked a military official, "is the slow accretion of frustration that can occur, the U.S. ignoring... Chinese proliferation." Until Delhi's so-called security compulsions were addressed, said one participant, "we were never going to have a meeting of the minds, much less any kind of agreements with them."

The South Asian experience tells us that if we want to shape nuclear weapons-related behaviour in the future, we need to anticipate how pertinent countries might evolve over time relative to US interests—that is, to plan policy based in part on the analysis of alternative scenarios about the future. Time after time, South Asian issues have been trumped by competing demands on the attention of American policymakers. Nonproliferation goals in the region, in particular, have been repeatedly subjugated to other priorities, such as driving the Soviets out of Afghanistan, bringing down the Taliban and fighting al Qaeda, and fortifying the U.S.-

India bilateral relationship. The regularity with which nonproliferation has been downgraded as a goal in South Asia has instilled a strong message that Washington will not sustain focus on this objective if it does not comport with current conceptions of realpolitik.

In South Asia, the United States has traditionally focused on addressing the symptoms of the conflict (i.e., nuclear weapons) rather than the conflict's root cause. However, one participant reminded the group that "the major reason for proliferation is insecurity," and, unfortunately, insecurity has been an enduring feature of the South Asian strategic landscape since 1947. A former senior official noted that, while the Talbott negotiations concentrated on four nonproliferation benchmarks, a fifth benchmark— resolving the dispute between the two countries— did indeed exist. There was an active debate within the administration about whether this benchmark should be tackled first (as the "trunk of the elephant") or last (as the "tail of the elephant"). In the end, the challenging task of addressing the underlying security situation in South Asia was set aside in the hope of achieving quick wins on the other benchmarks. Given the many other obligations of the United States around the globe at the time (including Kosovo and Iraq), to say nothing of the Lewinsky scandal at home, this decision might be seen as realistic and understandable. However, in view of the grave threat of a nuclear exchange between the two South Asian enemies, the decision might also be viewed as short-sighted.

Throughout the evening's discussion, it was stressed that, going forward, more U.S. attention would need to go toward preventing the use of nuclear weapons, rather than de-nuclearization, to include stepped-up educational campaigns about the risks of maintaining a deployed nuclear weapons force, the inherent vulnerabilities and uncertainties of command and control, and the high risk of even inadvertent escalation in the event of regional tensions. A major question raised during the meeting goes to the essence of American policy formulation: "how can we tell when our policies are not aligned with strategic realities?" If, as some participants suggested, the nuclear tests in 1974 and 1998 could not be stopped with the policies the U.S. attempted, was there enough policy momentum and intelligence to allow for the strategic goals of the United States vis-à-vis South Asia to be re-evaluated and adapted accordingly? Should the United States have stepped back and asked, "Are we advancing the ability of the United States to secure its interests and those of its allies with the non-proliferation strategy being employed at different times?" Or is it possible that U.S. policymakers were so fixated on a few specific objectives that they were unable to take into account the two governments' strategic priorities, tailoring policies accordingly? Beginning with the success of President Clinton's visit to India in March 2000—an event that marked a turning point in U.S.-India relations but with barely a mention of the nuclear issues dividing Washington and Delhi – a new strategic vision for India was introduced and has been sustained and even expanded in the Bush administration. The U.S.-India Civil Nuclear Agreement signals a new strategic relationship between the United States and India as well as a turning point in the U.S. approach to global non-proliferation. Most members of the group generally looked positively on the new level of strategic engagement with South Asia, but, as one former official expressed it, recent agreements heighten concern about the implications of U.S. Indian nuclear cooperation for both regional and global nonproliferation goals. As one expert put it, "I think one of the down-sides of the India civil nuclear deal is that countries around the world will get the impression that we're a good guy, a friend of the U.S., we can do this and we're not going to pay a cost." Another participant expressed doubt about the direction of India's future: "Our definition in the ten years ahead of what our national interests are may really... turn out to be very much at odds with those of India."

# 5

# Pakistani Nuclear Strikes on Tactical Targets

However, there is an undeniably close link between nuclear weapons and a nation's conventional military capabilities. If a nation's conventional capability is relatively low vis a vis a nuclear armed adversary, that nation is likely to adopt a 'first use' strategy to thwart a conventional military offensive that may threaten to undermine its territorial integrity and lead to its break up. This is the situation that Pakistan finds itself in at present. In such a case, the nuclear weapons to be used or threatened to be used would be 'tactical' nuclear weapons against India's mechanised forces inside Pakistani territory. While India may have no intentions of launching a major conventional offensive into Pakistan, given India's conventional superiority (no matter how slender the edge may be), Pakistan has based its national security strategy on the first use of nuclear weapons to prevent its comprehensive military defeat like in 1971 and, consequently, its disintegration as a nation. It is for this reason that Pakistan finds it difficult to accept India's offer of a bilateral no-first-use treaty as a confidence building measure.

In the Indo-Pak context, Indian advocates of tactical nuclear weapons pre-suppose that when pushed to the wall, Pakistan would not hesitate to use nuclear weapons against India's mechanised forces inside Pakistani territory as the 'opprobrium quotient', as General Sundarji called it, would be low since the use of nuclear weapons could be justified as a defensive measure of the last resort. They aver that in response India too should employ only tactical nuclear weapons on Pakistani forces, rather than raise the nuclear ante to full-scale retaliation. Though there is considerable merit in it, in India's overall strategic equation with Pakistan it is a dangerous argument and would completely degrade the potential not only of India's nuclear deterrence but also of India's conventional superiority.

According to the army doctrine published recently by the Army Training Command (ARTRAC), "the Indian Army believes in fighting the war in enemy territory. If forced into a war, the aim of our offensive(s) would be to apply a sledgehammer blow to the enemy. The Indian Army's concept of waging war is to ensure a decisive victory and to ensure that conflict termination places us at an advantageous position."16 In a future Indo-Pak war in the plains, should India pursue a pro-active strategy and launch an offensive with one or more Strike Corps across the international boundary, supported massively by the IAF, India's mechanised spearheads are likely to achieve major operational level gains in three to five days and strategic gains soon thereafter. Pakistan may then be forced to commit its strategic reserves, that is, either or both the Army Reserves North (ARN) and South (ARS) and risk their destruction in detail or exercise its nuclear option.

Indian analysts are inclined to believe that Pakistan is likely to resort to the early use of nuclear weapons, especially when it can justify their use as a defensive measure of the last resort on its own soil against Indian mechanised forces. If this logic is accepted, India's conventional superiority against Pakistan will stand negated and the Indian military leadership will either have to run the risk of accepting the consequences of a nuclear strike from Pakistan or plan to launch only tactical level limited offensives with shallow objectives so as to avoid crossing Pakistan's perceived nuclear threshold.

Such a course of action would naturally play straight into Pakistan's hands and give that country the freedom to continue to interfere in India's internal affairs through its 'proxy war' in J&K, including the launching of Kargil-type misadventures, without the fear of massive Indian retaliation with conventional forces.

Pakistan may even resort to launching trans-international boundary operations in areas such as the Rann of Kutch on one pretext or the other, as it did in the summer months of 1965. The safety provided by India's doctrine of 'no-first-use' of nuclear weapons would further embolden Pakistan to seek tactical advantage.

The Indian army would be left with the option to plan to seize a long though narrow strip of Pakistani territory virtually all along the front without ringing Pakistan's nuclear alarm bells by launching a number of limited, shallow objective offensives.

However, this capability is unlikely to dissuade Pakistan from practicing its peculiar brand of jihad through a cocktail of terrorism and aggressive actions across the LoC a la Kargil. The only sensible option may perhaps be to call Pakistan's nuclear bluff and plan to launch Strike Corps operations to achieve strategic gains in as early a time frame as is militarily possible. This approach will need to be combined with a declaratory policy that a nuclear strike against Indian soldiers, even if they are deep inside Pakistani territory, will constitute the use of nuclear weapons against India and will invite massive counter value and counter force punitive retaliation against Pakistan. General Sundarji wrote in 1992 that, "If the damage suffered by Indian forces (due to a Pakistani nuclear strike) is substantial, national and troop morale would demand at least a quid pro quo response. There might even be a demand in some quarters for a quid pro quo plus response."17 However, after over a decade of Pakistan's proxy war and particularly after that country's perfidious intrusions into the Kargil district of J&K in the summer months of 1999, the national mood is much different. Indian public opinion will accept nothing short of the final dismemberment of Pakistan in case that country chooses to cross the nuclear Rubicon and launches a nuclear strike, even if it is on Indian forces.

## PAKISTAN-CHINA NUCLEAR DEAL AND NON-PROLIFERATION

Pakistan-China nuclear cooperation has always been under the certain obligations to non-proliferation concerns. It has been ensured from the very first day of cooperation between the two countries that mutual cooperation shall be only for peaceful purposes and will be subject to IAEA safeguards, which is evident by the *Article V(1&2)* of the Nuclear Cooperation agreement 1986 that *"The cooperation pursuant to this Agreement shall be solely for peaceful purposes and the two Governments agree that the recipient country shall request the International Atomic Energy Agency to apply its safeguards."* Moreover, all reactors provided by international community to Pakistan are safeguarded by IAEA. China has been a time-tested friend of Pakistan who has always been the sole supporter of Pakistan in any event of trouble. In spite of a huge criticism by international community, China has extended its cooperation with Pakistan, which is in line with the international obligations; therefore Pakistan would never create an awkward position for China before the international community by misusing any technology or equipment provided by China. Pakistan has also faced a lot of loss due to the so-called AQ Khan story and would not be able to face another incident like the earlier if happens; therefore, it has strengthened the security of its nuclear program according to international standards. Now, there is no chance of nuclear embezzlement in Pakistan.

The non-proliferation concerns of international community on Pakistan-China nuclear deal can be mitigated through the credible domestic legislation in both countries. According to NTI website, Chinese nuclear exports are governed by some certain principles, i.e. "(1) acceptance of IAEA safeguards; (2) peaceful use only; and (3) no re-transfers to a third country without China's prior consent. China has also promulgated domestic laws regulating nuclear and dual-use exports." (China's Nuclear Exports and Assistance to Pakistan 2003)

Pakistan has also adopted credible measures in this regard. Pakistan is member of multiple non-proliferation conventions at international level and it has sufficient controls on its nuclear related entities.

Recently Pakistan has given its stance about the efforts to promote non-proliferation at Nuclear Security Summit in Washington DC held on 12-13 April 2010, and assured the world community about the establishment of effective Command &

Control system, Strict Regulatory Regimes, Extensive Export Control Regime and International Cooperation consistent with its National Policies.

Pakistan government has also taken credible legislative measures domestically against proliferation including nuclear, chemical, and biological transactions, which can provide an assurance to international community about Pakistan's commitment to non-proliferation. Pakistan has taken multiple measures which are supported with rules regarding licensing, diversion and 'catch all clause' providing heavy penalties of imprisonment up to 14 years or Rs. 5 million fines, or both, or confiscating the property of the convict inside Pakistan or outside Pakistan, depending upon the nature of the crime. (IAEA 2004) A brief view of these measures is given below

- Pakistan Nuclear Safety and Radiation Protection (PNSRP) Ordinance, 1984 and PNSRP Regulation, 1990. Controls the transaction of radioactive materials and nuclear substances.
- Statutory Notification No. SRO-782 (1), 1998 provides controls over the export of fissionable material.
- Chemical Weapons Convention Implementation Ordinance, 2000 (Ordinance No.LIV of 2000). Regulates the transaction of chemicals under chemical weapons convention obligations.
- Pakistan Nuclear Regulatory Authority Ordinance, 2001. Ordinance. PNRA is established to regulate all kinds of imports and exports of radioactive materials and sources of radiation.

Berkeley Journal of Social Sciences Vol. 1, Issue 3, March 2011

- Export Control Act 2004, "The materials, equipment and services which could contribute to the designing, development, production, stockpiling, maintenance or use of nuclear and biological weapons and their delivery systems shall be subject to the provisions of this law." (Hussain 2006)
- Biological Weapon Bill 2010 (Proposed), It is proposed by the ministry of foreign affairs Pakistan to enact a law

against the Biological weapon offenders, and suggests a death penalty for those who use or attempt to use Biological weapons, and suggests life imprisonment for those who develop, manufacture, import, export, or possess them. (News 2010)

An evaluation of the elements of effective export control system and its presence in Pakistan has been evaluated by Nazir Hussain, According to an analysis of Pakistan India laws about prevention of proliferation at Stimson centre, "India's and Pakistan's export control legislation nearly mirror one another in substance and structure. Both pieces of legislation explicitly define relevant terms, and there is near symmetry in the layout and organization of the various provisions." (Saha, Ziad Haider and Souvik 2009)

Pakistan's nuclear posture also shows that it has adopted a strategy of 'minimum credible deterrence' with lower nuclear threshold. Following its MCD strategy, Pakistan does not need to have a huge number of nuclear weapons, therefore, Pakistan need not to clandestinely divert peaceful civilian nuclear technology to the military purposes. Moreover, Pakistan's nuclear program is Uranium based, which was developed purely through indigenous means. Pakistan has its own Uranium enrichment plants and sufficient natural Uranium reserves at its own soil; therefore, it does not need international resources for the development of its nuclear weapon program that may invite huge undue international concerns. The Khaleej Times editorial suggests that "the US needs to realize that it cannot control or dictate developments between third states no matter how distasteful they may be. It must not forget that China would not have done this if it was not comfortable with controls and security measures implemented by Pakistan. It is also a good opportunity for Pakistan to alleviate previous concerns about proliferation and prove it is a responsible nuclear state, one that deserves due respect." (Pakistan-China civilian nuclear deal 2010)

The so called allegations of nuclear terrorism regarding Pakistan's nuclear weapon, is also a part of international propaganda against Pakistan's nuclear arsenal. One should be aware that stealing, manufacturing, and launching a nuclear weapon is not a task that can be fulfilled by some terrorists. Nuclear weapons are high-tech weapons which involve a complex mechanism for explosion. Such kind of knowledge cannot be obtained or used without having an organized institutional support. Moreover, Nuclear weapons are useless in the absence of credible delivery system, which is also very complicated and impossible to be designed, manufactured, and launched. Nuclear weapons cannot be launched through simple rocket launchers. Without having the involved technical equipments and the knowledge about their complicated operations, it is impossible for any group to use those weapons. It takes a lot of time and efforts to become capable of acquiring and launching nuclear weapons, which is even more difficult for sovereign states to obtain despite having huge resources and capabilities. In this scenario, how it is possible that Pakistan's nuclear weapons can fall into the hands of terrorist. The whole debate in this regard is baseless and just meant for the purpose of creating fuss against Pakistan.

## THE PAKISTAN-CHINA-INDIA DYNAMIC

### *The Problem of Pakistan*

India's geographically closest and most frequently problematic relationship is with its neighbour and prodigal twin, Pakistan. India's rise as a great power will have its most immediate impact on the extremely dangerous stalemate which exists between the two states. Many security concerns converge in Pakistan, as: the state has been a key supporter of the Taliban in Afghanistan, factions of which the Pakistani Army is now fighting in a de facto civil war; elements within the state support Islamic terrorist organisations that periodically attack India, provoking regional crises; and, the Pakistani Army has a growing nuclear arsenal, which could be vulnerable to misuse by malicious elements within the state. India and Pakistan engaged in wars in 1965 and 1971, with crises about continuing Pakistani support for insurgents in the disputed Indian state of Jammu and Kashmir erupting periodically, and threatening war in 1990. Following Indian and Pakistani nuclear tests in May 1998, Pakistani incursions across the Line of Control in the Kargil region of Kashmir led to another limited war, and the veiled nuclear threat by Pakistani Foreign Secretary Shamshad Ahmed that, 'We will not hesitate to use any weapon in our arsenal to defend our territorial integrity.' Major terrorist attacks in Jammu and Kashmir on 1 October 2001 and in the Indian capital Delhi on 13 December 2001 again threatened war, though merely resulted in major military manoeuvres by India, code-named *Operation Parakram*. The lack of military retaliation by India despite grave provocation seems to suggest that India is successfully deterred by Pakistan's nuclear capability, and this in turn only fuels the eagerness of some elements within Pakistan to provoke India. Pakistan has adopted an "asymmetric nuclear escalation posture", which has deterred Indian conventional military power and thus enabled Pakistan's 'aggressive strategy of bleeding India by a "thousand cuts" with little fear of significant retaliation.'

India is four times larger and seven times more populated than Pakistan. As Pakistan averages only 300 miles in width, it is susceptible to a central assault that would split the country in two. A number of important Pakistani cities also lie close to the international border in the Indus River basin. As Pakistan is thus extremely vulnerable to conventional attack by India's larger military, it defines such an attack as an existential threat to the Pakistani state. Pakistani Lt. Gen. Khalid Kidwai thus outlined that Pakistan would use its nuclear weapons if: India attacks Pakistan and conquers a large part of its territory; India destroys a large part of Pakistan's land or air forces; India blockades Pakistan in an effort to strangle it economically; or, India pushes Pakistan into a state of political destabilisation. This asymmetric escalation posture is designed for a rapid first use of nuclear weapons against conventional attacks, thus leaving India without the ability to punish terrorist attacks through conventional retaliation. As elements within Pakistan continue to provoke India, this creates an extremely dangerous imbalance reliant on India's restraint to maintain peace.

Vipin Narang notes that, 'Scholars who study the South Asian nuclear balance have argued that if a limited clash between India and Pakistan were to expand into a full-scale conventional war, escalation to the nuclear level would likely result.'4 Most of the "war-game" scenarios played out by the US military also foresee any conventional conflict between India and Pakistan escalating to the use of nuclear weapons within the first 12 days.

New analyses of this eventuality reveal that a conflict between India and Pakistan, in which 100 nuclear bombs were dropped on cities and industrial areas within the two countries, would kill more than 20 million people from the blasts, fires and radioactivity. In addition, the explosions could produce enough smoke to cripple global agriculture. Smoke generated by burning cities could create a climatic response that immediately reduces sunlight, cools the planet, and reduces precipitation worldwide. This "nuclear winter" would reduce or eliminate agricultural production over vast areas, simultaneously decreasing crop yields nearly everywhere. Approximately one billion people worldwide today live on marginal food supplies and would be directly threatened with starvation. While some analysts maintain that nuclear weapons would be used in only a measured way, the chaos, fear and interruption of communications that would follow nuclear war's commencement leads some to doubt that attacks would be limited in any rational manner. Additionally, Pakistan could face a decision to use its entire nuclear arsenal quickly or lose it to Indian forces which seize its military bases. Thus, unrestrained nuclear war in South Asia potentially has cataclysmic regional and global consequences.

Following the terrorist attack by Kashmiri militants in December 2001 and the subsequent military standoff with Pakistan in *Operation Parakram*, the Indian Army announced a new limited war doctrine in April 2004 called the Cold Start doctrine, which aims to allow conventional retaliation without posing an existential threat to Pakistan. Under Cold Start, the Indian army would avoid delivering a catastrophic blow to Pakistan, and instead make shallow territorial gains, 50-80 kilometres deep, that could be used in post-conflict negotiations. This doctrine aims to deny Pakistan the justification of "regime survival" for employing nuclear weapons in response to a conventional Indian attack. However, Walter C. Ladwig III foresees that, 'An operational Cold Start capability could lead Pakistan to lower its nuclear red line, put its nuclear weapons on a higher state of readiness, develop tactical nuclear weapons, or undertake some equally destabilising course of action.' The danger of escalation is further compounded by the relatively immature "command and control" and early warning systems of both the Indian and Pakistani nuclear arsenals. There also remains the danger of nuclear accident as, if one nation accidentally detonates a nuclear warhead on one of its own military bases, it probably will not have adequate surveillance intelligence to know that it has not been attacked by its enemy, and thus may falsely "retaliate" against the other country.

Meanwhile, in the context of the continuing conflict in Afghanistan, Pakistan believes that the United States would intervene to prevent war, as it relies on Pakistani troops along the Afghan border and supplies for American forces are transported through Pakistan. Thus, Pakistan believes the only potential military action available to India is air-strikes against Islamist training camps, which itself is not a serious problem, and may actually help Islamabad by killing destabilising jihadists while generating massive support among

Pakistanis for their government. The dual problems of nuclear escalation and American reliance on Pakistan for counter-insurgency meant that following terrorist attacks in Mumbai by Pakistani group Lashkar-e-Taiba on 26 November 2008, which killed 163 people, India was unable to respond with conventional military strikes. Any attack by India might either destabilise the Pakistani Government, or escalate the conflict to nuclear exchange. In the event of state disintegration, Pakistani nuclear weapons could fall into the hands of militant elements who would attempt to use those weapons against India or the West.

Unfortunately, there is no easy path to stabilising reform within Pakistan. Pakistan essentially has a feudal political establishment, run by a civilian aristocracy of wealthy agricultural landowners and industrialists, and the Army. The civilian political parties primarily function as patronage networks, without deep-seated ideological differences, and merely struggle to control state resources.

As a key aim of the agricultural and industrial élites is to avoiding paying income taxes, the Pakistani Government is also chronically in debt. The Army is seen by most Pakistanis as the primary defender of the nation and the ultimate guarantor of domestic stability. The ever-present threat of India is used to justify the Army's disproportionate share of national resources, and the Army itself also owns and manages a large agricultural and industrial empire. Domestically, the Army is the ultimate power-broker between the political parties, and has acted on several occasions to remove the party in power. As successive governments have received bailouts from international financial institutions, neither the civilian political élites nor the Army have felt any real incentive to institute fundamental change.

For the time-being, the Army is objectively the most stable and responsible force to control the country. The Pakistani military is the only state institution that works effectively, and without it Pakistan would probably have disintegrated long ago. The dire alternatives are representatives of the rising wave of radical Islam who arose from the madrassas under the patronage of General Zia ul-Haq, and gained their training in the US-backed *mujahedeen* struggle against the Soviet occupation of Afghanistan. These elements, and more recent jihadist recruits, are currently involved in Kashmiri terrorist organisations like Jaysh-e-Mohammad, and Lashkar-e-Taiba, as well as in the Afghani and Pakistani Taliban which occupy Pakistan's border provinces. While the Pakistani Army and intelligence services are often unwilling to directly challenge these forces (and, indeed, currently cultivate relations with the Kashmiri groups and the Afghani Taliban), and external (and, particularly, American) attempts to move forces into Pakistani territory would almost certainly make things worse, this unstable situation is likely to continue.

As India's power increases, so will its ability to strategically encircle Pakistan, through relations with Iran and Afghanistan, and via naval power. At the same time, India's patience for Pakistan's continuing terrorist provocations will probably lessen. Nevertheless, Pakistan's deterrent capabilities remain, as attacks on the Pakistani state – either unsuccessful or successful – are likely to result in either nuclear exchange or widespread chaos and bloodshed. If India continues restraint, however, and reaches out to more moderate elements within the military and civilian political parties, it could leverage its growing economic strength to gradually help a more moderate Pakistani state develop.

## THE CHALLENGE OF CHINA

On a grander strategic level, relations between India and China will be highly significant as India emerges as a great power. There is a growing interdependence between the two Asian giants, as China is now India's number-one trading partner, with more than $52 billion in bilateral trade, and estimates are that China-India trade will surpass US-China trade by 2020. China's powerful manufacturing sector complements India's combination of a raw materials and cutting-edge technology economy. Strategically, a strong and influential India helps to create a more multipolar world, consistent with Chinese interests, although China increasingly regards India as its main Asian rival. China is thus involved in a complex game of encirclement with India. China has armed Pakistan with nuclear weapons and ballistic missile technology, and has built 'strong military-to-military ties with Burma, Pakistan, Nepal, Bangladesh, and Sri Lanka as part of what Indians see as a strategy to tie India down, Gulliver-like, in its region.'[9] China is also developing deep-water ports throughout the Indian Ocean to support its projected blue-water naval capacity.

Meanwhile, on the border, China continues to press its claims to vast tracts of Indian territory. Over the past years, increased friction in the border area between India and China has led to incursions by Chinese troops, the wounding of several Indian border police, and a build-up of military forces on both sides, as Beijing has been uncharacteristically assertive in its claims to sections of India's Arunachal Pradesh state. The Indians responded by moving 30,000 troops and their latest warplanes into the area, leading some analysts to predict a China-India war within five years.

China rejects the McMahon Line that forms the border, and places the traditional Sino-Indian border at the base of the

Himalayan foothills. Stratfor's George Friedman argues that, for China, control of Tibet is of vital strategic importance, providing a barrier against its populous and economically and militarily-advancing neighbour. The high mountain passes of Tibet provide virtually impenetrable terrain which is easy to protect militarily. Along the frontier directly south of this border, in India, is one of the largest population concentrations in the world. If China were to withdraw, Beijing fears that this population could migrate into Tibet, and Tibet could gradually turn into a beachhead for Indian power that would directly abut Sichuan and Yunnan provinces. The Chinese thus see control of Tibet as a matter of fundamental national security. They also see the 1959 decision by Indian Prime Minister Jawaharlal Nehru to give asylum to the Dalai Lama, and the continuing support for the Tibetan government-in-exile, as perpetuating this threat. Thus, 'Beijing's price for a border settlement and for normalisation of ties with India, appears to be that India dismantle the Tibetan settlement in Dharamshala and request the Dalai Lama take up residence in another country.'On a broader front, 80 per cent of China's oil and gas supplies transit the Indian Ocean and South China Sea, so the Chinese navy is increasingly making its presence felt in the area in order to secure its lines of supply.

For China, like India, the steady flow of imported resources is not just an issue of economic growth, but also of the longevity of the Chinese Communist Party. Chinese leaders increasingly fear that adversaries could blockade sea lanes and strategic bottlenecks such as the Strait of Malacca, and are thus moving to an offshore defence policy that will include "distant ocean defence". China's actions, however, may impinge upon India's interests and destabilise relations.

Jason Blazevic argues that, following "defensive realist" strategies, each nation will attempt to gain power for self-preservation and other nations will see this move as a strategic threat, thus decreasing collective security. As part of this competition, China has been developing a so-called "string-of-pearls" strategy, expanding influence into ports in Burma, Sri Lanka and Pakistan. According to a report by US defence contractor

Booz Allen Hamilton, 'China is building strategic relationships along the sea lanes from the Middle East to the South China Sea in a way that suggests defensive and offensive positioning to protect China's energy interests.' China emerged as the biggest military spender in the Asia-Pacific in 2006, and now has the fourth-largest defence expenditure in the world. Its navy is also considered the third-largest in the world behind only the US and Russia, and is superior to the Indian Navy. In this context, India perceives Chinese actions as power maximisation, and fears that China's forward-basing strategy will be used to contain India and rapidly achieve hegemony in the Indian Ocean.

Meanwhile, China and India have adopted nuclear "assured retaliation" postures (what they sometimes refer to as "credible minimum deterrence"), which rely on a small but secure and survivable nuclear force that assures a retaliatory strike against a primary opponent. In many ways, this seems like the most stable aspect of the competition between India and China, though it is yet to be seen what reaction a new generation of *Surya* missiles might provoke in China. Meanwhile, analysts like Stephen Walt expect that China will follow a consistent but non-provocative build-up of its military capabilities and diplomatic alliances over the long-term, aiming to gradually edge the United States out of a hegemonic position. India is likely to mirror this build-up and thus tension, and possible low-level confrontation, may result on the India-China border and in the Indian Ocean region.

## THE PERIL OF PRESTIGE IN NUCLEAR POWER

The cost-benefit analyses with regard to fuel cost for nuclear energy is particularly troubling. In most cases, the capital costs are the major component of such analysis whereas operating and maintenance costs and fuel costs are frequently underestimated. The price of uranium fuel can fluctuate dramatically as we can see from observing the past five years of the price of uranium oxide which was around $6 per pound in 2001 and has jumped to over $40 per pound in 2006.[9] Furthermore the cost of appropriate disposal of nuclear wastes is frequently neglected. While reprocessing is often presented as an alternative, in reality reprocessing does not reduce waste but can only reduce the amount of mined uranium. France, among the world's leading nuclear energy users, spends about $1 billion extra per year on reprocessed plutonium fuel compared to uranium fuel. Even the relatively promising thorium reactors for which India has the second-largest ore reserves of monazite in the world, first require the thorium to be converted to fissionable uranium (233).

Plutonium fuel obtained by reprocessing (also called mixed-oxide fuel or MOX) is two to three times more costly than uranium fuel. Apart from the prestige of being a nuclear energy producer, increased investment in nuclear power makes little economic sense. By playing around with discount rates proponents of nuclear energy can sometimes come up with ostensibly cost-effective comparisons with other fuels but there is little doubt that the construction cost of a nuclear power plant is inordinately more than any other source. In a recent study by the Massachusetts Institute of Technology, the all-inclusive cost for a nuclear power plant operating over 40 years is 6.7 cents per kilowatt-hour, which is almost twice the cost for natural gas at current prices.

And all these arguments bode negatively for nuclear even without considering its environmental and human health impact. Nuclear energy is also not very reliable at this stage since plant upgrades can take years to accomplish. For example, Pakistan's only nuclear generator, the Karachi Nuclear Power Plant (KANUPP) was shut down for refurbishment in December 2002 after exhausting its 30 year design life and is still undergoing upgrades before being ready to reach capacity again.

The environmental challenges of managing radioactive mining has become evident by the recent case of the village of Baghhalchur in rural Punjab, Pakistan. From 1978 to 2000 this region provided the Pakistani Atomic Energy Commission (PAEC) with yellow cake for the country's nuclear program. The half a million tribesmen in this region near Dera Ghazi Khan, many of whom are Baluchi, have leukemia rates that are six times the national average. Even former employees of the PAEC, such as Professor Khalid Rashid of Bahria University have publicly acknowledged that there are legitimate concerns of radioactive pollution that need to be investigated. In a rare show of support for environmental enforcement the Pakistani supreme court agreed to hear the petitions of the residents of the area in March, 2006 and a decision is pending.

The ostensible benefit of nuclear energy in terms of reduced greenhouse gas emissions is also misleading since the energy required to mine uranium and the maintenance of reactors shows that there is indeed a net contribution of greenhouse gases from nuclear energy as well. While Pakistan and all other countries should keep the nuclear option open it must always be a last resort and probably requires several more decades of research on waste management solutions and cost efficiency before being viable at a large scale.

### *Humbling the Hysteria over Hydropower*

The prestige factor with large-scale hydropower also appears to be resonating with the Pakistani government. While the advantages of dams such as Tarbela and Mangla at the time of construction are widely appreciated, the long-term viability of these projects remains questionable. In its case study on Tarbela dam, the World Commission on Dams generally concluded that the dam had made a positive contribution to the Pakistani economy, particularly the energy sector. However, what is less clear is whether the dam and other such large irreversible hydropower projects can sustain benefits over the longrun in comparison with alternative energy sources. The useful life of a dam such as Tarbela is about 100 years for which around 100,000 people were displaced, not to mention the inundation of 23,000 hectares of arable land. Even the increase in cultivable land requires further ecological study in cost-benefit analyses since in many cases mismanagement of the irrigation schemes led to salinity and water-logging and eventual loss of arable capacity in 22% of the Indus basin. Evaporation losses can greatly diminish irrigation benefits as well, and the flood control advantage of dams must be balanced with the risk of dam failure in high risk zones.

In particular seismic hazards and the vulnerability of such sources in times of armed conflict and droughts also needs to be considered, specially following the Kashmir earthquake of October 2005. The vulnerability of dams to earthquakes remains considerably high throughout this region as exemplified by numerous studies of faults in the area. A large dam failure can be utterly catastrophic as illustrated by China's experience with the collapse of the Banqiao reservoir dam in 1975 which killed over 175,000 people and displaced 11 million residents. Even though China is proceeding with the Three Gorges project on the Yangtze river, despite the refusal of the World Bank to fund, the Chinese are having second thoughts about some of their other dam projects including a moratorium on 13 proposed dams on the Nu River.

Indeed, even the positive impacts of reduced greenhouse gas emissions of large dams is being questioned since there is potential for methane generation from dam reservoirs. It is for this reason that dams above 10MW generating capacity were initially excluded from the list of eligible renewable energy sources presented by the European Union to the Intergovernmental Panel on Climate Change in 2000. While this list was subsequently not accepted by all countries, the World Bank has admitted that hydropower projects greater than 10MW have "declining commitments" from the international community. It is thus alarming that the Pakistani government is now considering five new large hydropower projects. The Bhasha (Diamir) Dam whose construction has already been inaugurated by President Musharraf would be comparable in MW capacity to Tarbela at around 3500MW. Extensive community opposition is already palpable around this project, reminiscent to earlier concerns over the Kalabagh dam, and there are growing concerns that the conflicts at the micro-level as well as distributional concerns between provinces may further destabilize the country.

As compared to large-scale hydropower, small-scale hydropower is a highly attractive renewable solution and must be encouraged across Pakistan. Such dams have the advantage of being more flexible to engineering redesign or removal if necessary as they age. There are indeed promising possibilities in this regard for smaller rivers across Pakistan such as the Kunhar, the Swat, and Chitral. While aggregate hydropower capacity from these rivers might not ostensibly match the potential from large projects, the overall efficiency in distribution systems can often make them more attractive. There is much to be gained from pursuing a sensible policy on hydropower so long as we remember that "bigger" is not always "better."

## AN AGENDA FOR CHANGE

Despite the aforementioned grim critique there are some relatively quick policy interventions and compliance measures which can be undertaken to improve Pakistan's energy prospects. The country has adequate human and natural resources to meet these demands for the foreseeable future. As relations improve with its neighbors and regional security the long-term outlook can indeed be very positive as the following measures are considered domestically:

### *Auditing Energy Consumption*

The first step to solving any technical problem to is to have a better estimate of the status quo. At present there is hardly any data available on the energy performance of Pakistan's industry. Therefore a detailed audit of industries and households in urban and rural areas is needed. A modest study of energy conservation potential including audits was performed by the government in the late eighties which included industrial units, residential and commercial buildings and appliances, turbines and tractors in agriculture and passenger and freight vehicles. Apparently there is renewed interest from the Asian Development Bank and the German development agency (GTZ) to revise this study which should subsequently be an important tool for energy policy-makers in Pakistan.

Individual studies of energy consumption, particularly in rural areas of Pakistan have revealed some counterintuitive insights which the government might also consider. For example, one doctoral study of rural energy consumption in Punjab found that electricity is only used for lighting which is a negligible proportion of the total household energy consumption, and the researcher concluded that ""a route of supply side energy policy that only encourages increasing the supply of energy resources, most often based on inaccuracies extrapolations of past growth or historic elasticity of energy supply. Food preparation, water heating and animal-warming are main demand areas in rural areas and traditional fuels continue to be preferentially used even when grid power is made available. Some of these fuels may indeed be very problematic when used in crude form, such as dung, but quite workable with small technological innovations that filter out pollutants such as inexpensive "clean" stoves that have been used in Mexico and China. A comprehensive energy audit would reveal the details necessary to implement such technological efforts and provide more effective and targeted solutions.

Creating proper economic incentives to ensure conservation behaviour on the part of consumers is an essential ingredient to effective energy policy. First there needs to be effective enforcement of energy usage to prevent theft and "free riding" of the system. The government has begun to enforce laws against such thefts but considerably more compliance assurance is needed through police action and prosecution where necessary.

Furthermore, recent analyses conducted at the Lahore University of Management Sciences has revealed that there is allocative inefficiency in Pakistan's manufacturing sector characterized by "the absence of equality between marginal rates of substitution and factor price rations." In other words the pricing of energy in Pakistan's manufacturing sector is leading firms to use resources inefficiently. Ensuring that such pricing concerns are addressed will reduce the load on the system considerably and be a win-win solution for industry as well that will have more dependable supply.

### *Using Technology to Overcome losses in the System*

By one estimate of Pakistan's private energy systems, thermal efficiency in energy generation system tends to be around 32-35% when the global average is around 54%.24 We could thus have a 60% improvement in energy generation by simply switching to newer production technologies. Distribution losses in these systems tend to be around 23%, whereas the technical losses should be no more than 3%. By this estimate Pakistan could increase its energy availability by a staggering 80% simply through more efficient distribution systems that could be updated at a fraction of the cost of mega-energy generation projects being proposed. Furthermore, these numbers do not even account for energy conservation measures in buildings and factories that would result from proper energy audits across sectors mentioned earlier. There are some glimmers of improvement in the improvement of energy efficiency through more effective harnessing of biofuels as revealed by one comparative study of the region which compared Pakistan, India, Bangladesh and Thailand. Indeed there are many lessons on efficient technological applications, specially at the rural scale which can be gleaned from such comparisons.

### *Giving Precedence to Renewable Sources*

Apart from natural gas, there is tremendous potential for wind and solar energy across South Asia that has hardly been explored. With funding from the Asian Development bank, Pakistan's government has set a target of generating 10 percent of its electricity needs using renewable energy resources (approximately 2,700 MW) by 2015. The government has established an Alternative Energy Development Board (AEDB) and will launch a Renewable Energy Project that will invest in developing electricity sources for rural areas. However, this target is woefully inadequate based on.

Based on comparative data from India, Pakistan as the potential for solar and wind energy that far exceeds this goal. There is tremendous potential for wind and solar energy across South Asia that has hardly been explored. According to Winrock International, less than 10 percent of India's estimated wind energy generation potential of 45,000 MW has been harnessed so far. Solar energy potential — an estimated 300 days per year of full solar exposure in many areas of the country — is enormous as well. While the Pakistani government has started to develop some wind and solar projects in Sindh and Baluchistan as highlighted by Chapter X (Pandey) in this volume, these projects continue to be relegated to the periphery rather than being given precedence over the larger infrastructure projects.

There has also been a renewed interest in mining coal in Pakistan. While coal is abundant in Baluchistan and parts of Sindh, the quality of the deposits is a matter of great concern. The contribution of coal to Pakistan's electricity generation has declined from 60% in 1947 to 8% currently but this should not be a cause for lament by the government. Some high quality coal deposits when harnessed with appropriate technologies are indeed viable. However, there must first be appropriate regulatory safeguards for safety and health in mining the coal as well as protection for sensitive ecological areas such as Kirthar National Park. At present Pakistan has not been part of numerous industry-wide efforts to improve the performance of the mining sector such as those launched by the World Business Council on Sustainable Development. Any new mining projects must adhere to such standards before being rushed through for approval.

## PAKISTAN'S STRATEGIES IN CENTRAL ASIA

Pakistan took due notice of the geo-strategic importance of Central Asian states in the changed security paradigm after the end of the Cold War. Initial efforts by Pakistan to make some inroad into Central Asia may not have succeeded because of its unclear foreign policy objectives, but Pakistan remains an important player in the region. In fact, its geo-strategic location makes it difficult for Central Asian regimes to ignore Pakistan. In recent years, Pakistan's relations with the Central Asian Republics (CARs) have improved. In the unfolding geo-political situation, the current Central Asian regimes are trying to build new equations with Islamabad.

Analysis of Pakistan's strategies in the Central Asian region constitutes the principal focus of this book. It argues that various economic and geo strategic factors have shaped Pakistan's policy towards Central Asia, but fear of India's influence in this region remains a predominant factor in the formulation of its strategies. In fact, Pakistan's foreign policy, since its very inception, has been conditioned by two interrelated factors, i.e., the fear of India and an urge to seek a strategic balance with India. Another important element of its foreign policy has been its self-proclaimed strong attachment to Islamic ideology. These strands determine

Islamabad's policy towards Central Asia as well. Therefore, Pakistan's relation with the CARs needs to be examined in the context of its overall foreign and military policies. Pakistan's adversarial relations with neighbouring India play a vital role in the formation of its national security plans. Time and again this has been articulated within Pakistan. Its policy towards the United States (US) has always been premised on the consideration that military assistance from the US would help Pakistan attain parity with India. Its strong politico-military ties with China also seek to counterbalance India's influence in the region. At another level, its desire to be the leader of the Islamic bloc is premised on the consideration that this would enhance Pakistan's influence in the Islamic bloc, which, in turn, can be used against India. Pakistan has always tried to project itself as the only country that can stand up to India in the region. This has been the cornerstone of Islamabad's strategic thinking.

Pakistan's foreign policy-making is highly personalised and centralised, but the army plays a big role in setting the parameters within which Islamabad conducts its relations with the outside world. The military has a significant influence that even elected governments cannot ignore. The role of the intelligence agencies, particularly the Inter-Services Intelligence (ISI), is equally significant. Also, the religious orientation of the state accords a special legitimacy to the role of religion in the training of the military personnel. There is, hence, a curious blend of loyalties of the armed forces to the state of Pakistan and the religion of Islam that serves as the ideological glue. Some scholars believe that "religion is very-very central to the Pakistan's military strategic thinking."

A few scholars have argued that Pakistan's foreign policy-making process is influenced by three contending schools of thought but that are united in their hostility towards India. They differ on the strategy to be pursued by them to counter India. The first school of thought lays emphasis on'surrender' and believes in a uni-polar world. It maintains that Pakistan has little choice but to rely on and surrender its policy options to the US as a balancer. The second school of thought advocates 'independence' and has a multipolar worldview. While acknowledging the importance of the US, it wants Pakistan to reach out to and benefit from its relationship with other major powers like Japan, China and Russia. This school argues that such a relationship would offer Islamabad considerable flexibility. The third school of thought emphasises on 'Islam' and the Islamic nature of the Pakistani state. It also subscribes to the unipolar worldview and argues for alliances based on Pakistan's ideological and religious interests.

It is also often argued that within the Pakistani establishment there are either "hawks or liberal pacifists, but no realists". These varied nuances demand serious consideration. It is important to note that Pakistani rulers and the military in particular, at some point of time, have been influenced by these three schools of thought while formulating Pakistan's policy towards the CARs. Before examining Pakistan's present-day strategies in the CARs, it is important to understand its involvement in Central Asia and Afghanistan prior to the emergence of the independent Central Asian states in 1991.

## BACKGROUND

Pakistan's quest for security led to its involvement in Central Asia much before the CARs emerged as independent states in 1991. The military regime under President Muhammad Zia-ul-Haq encouraged the Afghan mujahideen to spread out to the erstwhile Central Asian republics within the then Soviet Union and the CIA supplied arms to the mujahideen through the ISI to conduct these forays. The fear of expanding Soviet influence in Afghanistan and beyond led to Pakistan's involvement in Afghanistan and Central Asia.

The Soviet intervention in Afghanistan in 1979 added a new dimension to Pakistan's existing threat perception. It was of the view that after consolidating its position within Afghanistan, Moscow would try to access the 'warm waters' of the Arabian Sea through Pakistan. Islamabad was able to sell this idea to Washington and after the Soviet invasion of Afghanistan, it became a 'frontline' state for the US. This threat perception was crafted by the Pakistani leadership to cement its ties with Washington, which otherwise was at an all-time low since the military takeover in 1977. It also helped Pakistan achieve its larger strategic goal of acquiring more military and economic aid from the US so as to attain parity with India. To counter India's influence in Afghanistan, because of its earlier ties in Kabul, Pakistan always wanted to see a friendly Pashtun government in Kabul since the 1950s. And since the 1980s, Pakistan projected Afghanistan as a source of its "strategic depth" in the event of war with India.

As part of a strategy to destabilise the Soviet Union, a conscious policy was adopted by Pakistan to encourage Islamic influence in and infiltrate Islamist mujahideen into the Central Asian states. In 1984, Afghan groups trained by Pakistani intelligence sent 5,000 copies of the Koran across the border. This group had drawn in people living in northern Afghanistan– mainly Uzbeks. Moreover, the base camps of groups entering Soviet territory were located north of Peshawar in Chitral district on the border with Afghanistan. In fact, the policy of exporting jihad to Central Asia had an impact there during the Soviet era, which was visible in the immediate aftermath of the Geneva Agreements of April 1988 and the withdrawal of Soviet forces from Afghanistan. The Tajik civil war broke out immediately after the Central Asian republics gained independence in 1991.

In the late 1970s, dissident Islamic underground parties had began to form in Tajikistan, and the Tajik nationalists were seen to be gaining in popularity and influence by the end of the 1980s. However, real disturbances did not occur until the early 1990s. The Soviet Union collapsed in 1991, and Tajikistan declared its independence in 1991. The Tajik civil war started in 1992 and continued till 1997.

Islamabad did not make any change in its military-political strategy during Benazir Bhutto's period. Reports of the Pakistani intelligence services and their role in promoting Islamic radicalism in Central Asia appeared in the writings of General A.A. Liakhovskii, a participant in the Afghan war. According to him, the organisation "Islamic Union of the Northern Peoples of Afghanistan" (Islamskiisoiuz severnykh narodov Afghanistan), created in 1988, launched subversive activities in areas of Central

Asia contiguous with Afghanistan, with the goal of liberating Soviet Muslims and creating a "free Turkestan". Azad Beg headed this organisation, which had its headquarters in Peshawar. According to Liakhovskii, the field commanders of this organisation shipped narcotics, weapons, and subversive (mainly Islamic) literature to the USSR.

However, the Soviet withdrawal from Afghanistan and the end of Cold War considerably altered the geo-strategic scenario in the region. Pakistan lost its role as a 'frontline state' thus losing its strategic relevance to the US. The Gulf War further dented Pakistan's geo-strategic advantage with Washington reinforcing its links with the Persian Gulf region. This period also witnessed improved relations between India-US and India-China. Therefore, the 1990s offered a very different geo-strategic configuration. Another important development during this period was the emergence of the Taliban and its strong ties with Pakistan. The Taliban connection was used by Islamabad to sponsor cross-border terrorism in Jammu and Kashmir. Pakistan and Afghanistan became the hub of terrorist activities. These developments had serious implications for the newly independent countries of Central Asia. Jihadi elements from Afghanistan and Pakistan started infiltrating into the neighbouring Central Asian states of Tajikistan, Uzbekistan and Kyrgyzstan.

The events of 9/11 once again changed the geo-political landscape with new alignments and realignments taking shape in Central Asia. For the US and Pakistan, Central Asia became an area of great strategic significance. Islamabad, while forced to cooperate with Washington in its global war against terrorism, could manage much-needed economic and military aid for its services in Afghanistan and its sudden reversal of policy towards that country. Post-9/11, Pakistan tried to make inroads into Central Asia with an improved image. It offered shorter routes for Central Asian goods and connectivity with the rest of the world.

## PAKISTAN'S OBJECTIVES IN CENTRAL ASIA

Pakistan's objectives in Central Asia are determined by its political and security imperatives; its economic and commercial gains; countering India's influence and its desire to be an energy transit-corridor in South Asia and the Asia-Pacific region. Pakistan has always desired to expand its influence in Afghanistan and beyond. Central Asia is seen as an area of natural expansion for Pakistan. Hafeez Malik believes that Central Asia presents Pakistan with a new security environment "...freed from the nutcracker squeeze the Soviet Union had created through an alliance between Afghanistan and India."

Related to Pakistan's ambition to expand its influence is the desire to be the leader of the Islamic bloc. Albeit this idea has not crystallised, but it has always dominated the thinking of the Pakistani leadership, including Prime Minister Bhutto in the 1970s and Gen. Zia in the 1980s. The debate still remains pertinent to Pakistan's geo-strategic formulations. The Islamic groups and parties viewed Central Asia as paving the way for an Islamic bloc thus providing an opportunity to unite Muslims in the CARs, Iran, Turkey, Pakistan and Afghanistan. It was felt that such a strategic bloc would acquire a central role in securing strategic interests vis-a-vis India or even the Christian-Jewish threat. The emergence of the CARs were perceived as an opportunity to form a large regional grouping stretching from the Arabian Sea in the south to the Black Sea in the west based on the common religious identity of Islam. Importantly, it was seen to offer a huge political and economic benefit to Pakistan.

In fact, Central Asia does provide Pakistan with numerous opportunities in terms of trade in raw material and manufactured goods, contracting for regular power supply and opening up communications. The resource rich Central Asia is seen as a future source of energy for Pakistan.

## CONSTRAINTS ON U.S. ASSISTANCE

Constraints on U.S. assistance can be grouped into three categories. The first category encompasses legal prohibitions, embodied in international treaties and U.S. domestic law. While domestic laws can be changed, or provisions can be waived, international treaties are more difficult to amend. The second category includes technical limitations, given what little we know about Indian and Pakistani nuclear weapons and their secret nuclear facilities. In addition, assistance should be guided by the impact it would have on the technical capabilities of the Indian and Pakistani nuclear arsenals — that is, assistance should not advance the nuclear weapon programs of India and Pakistan, nor should it encourage testing, deployment or increased operational readiness. The third category covers political limitations, including Indian and Pakistani willingness to engage in cooperation and the impact of assistance on the nonproliferation regimes.

### *International Legal Constraints*

The primary treaty constraint on the United States is found in Article I of the NPT. Article I requires nuclear weapon states to commit: Under Article I, the United States is prohibited from transferring to any state (nuclear weapon state, non-nuclear weapon state, party or non-party to the Treaty) nuclear weapons, nuclear explosive devices or control over such weapons or devices, directly or indirectly. It is not readily apparent what is meant by "control" over such weapons; a narrow interpretation would focus on the ability of another state to use such a weapon. The history of NPT negotiations reveals that concerns over transferring "control" over such weapons focused primarily on allies (e.g. NATO) being able to make command and control decisions for U.S. nuclear weapons deployed in Europe.

The second part of the obligation lies in not assisting, encouraging or inducing non-nuclear weapon states to manufacture or otherwise acquire nuclear weapons or other nuclear explosive devices or control over such weapons or explosive devices. The negotiating history reveals that negotiators intended to interpret "manufacture" broadly, from the beginning of the acquisition cycle to the end. Non-nuclearweapon states party to the NPT are obligated not to seek or receive any assistance in the manufacture of such weapons under Article II. Presumably, this would cover assistance that enhanced command and control of weapons, including permissive action link (PAL) technology. However, India and Pakistan, while they are legally non-nuclear weapon states, are not party to the NPT, and so are not bound by such an obligation.

As defined by paragraph 3, Article IX of the NPT, India and Pakistan are considered to be non-nuclear weapon states because they did not explode a nuclear device before 1967. In the case of providing assistance to Russia, there was no parallel concern because Russia is a nuclear weapon state under the NPT. It is difficult to interpret what might constitute a violation of Article I under the NPT. In the ratification hearings before Congress in 1968, U.S. administration officials noted that the treaty does not specify what can be done, but rather what cannot be done. There is no currently publicly available legal view from the State Department on what might constitute a violation of Article I, but legal advisors have considered this question by examining precedents in the application of U.S. domestic law. In general, the closer assistance is attached to the nuclear weapons programs, the more likely that it could run afoul of U.S. legal obligations, both under international treaty obligations and domestic law. Thus, some kinds of aid (e.g., food or humanitarian aid) could be considered, in the extreme, to be assisting or encouraging a nuclear weapons program because they free up resources that the target government can put towards a nuclear weapons program but are permitted in practice because they do not have a close association with a nuclear weapons program. If assistance took the form of transferrable funds, however, the possibility of linkage to a nuclear weapons program might be considered to be greater.

## Domestic Legal Constraints

As noted earlier, U.S. domestic law covers restrictions in the following areas: nuclear weapons cooperation, nuclear material trade, and dual-use exports. U.S. domestic laws have incorporated significant nonproliferation requirements over the years, which complicate cooperation with India and Pakistan. The Atomic Energy Act. (as amended; 42 U.S.C. 2011 and following) governs the military and civil uses of nuclear energy, including those related to international cooperation. Prior to the development of international safeguards, U.S. law required that states receiving U.S.-origin nuclear material or equipment not retransfer it and place it under adequate physical security. The 1978 Nuclear Nonproliferation Act amended the AEA to require that significant cooperation, regardless of the purpose, requires an Agreement for Cooperation. The United States does not currently have an Agreement for Cooperation with India or with Pakistan.

*Releasing Sensitive Information.* Section 144 of the AEA covers the release of sensitive nuclear information. The Secretary of Energy may release Restricted Data on various aspects of the nuclear fuel cycle except those related to the design or fabrication of atomic weapons. The Secretary of Defence may exchange Restricted Data if it is necessary to a) develop defence plans; b) train personnel in employing and defending against nuclear weapons; c) evaluate the capabilities of potential enemies in employing nuclear weapons; d) develop compatible delivery systems for nuclear weapons. It is unlikely that any of these circumstances would develop in the case of cooperation with India or Pakistan.

The President can authorize the Secretary of Energy, with the assistance of the Department of Defence, to exchange Restricted Data on atomic weapons with another country provided that a) communication of Restricted Data is necessary to improve that nation's nuclear weapon design, development, or fabrication capability; AND b) that nation has made "substantial progress in the development of atomic weapons." When the language on "substantial progress" was added in 1954, the only nation that met the qualification was the United Kingdom. In general, most weapons related data, including some on safety, security, fuze and firing, are classified as restricted data or formerly restricted data. Since it is not in the U.S. interest to improve India or Pakistan's nuclear weapons capability.

*Agreements for Cooperation.* The Atomic Energy Act was amended in 1978 by the Nuclear Nonproliferation Act (NNPA). Section 123 of the NNPA requires states with which the United States conducts significant nuclear trade to sign an Agreement for Cooperation. Examples of significant nuclear trade include provision of nuclear reactors, nuclear material or major reactor components. The Nuclear Regulatory Commission regulates significant nuclear trade; the Department of Energy regulates the transfer of know-how, technology and technical services. Section 123 of the NNPA requires recipient states that are "non-nuclear-weapon states" to maintain IAEA safeguards on "all nuclear materials in all peaceful nuclear activities on their territory." Unless cooperation falls under the category of sale, lease or loan of non-nuclear parts of atomic weapons (which would require that the recipient nation has made "substantial progress in the development of atomic weapons" and that the transfer would not contribute significantly to that nation's atomic weapon design, development, or fabrication capability), the recipient state must guarantee that "no nuclear materials and equipment or sensitive nuclear technology transferred under the agreement will be used for any nuclear explosive device, or for research on or development of any nuclear explosive device or for any other military purpose. In addition, the Secretary of State, who negotiates the Agreements for Cooperation, must provide a nuclear proliferation assessment statement (NPAS) to the President. The NPAS must analyse whether the proposed agreement is consistent with each of the criteria contained in Section 123 of the AEA and whether safeguards and other control mechanisms and the peaceful use assurances in the agreement for cooperation are adequate to ensure that any assistance furnished will not be used to further any military or nuclear explosive purpose.

The President may exempt a proposed agreement for cooperation from any of the specified requirements if he determines that including such requirements would be seriously prejudicial to achieving U.S. nonproliferation objectives or otherwise "jeopardize the common defence and security." There is no precedent for exempting an agreement from the full-scope safeguards requirement.

Section 128 of the NNPA describes the conditions for terminating U.S. cooperation. It states that, No nuclear material and equipment or sensitive nuclear technology shall be exported to: (1) any non-nuclear-weapon state that is found by the President to have, at any time after March 10, 1978 a) detonated a nuclear explosive device; or b) terminated or abrogated IAEA safeguards; or c) materially violated an IAEA safeguards agreement; or d) engaged in activities involving source or special nuclear material and having direct significance for the manufacture or acquisition of nuclear explosive devices, and has failed to take steps which, in the President's judgment, represent sufficient progress toward terminating such activities...

Export Regulations. Transfers of nuclear-related equipment or nuclear material that do not meet the requirement for an agreement of cooperation could possibly still require full-scope safeguards as a condition of supply under the Nuclear Suppliers' Group (NSG) guidelines. Since 1992, NSG member states have required full-scope safeguards as a condition for supplying items on the NSG "trigger list." In addition, the Department of Commerce requires a license for exporting items on the NSG's dual-use list (those with nuclear and other applications) to states outside the NSG. Neither India nor Pakistan is a member of the NSG.

U.S. export regulations function in several tiers. The Commerce Control List specifies what items are regulated and why, but an equally important consideration is the question of the end-user. One technique for streamlining the export control system and making it more understandable for exporters was the development of the entities lists. The Department of Commerce maintains a list of entities subject to license requirements. At present, the entities of proliferation concern are located in China, India, Israel, Pakistan, and Russia. In response to the sanctions imposed on India and Pakistan after the 1998 nuclear tests, the number of Indian and Pakistani organizations listed on the entities list grew dramatically. At the time, the Department of Commerce policy was to deny licenses for exports to India and Pakistan of items controlled for nuclear nonproliferation or missile technology reasons, and presume to deny items on the Commodity Control List to Indian and Pakistani military entities. In 2001, these restrictions were lifted when the President determined that sanctions were not in the national security interest of the United States. Exports of items controlled for nuclear proliferation and missile technology reasons are reviewed on a case-by-case basis.

Currently, Indian nuclear-related facilities on the entities list include:

- Bhabha Atomic Research Centre (BARC)
- Indira Gandhi Atomic Research Centre

- Indian Rare Earths
- Nuclear reactors, fuel reprocessing and enrichment plants, heavy water production facilities and their co-located ammonia plants.

The Pakistani nuclear-related facilities that currently appear on the entities list include:

- AQ Khan Research Laboratories
- Pakistan Atomic Energy Commission (PAEC) and subordinate entities, including National Development Complex, nuclear reactors, fuel reprocessing and enrichment facilities, all uranium processing, conversion and enrichment facilities, heavy water production facilities and any co-located ammonia plants, Pakistan Institute for Nuclear Science and Technology (PINSTECH).

It appears that equipment, material or information exported for the purposes of cooperative nuclear threat reduction would need to be licensed if it was destined for the facilities listed above. All of the facilities are unsafeguarded and all are sensitive sites. On the other hand, such sites may have good security already, since they are associated with the nuclear weapons programs.

A potentially greater concern is how the United States' unwritten policy of not supplying any items to unsafeguarded nuclear facilities would fit with exports to India and Pakistan under a CTR-like program. Under the 1990 Enhanced Proliferation Control Initiative (EPCI), the Department of Commerce can impose licensing requirements on exports and reexports of goods and technology that would normally be uncontrolled where there is an unacceptable risk of diversion to activities related to nuclear, chemical or biological weapons or missile proliferation. U.S. exporters are required to apply for a license if they have knowledge of or have reason to know that such exports will be used directly or indirectly in any one of the following activities: nuclear explosive activities, unsafeguarded nuclear activities, or safeguarded and unsafeguarded activities to produce special nuclear material (through reprocessing or enrichment), produce heavy water or fabricate nuclear fuel that uses plutonium. Section 744.2 of the Export Administration Regulations provides eight criteria for assessing license applications. Potentially, the most significant of these criteria is the nonproliferation credentials of the importing country, which include whether the state adheres to the NPT, has full-scope safeguards, and has an agreement for cooperation with the United States and whether the actions, statements, and policies of the state support nuclear nonproliferation.

### Technical Constraints

Descriptions of the Indian and Pakistani nuclear weapons programs are incomplete and their accuracy is not reliable. Although the two states have exchanged lists of nuclear facilities since 1991 as part of a confidence-building effort, critics charged that the lists initially were incomplete.

More is known about fissile material production sites than weapons machining or assembly sites, but overall there is a high level of secrecy attached to both nuclear weapons programs. Without knowledge of where vulnerabilities lie, it will be difficult to target even the most rudimentary assistance.

In the case of Russia and the NIS, U.S. government officials have complained for years that Russia has not provided the kinds of access necessary for the United States to ensure that its goals are being met. With respect to the material protection, control and accounting programs, most of the material, according to one report, remains outside of the program because the United States cannot gain access to sensitive facilities.

A significant concern is whether U.S. assistance, if it is targeted at making nuclear weapons more secure from unauthorized use, would improve Indian or Pakistani nuclear weapon capabilities.

Permissive action links, which were developed by the United States in the 1960s, were designed so that unauthorized users would not be able to produce a nuclear yield from the weapon.

As one observer has remarked, however, another intended consequence is that weapons with PALs on them are more deployable. One of the goals of U.S. nonproliferation policy presently is to keep India and Pakistan from deploying their weapons.

## *Political Constraints*

U.S. assistance is likely to be a sensitive issue for the Indian and Pakistani governments. Neither state will want to be seen as needing assistance. India has refused to participate in technical cooperation programs with the IAEA except on a regional basis precisely for this reason. On the other hand, India has welcomed talks with the United States on reactor safety and a U.S. delegation travelled to India in 2003 for meetings on that topic. It may be possible to make such assistance less sensitive if it is focused on physical security of the nuclear fuel cycle and not linked to nuclear weapon capabilities.

Pakistani officials have been quite vocal in insisting that their nuclear assets are safe and secure and that U.S. assistance is not required. However, one Indian report noted that the Pakistani Foreign Office spokesperson Aziz Ahmed Khan admitted that the U.S. had offered to train Pakistani personnel on safety and security of nuclear assets.

A Pakistani report in early February 2003 stated that "General Musharraf's decision to assume control of the Nuclear Command Authority has prompted the Bush Administration to ask Islamabad for installation of U.S. nuclear weapon command and control." According to some government officials, U.S. assistance needs to have a low profile in order to succeed.

Another constraint is the current level of cooperation between the United States and India and Pakistan. Although Pakistan has been cooperating closely with the United States in the war on terrorism, the United States has been pushing for both nations to give up their nuclear programs for almost thirty years. Perceptions of mistrust may be difficult to overcome, impeding the level of cooperation that may be needed.

Following Operation Enduring Freedom in Iraq, some in Pakistan apparently are wondering whether Pakistan could be the next target of U.S. counter proliferation efforts. Qazi Hussain Ahmed, leader of Pakistan's largest Islamist party, told Reuters in April 2003 that "Thinking that our turn will not come is like closing your eyes to the truth." On the other hand, the Bush

Administration did not impose sanctions on Pakistan for aiding North Korea's clandestine uranium enrichment program, and has not pressed the Pakistani government for direct access to A.Q. Khan, both of which could be interpreted by Pakistan as reluctance by the Bush Administration to upset relations. In addition, the designation of Pakistan in 2004 as a major non-NATO ally has probably also bolstered Pakistan's confidence in the United States. On the whole, despite some progress in Kashmir, there are still few indications that India or Pakistan would want to enhance transparency to build confidence, either with each other or with the United States. Between the two states, there appears to be more interest in threat enhancement than threat reduction. In addition, Pakistan's reliance on foreign procurement sources could also make transparency measures difficult. A culture of secrecy for India and Pakistan, not easily overcome in the case of Russia, may be difficult to transcend. On the other hand, professional pride in their accomplishments may provide some leverage for scientists' or military officials' cooperation.

## *Policy Options*

The legal, technical, and political constraints described above appear to foreclose assistance that would directly involve a) access to nuclear weapons; b) measures that would enhance operational capabilities of nuclear weapons; c) direct access to sensitive nuclear facilities. Senator Lugar suggested in November 2004 that "We can promote exchanges between Pakistani and Indian security experts, and offer assistance on export controls, border security, and the protection, control and accounting of nuclear arsenals. This will require some diplomatic and administrative skill to stay within our NPT obligations." The measures outlined below are limited but feasible and could help mitigate some aspects of the nuclear threat in India and Pakistan.

## *Site Security*

Improving site security would help guard against the threat of weapons or materials or components leaving a sensitive site either through theft by someone within the facility (a worker) or from outside theft. Perimeter security measures, such as gates and other barriers like barbed wire and personnel identification systems, can help minimize the threat of unauthorized entry. Sensors to detect unauthorized actions (movement, tampering) can help against both insider and outsider threats. Measures to protect against inside theft include checks on personnel leaving facilities (typically onerous without technical detection measures for material or components), cameras in sensitive areas and accounting and access procedures. Armed guards could help, as would operational and administrative controls.

In the Russian case, U.S. officials toured sites and conducted vulnerability assessments. Even perimeter visits would likely be viewed as too sensitive by India and Pakistan. However, the United States could offer information or briefings on how security is conducted at sensitive (not necessarily nuclear) facilities in the United States. Ideally, assistance could cover types of requirements for personnel vetting and training and development of a security culture. As noted above, assistance of this kind has been provided under IAEA auspices. If materials, such as cameras or sensors, were intended to be installed at unsafeguarded facilities, they would likely require licenses. It is likely, however, that commercial versions of security systems would be cheaper and more palatable for India and Pakistan to install themselves if they are not already present.

## *Material Security*

Measures to enhance material security generally fall into the category of material protection, control and accounting (MPC&A). In some cases, securing material in a storage site with tamper-proof seals, cameras, and other monitoring techniques is adequate, but most often the material is intended to be used in processes (like enrichment or reprocessing, or fuel fabrication). This requires a system of accounting and control that can follow material flows. International safeguards rely heavily on state systems of accounting and control (SSACs) in measuring physical inventories of materials. Some technical exchanges in these areas may be possible. Some new techniques for securing material in place could be shared (one innovative approach used in Russia was placing heavy cement blocks over plutonium containers). Pakistan's and India's participation in multilateral programs on physical protection of material could be encouraged as well as their participation in experts' training sessions conducted by Sandia National Laboratory on physical protection (Indian experts attended one in May 2002). It is also possible to provide equipment for physical protection (cameras, seals, locks, or barriers) under license.

### Nuclear Weapons Security

Assistance on nuclear weapons security would be extremely limited if it were considered desirable. The objective of such measures would be to ensure that weapons could not be stolen or detonated by an unauthorized person. Again, the simplest measures are armed guards; undoubtedly both India and Pakistan are aware of the advantages of protecting their nuclear weapons. Advice or equipment to ensure no unauthorized use of nuclear weapons, such as PALs, would require access to nuclear weapons. General information on permissive action links, such as concepts or approaches, is publicly available and would not require access to weapons. In all likelihood, however, both India and Pakistan have probably exhausted public sources of information on that topic. Beyond the warheads themselves, measures to ensure that command and control systems work would also help ensure no unauthorized use, but could possibly enhance operational capabilities.

### Personnel Security

The types of measures for personnel security that could be implemented absent Pakistani and Indian disarmament are limited. Obviously, if there are ongoing nuclear weapons programs, the two governments are unlikely to welcome proposals to divert their scientific expertise into civilian enterprises. However, there are clearly training programs in physical security and personnel vetting that could provide more security to those nuclear programs without enhancing their nuclear deterrents in a way that would contravene the NPT. Strictly civilian cooperation could have a positive spillover effect. On January 12, 2004, President Bush announced a new strategic partnership with India, to cooperate in three areas: civilian nuclear technology, space technology and high-technology trade. U.S. officials reportedly stated that any civilian nuclear technology must not be used in India's nuclear weapons program, although it is unclear how that would be achieved. Reportedly, cooperation has allowed for exports to safeguarded nuclear facilities. This program might have the potential to develop relationships with Indian scientists that would benefit any future, more intrusive cooperative threat reduction program. With respect to Pakistan, assistance may be more difficult. Pakistan has denied U.S. officials direct access to AQ Khan, and although this might be an exception because of Khan's unique status, it could also become the rule. Pakistani officials, both with respect to the nuclear arsenal and nuclear scientists, appear to have taken a "hands-off" attitude.

## Issues for Congress

### Costs

India's and Pakistan's nuclear programs are far smaller than Russia's and unlikely to incur the kinds of costs that the CTR program has thus far incurred. On the other hand, data are scarce on the state of nuclear materials in India and Pakistan, so it is difficult to determine the scope and time frame of any such program. At a minimum, however, such a program is likely to be incrementally implemented. Costs could be minimal if a quick-fix, low-technology, information-oriented approach is taken or they could be more substantial if a sophisticated, high-technology approach is taken that would incorporate cameras, encryption, remote monitoring, and other means.

### Certifications

In 1991, the legislation that created the Nunn-Lugar program stipulated that U.S. assistance in destroying nuclear and other weapons may not be provided to the Soviet Union, any of its republics or successor entities unless the President certifies to the Congress that the proposed recipient is committed to:

- making a substantial investment of its resources for dismantling or destroying such weapons;

- forgo any military modernization that exceeds legitimate defence requirements or is designed to replace destroyed WMD;
- forgo the use of fissile materials and other components from destroyed nuclear weapons in new nuclear weapons;
- facilitate U.S. verification of weapons destruction that uses U.S. money;
- comply with all relevant arms control agreements; and
- observe internationally recognized human rights, including the protection of minorities.

Initially, Presidents George H. W. Bush and Clinton certified that the recipient nations — Russia, Ukraine, Belarus, and Kazakhstan — met those conditions. The Clinton Administration withdrew its certification of Belarus for human rights abuses in FY1998 and the George W. Bush administration withdrew its certification of Russia in 2002 for its failure to comply with arms control agreements, namely, the Chemical Weapons Convention and the Biological Weapons Convention. The Bush Administration subsequently requested a waiver from Congress for the certification. It is not clear whether Congress would opt to apply the same certification requirements to recipient states outside the former Soviet Union. However, S. 2980, which was introduced by Senator Lugar in the 108th Congress, sought to remove the need for certifications, as well as other restrictions. The 109th Congress may consider this issue more fully if legislation is once more introduced.

# 6

# Pakistan's Nuclear Program

Pakistan's nuclear weapons program was established in 1972 by Zulfiqar Ali Bhutto, who founded the program while he was Minister for Fuel, Power and Natural Resources, and later became President and Prime Minister. Shortly after the loss of East Pakistan in the 1971 war with India, Bhutto initiated the program with a meeting of physicists and engineers at Multan in January 1972.

India's 1974 testing of a nuclear "device" gave Pakistan's nuclear program new momentum. Through the late 1970s, Pakistan's program acquired sensitive uranium enrichment technology and expertise. The 1975 arrival of Dr. Abdul Qadeer Khan considerably advanced these efforts. Dr. Khan is a German-trained metallurgist who brought with him knowledge of gas centrifuge technologies that he had acquired through his position at the classified URENCO uranium enrichment plant in the Netherlands. Dr. Khan also reportedly brought with him stolen uranium enrichment technologies from Europe. He was put in charge of building, equipping and operating Pakistan's Kahuta facility, which was established in 1976. Under Khan's direction, Pakistan employed an extensive clandestine network in order to obtain the necessary materials and technology for its developing uranium enrichment capabilities.

In 1985, Pakistan crossed the threshold of weapons-grade uranium production, and by 1986 it is thought to have produced enough fissile material for a nuclear weapon. Pakistan continued advancing its uranium enrichment program, and according to

Pakistani sources, the nation acquired the ability to carry out a nuclear explosion in 1987.

## NUCLEAR TESTS

On May 28, 1998 Pakistan announced that it had successfully conducted five nuclear tests. The Pakistani Atomic Energy Commission reported that the five nuclear tests conducted on May 28 generated a seismic signal of 5.0 on the Richter scale, with a total yield of up to 40 KT (equivalent TNT). Dr. A.Q. Khan claimed that one device was a boosted fission device and that the other four were sub-kiloton nuclear devices.

On May 30, 1998 Pakistan tested one more nuclear warhead with a reported yield of 12 kilotons. The tests were conducted at Balochistan, bringing the total number of claimed tests to six. It has also been claimed by Pakistani sources that at least one additional device, initially planned for detonation on 30 May 1998, remained emplaced underground ready for detonation.

Pakistani claims concerning the number and yields of their underground tests cannot be independently confirmed by seismic means, and several sources, such as theSouthern Arizona Seismic Observatory have reported lower yields than those claimed by Pakistan.

Indian sources have also suggested that as few as two weapons were actually detonated, each with yields considerably lower than claimed by Pakistan. However, seismic data showed at least two and possibly a third, much smaller, test in the initial round of tests at the Ras Koh range. The single test on 30 May provided a clear seismic signal.

| *DEVICE* | *DATE* | *YIELD [announced]* | *YIELD [estimated]* |
|---|---|---|---|
| [boosted device?] | 28 May 1998 | 25-36 kiloton | Total 9-12 kiloton |
| Fission device | 28 May 1998 | 12 kiloton | |
| Low-yield device | 28 May 1998 | sub-kiloton | — |
| Low-yield device | 28 May 1998 | sub-kiloton | — |
| Low-yield device | 28 May 1998 | sub-kiloton | — |
| Fission device | 30 May 1998 | 12 kiloton | 4-6 kiloton |
| Fission device | not detonated | 12 kiloton | — |

The nuclear tests that Pakistan claims to have carried out in May 1998 as well as the announced yields. Other sources have reported lower yields than those claimed by Pakistan. The Southern Arizona Seismic Observatory reports that the total seismic yield for the May 28th tests was 9-12 kilotons and that the yield for the May 30th tests was 4-6 kilotons.

According to a preliminary analysis conducted at Los Alamos National Laboratory, material released into the atmosphere during an underground nuclear test by Pakistan in May 1998 contained low levels of weapons-grade plutonium. The significance of the Los Alamos finding was that Pakistan had either imported or produced plutonium undetected by the US intelligence community. But Lawrence Livermore National Laboratory and other agencies later contested the accuracy of this finding. These tests came slightly more than two weeks after India carried out five nuclear tests of its own on May 11 and 13 and after many warnings by Pakistani officials that they would respond to India.

Pakistan's nuclear tests were followed by the February 1999 Lahore Agreements between Prime Ministers Vajpayee and Sharif. The agreements included confidence building measures such as advance notice of ballistic missile testing and a continuation of their unilateral moratoria on nuclear testing. But diplomatic advances made that year were undermined by Pakistan's incursion into Kargil. Under US diplomatic pressure, Prime Minister Sharif withdrew his troops, but lost power in October 1999 due to a military coup in which Gen. Pervez Musharraf took over.

## NUCLEAR INFRASTRUCTURE

Pakistan's nuclear program is based primarily on highly enriched uranium (HEU), which is produced at the A. Q. Khan research laboratory at Kahuta, a gas centrifuge uranium enrichment facility. The Kahuta facility has been in operation since the early 1980s. By the early 1990s, Kahuta had an estimated 3,000 centrifuges in operation, and Pakistan continued its pursuit of expanded uranium enrichment capabilities.

In the 1990s Pakistan began to pursue plutonium production capabilities. With Chinese assistance, Pakistan built the 40 MWt (megawatt thermal) Khusab research reactor at Joharabad, and in April 1998, Pakistan announced that the reactor was operational. According to public statements made by US officials, this unsafeguarded heavy water reactor generates an estimated 8-10 kilotons of weapons grade plutonium per year, which is enough for one to two nuclear weapons. The reactor could also produce tritium if it were loaded with lithium-6. According to J. Cirincione of Carnegie, Khusab's plutonium production capacity could allow Pakistan to develop lighter nuclear warheads that would be easier to deliver with a ballistic missile.

Plutonium separation reportedly takes place at the New Labs reprocessing plant next to Pakistan's Institute of Nuclear Science and Technology (Pinstech) in Rawalpindi and at the larger Chasma nuclear power plant, neither of which are subject to IAEA inspection.

## *Nuclear Arsenal*

The Natural Resources Defense Council (NRDC) estimates that Pakistan has built 24-48 HEU-based nuclear warheads, and Carnegie reports that they have produced 585-800 kg of HEU, enough for 30-55 weapons. Pakistan's nuclear warheads are based on an implosion design that uses a solid core of highly enriched uranium and requires an estimated 15-20 kg of material per warhead. According to Carnegie, Pakistan has also produced a small but unknown quantity of weapons grade plutonium, which is sufficient for an estimated 3-5 nuclear weapons.

Pakistani authorities claim that their nuclear weapons are not assembled. They maintain that the fissile cores are stored separately from the non-nuclear explosives packages, and that the warheads are stored separately from the delivery systems. In a 2001 report, the Defense Department contends that "Islamabad's nuclear weapons are probably stored in component form" and that "Pakistan probably could assemble the weapons fairly quickly." However, no one has been able to ascertain the validity of Pakistan's assurances about their nuclear weapons security. Pakistan's reliance primarily on HEU makes its fissile materials particularly vulnerable to diversion. HEU can be used in a relatively simple gun-barrel-type design, which could be within the means of non-state actors that intend to assemble a crude nuclear weapon.

The terrorist attacks on September 11th raised concerns about the security of Pakistan's nuclear arsenal. According to press reports, within two days of the attacks, Pakistan's military began relocating nuclear weapons components to six new secret locations. Shortly thereafter, Gen. Pervez Musharraf fired his intelligence chief and other officers and detained several suspected retired nuclear weapons scientists, in an attempt to root out extremist elements that posed a potential threat to Pakistan's nuclear arsenal.

Concerns have also been raised about Pakistan as a proliferant of nuclear materials and expertise. In November, 2002, shortly after North Korea admitted to pursuing a nuclear weapons program, the press reported allegations that Pakistan had provided assistance in the development of its uranium enrichment program in exchange for North Korean missile technologies.

## Foreign Assistance

In the past, China played a major role in the development of Pakistan's nuclear infrastructure, especially when increasingly stringent export controls in western countries made it difficult for Pakistan to acquire materials and technology elsewhere. According to a 2001 Department of Defense report, China has supplied Pakistan with nuclear materials and expertise and has provided critical assistance in the construction of Pakistan's nuclear facilities.

In the 1990s, China designed and supplied the heavy water Khusab reactor, which plays a key role in Pakistan's production of plutonium. A subsidiary of the China National Nuclear Corporation also contributed to Pakistan's efforts to expand its uranium enrichment capabilities by providing 5,000 custom made ring magnets, which are a key component of the bearings that facilitate the high-speed rotation of centrifuges.

According to Anthony Cordesman of CSIS, China is also reported to have provided Pakistan with the design of one of its warheads, which is relatively sophisticated in design and lighter than U.S. and Soviet designed first generation warheads.

China also provided technical and material support in the completion of the Chasma nuclear power reactor and plutonium reprocessing facility, which was built in the mid 1990s. The project had been initiated as a cooperative program with France, but Pakistan's failure to sign the NPT and unwillingness to accept IAEA safeguards on its entire nuclear program caused France to terminate assistance.

According to the Defense Department report cited above, Pakistan has also acquired nuclear related and dual-use and equipment and materials from the Former Soviet Union and Western Europe.

### *Intermittent US Sanctions*

On several occasions, under the authority of amendments to the Foreign Assistance Act, the U.S. has imposed sanctions on Pakistan, cutting off economic and military aid as a result of its pursuit of nuclear weapons. However, the U.S. suspended sanctions each time developments in Afghanistan made Pakistan a strategically important "frontline state," such as the 1981 Soviet occupation and in the war on terrorism.

## PAKISTAN'S NUCLEAR DOCTRINE

Several sources, such as Jane's Intelligence Review and Defense Department reports maintain that Pakistan's motive for pursuing a nuclear weapons program is to counter the threat posed by its principal rival, India, which has superior conventional forces and nuclear weapons.

Pakistan has not signed the Non-Proliferation Treaty (NPT) or the Comprehensive Test Ban Treaty (CTBT). According to the Defense Department report cited above, "Pakistan remains steadfast in its refusal to sign the NPT, stating that it would do so only after India joined the Treaty. Consequently, not all of Pakistan's nuclear facilities are under IAEA safeguards. Pakistani officials have stated that signature of the CTBT is in Pakistan's best interest, but that Pakistan will do so only after developing a domestic consensus on the issue, and have disavowed any connection with India's decision."

Pakistan does not abide by a no-first-use doctrine, as evidenced by President Pervez Musharraf's statements in May, 2002. Musharraf said that Pakistan did not want a conflict with India but that if it came to war between the nuclear-armed rivals, he would "respond with full might." These statements were interpreted to mean that if pressed by an overwhelming conventional attack from India, which has superior conventional forces, Pakistan might use its nuclear weapons.

## DILEMMAS OF SMALL NUCLEAR FORCE IN THE SECOND ATOMIC AGE

Dilemmas of Small Nuclear Forces, 4-series of articles highlighting the Nuclear Doctrine of Pakistan, its command and control system. The series contain 3 articles: First article (below) explore the Rise of Nuclear Deterrence, Second: is subjected to Post-1998 Doctrinal Contemplation,Third: Confidence-Building Measures between India and Pakistan, andFourth: concludes with the military objectives of Pakistan's nuclear weapons and highlights from the Nuclear Security Summit 2010.

A doctrine could be defined as a set of principles formulated and applied for a specific purpose, working towards a desired goal or aim. A nuclear doctrine would consequently consist of a set of principles, and instructions for the employment or non-employment of nuclear weapons and other associated systems. Until 2005, India and Pakistan were the only states outside the Nuclear Nonproliferation Treaty to declare, openly, their nuclear weapons capability. In 1998, they tested nuclear weapons and since then, deployed ballistic missiles, enunciated nuclear doctrine, and made organizational changes to their nuclear establishments. In 2002, they teetered on the brink of war in Kashmir. The factors that have conceived the concept which has formulated the nuclear doctrine of Pakistan. I certainly believe that in South Asia a balance of power cannot be maintained by conventional means alone. This chapter endeavours to construct a proto Pakistani nuclear use doctrine from its declaratory and operational postures, in particular from the statements and interviews of the Pakistani political and military leaders and government officials. Initially reflecting upon its pre-1998 nuclear strategy, which has got critical implications for the post-tests doctrinal contemplation.

Pakistan is believed to have been developing a nuclear capability since the early 1970s. In May 1998, Pakistan responded to India's nuclear tests by testing a series of nuclear weapons and declaring itself a nuclear weapon power. Pakistan, like India, has supported comprehensive disarmament proposals at the United Nations and Conference on Disarmament, but did not join the CTBT for similar reasons as India. Pakistan has proposed a number of bilateral or regional initiatives which India has not supported. These include a Nuclear Weapons Free Zone in South Asia and joining the NPT. India opposes these on the grounds that they do not address the nuclear threat India faces from China and the other NWS. Pakistan and India have concluded a number of bilateral confidence building measures including a hot-line agreement and an agreement not to attack each other's nuclear power facilities.

While all these (including Pakistan, India, North Korea and Israel) small nuclear powers are in the process of developing their nuclear force structures, two key questions that have arisen are: How, when and for what purposes do they plan to use nuclear weapons? And what command. The word "small" here distinguishes these nation and their doctrines from U.S.A, UK, France and Russia. Prime focus is to understand the emerging structure of Pakistan's Nuclear Doctrine.

In *The Myth of Independence*, Zulfikar Ali Bhutto (president of Pakistan in December 1971) argued that modern wars should be conceived of as total wars, and in this type of war Pakistan needed nuclear weapons. Bhutto's thinking, as will be analysed below, had far-reaching impacts on Pakistan's nuclear strategy, and on its doctrinal contemplation.

Soon after assuming Presidency of Pakistan on 20th December 1971 he took the decision to initiate a nuclear weapons project. This decision was taken against the backdrop of three specific factors: firstly, it was a direct consequence of the 1971 war where Pakistan's conventional inferiority was demonstrated for the third time, at the cost of almost half of its territory; secondly, Pakistani leaders in general (particularly Bhutto) were convinced that India was determined to build a nuclear arsenal; and thirdly, Bhutto believed that only nuclear weapons could guarantee the national survival of Pakistan against the Indian threat.8 It is evident that Pakistan's nuclear weapons project was initiated to deter Indian nuclear as well as conventional aggression, an aim that endured in the subsequent years and today constitutes one of the central pillars of Pakistan's nuclear use doctrine.

## BRASS TACKS CRISIS – FIRST NUCLEAR DETERRENCE POSTURE [1986-1987]

First employment of Pakistan's nuclear deterrent stratagy was during the 1986-1987 brasstacks crisis between India and Pakistan. With the crisis peaking in January 1987, India had deployed 400,000 troops, or about half the Indian army, within 100 miles of Pakistan. It began when India had launched the largest ever military exercises in the subcontinent, called Operation Brass Tacks. The exercise would take place not in India's far north, where the always tense state of Kashmir is located, but in the desert area of Rajastan, a few hundred miles from the Pakistani border, which, a the Pakistani government was sure to note, was and ideal location from which to launch a cross border operation into the Pakistani state of Sindh that could cut Pakistan in half. The exercises included bulk of Indian Army, and was comprised of the nine infantry, three mechanised, three armoured and one air assault divisions, and three armoured brigades under four corps HQ with all theparaphernalia for a real war, concentrated on Pakistan's sensitive border areas. This was bigger than any NATO exercise – and the biggest since World War II. Also planned was an ambitious amphibious operation by the Indian Navy with one division, in Korangi area of Karachi. Another feature of the exercise was a decision by General Sundarji to integrate Indias special weapons, including tactical nuclear into day-to day field maneuvers of the troops.

Pakistani military analysts saw Brass Tacks as a threatening exhibition of an overwhelming conventional force. Some even suspected that India wanted to launch swift surgical strikes at the Sikh terrorists' training and planning sites inside Pakistan. Pakistan responded with maneuvers of its own that were located close to India's state of Punjab. The crisis atmosphere was heightened when Pakistan's premier nuclear scientist Abdul Qadir Khan revealed in a March 1987 interview that Pakistan had manufactured a nuclear bomb. Although Khan later retracted his statement, India stated that the disclosure was "forcing us to review our option." Interview by Dr A.Q Khan's interview to Indian journalist, Kuldip Nayar records:

*what the CIA has been saying about our possessing the bomb is correct and so is the speculation of some foreign newspapers ... They told us that Pakistan could never produce the bomb and they doubted my capabilities, but they now know we have done it ... Nobody can undo Pakistan or take us for granted. We are there to stay and let it be clear that we shall use the 10 bomb if our existence is threatened.*

Formal and impromptu talks between the leaders of the two countries finally resulted in a number of new CBMs between India and Pakistan. These were important and covered a number of areas. For example, the Agreement on the Prohibition of Attack against Nuclear Installations and Facilities was signed on December 31, 1988, in Islamabad by the two foreign secretaries and witnessed by the two prime ministers, Rajiv Gandhi and Benazir Bhutto, respectively. Earlier fears of impending attack on the facilities resulting in an all-out war fed the need for the agreement.

## KASHMIR – SECOND NUCLEAR DETERRENCE POSTURE [1990]

Pakistan again advanced a nuclear deterrent posture in 1990 in the context of a spiralling crisis over the disputed territory of Kashmir, which developed against the backdrop of an acute separatist insurgency in the Indian. Reportedly, New Delhi planned for surgical air strikes against the militant training camps inside Pakistani territory, which prompted Islamabad to assemble a crude nuclear bomb and modify several American supplied F-16 aircrafts for its delivery. The crisis was eventually averted through diplomatic intervention from Washington, but Islamabad firmly believed that Pakistan's deterrence posture prevented India from carrying out the planned strike. This crisis also marked the emergence of a nascent mutual nuclear deterrence in the Indo-Pakistani context.

## COMMAND AND CONTROL OF NUCLEAR DETERRENCE

What did emerge during this period, primarily in the context of the 1986-87 Brasstacks crisis and the 1990 Kashmir episode, was a general notion of nuclear deterrence, which implied that Pakistan would use nuclear weapons to counter India's nuclear as well as conventional aggression. to build a robust nuclear command structure. However, former Army chief of staff General Mirza Aslam Beg has claimed that the Pakistani leadership realised the necessity of establishing a command structure, *given the tension, mutual mistrust and suspicion between India and Pakistan, it is dangerously tempting for each to launch an attack before being attacked which could escalate to a nuclear level.*

Bhutto had established a National Nuclear Command Authority (NNCA) in the 1970s, which institutionalised the nuclear decision-making and assumed the responsibility of developing a nuclear force structure and appropriate alert posture. ('NNCA Responsible for Safeguarding Nuclear Programme, The News, 2 June 1998).

## PAKISTAN NUCLEAR CAPABILITIES AND THINKING

Most observers estimate that Pakistan has enough nuclear material (highly enriched uranium and a small amount of plutonium) for 30 to 50 nuclear weapons. Like India, Pakistan is thought to have a small stockpile of nuclear weapons components and can probably assemble some weapons fairly quickly. Pakistan could deliver its nuclear weapons using F-16s (shown above) it purchased from the United States provided the appropriate "wiring" has been added to make them nuclear-capable. In the 1980s, Pakistan moved assiduously to acquire ballistic missile capabilities and now deploys short-range ballistic missiles and a small number of medium-range missiles. AQ Khan, former head of Khan Research Laboratories, maintained that only the medium-range Ghauri missiles would be usable in a nuclear exchange (given fall-out effects for Pakistan of shorter-range missiles). Other observers view the 30 to 50 Hatf2 short-range (300km) missiles (modified Chinese M-11s) as potential delivery vehicles for nuclear weapons. Ghauri missiles (1350 and 2300km), which reportedly are based on the North Korean No-Dong and Taepo-Dong-1, are capable of reaching New Delhi with large payloads.

On June 4, 2002, President Musharraf went a step further then his UN ambassador sna stated that: "The possession of nuclear weapons by any state obviously implies they will be used under some circumstances. In recent years, Pakistan apparently has taken steps toward refining command and control of nuclear weapons. In April 1999, General Musharraf announced that the Joint Staff Headquarters would have a command and control arrangement and a secretariat, and a strategic force command would be established. With some experience and the passage of time a degree of sophistication will certainly be introduced in Pakistan's nuclear doctrine of the first-use of nuclear weapons to provide the government more options in the use of nuclear weapons. This would also avoid unessential collateral damage to cities and other population centres in both countries. The object would be to employ nuclear weapons if attacked yet cause the least civilian casualties and damage to infrastructure.

## CREDIBLE NUCLEAR DETERRENCE AND DOCTRINE FOR PAKISTAN

Pakistan and India since May 11/28, 1998 have come into the atomic age, despite their status as non-weapon states under the NPT regime. There should be no doubt about this fact. In fact, the sooner this fact is realized and absorbed by both these countries and their leadership as well as the five members of the nuclear club, the better it is for all concerned individuals and states. Despite my advice, and a minority of other Pakistani origin academics that also urged the Pakistani leadership not to go nuclear, Pakistan, however, decided to match India at the nuclear level for a variety of reasons.

The nuclear genie has been unleashed; it can not be bottled back. Therefore, it is better to weaponise the respective nuclear detonations and deploy nuclear weapons with complete Command, Control, Communication, and Intelligence (C3I) systems in place for a stable nuclear deterrence between the two rival states of

South Asia. This nuclear factor is needed not so much as a peace maker, which is a misnomer, but more so for pure deterrence reasons. It guarantees against misadventure by any side. Now the need of the hour is to create a credible nuclear deterrence between India and Pakistan as well as to adopt a sound nuclear doctrine for Pakistan's armed forces. In order to stabilize the nuclear situation of the subcontinent, these countries must take a number of political, strategic, diplomatic, and tactical steps simultaneously. On the political and diplomatic front, there is a need to take a number of policy initiatives on the part of Pakistan.

First, Pakistan must immediately reassure the international community that Pakistani nuclear weapons are not for sale. This seems to have been done by both the Prime Minister and even more categorically by Pakistan's top foreign affairs bureaucrat, S.A. Khan. Second, Pakistan has already offered to sit down with India to discuss confidence building measures and the Kashmir affair. However, there should be a clear timeline, let's say by the end of 1999, to resolve this issue bilaterally. In case of a deadlock, which is bound to happen, the case should be submitted automatically to the UN with reference to its resolutions to ask Kashmiris to accede to either India or Pakistan as the logical and fair culmination of the unfinished business of the partition of the subcontinent. Including a third choice at this stage will not only complicate the matter more but also insult most Kashmiris like me. It is also necessary to avoid Kashmir becoming a point of conflict between extra-regional powers and China and Russia, especially if Kashmir is used as a listening post against them.

If India comes to terms on Kashmir, then the size of the Pakistan army could immediately be reduced. In order to preserve peace, the best guarantee would still be a strong Pakistan. An increase of expenditure on naval, airforce, and the nuclear deterrence capabilities for at least a decade or so would have to be taken by Pakistan to ensure that the transition to a less hostile environment in South Asia is smooth. After that period, one could reduce all elements of hostile military posturing.

In fact, what would be the need of having large standing armed and nuclear forces, if Pakistan's main bone of contention with India had been resolved amicably. Judging from the press coverage of diplomatic activities, Kashmir is back in the limelight in multilateral fora. However, Indian diplomacy will do its utmost to reduce this issue to the back burner but Pakistani diplomats must do their best to keep England, Japan and US committed to this issue at the multilateral level.

If India accedes on Kashmir, then Pakistan could reward India by nominating her for the UN Security Council's permanent seat. In fact, this offer should be made to the Indians during the Indo-Pakistani bilateral negotiations on Kashmir

Third, Pakistan must be quick to capitalize on its biggest assets; the nuclear and missile scientists. Pakistan must send her atomic scientists on goodwill missions from Indonesia and Malaysia to all the way to Western Sahara and Morocco in the same manner as the first U.S. astronauts travelled around the globe. Now that Pakistan has proven its scientific credentials, these countries will most likely want Pakistan as their friend. Most Muslim countries, with the exception of the oil rich Gulf sheikhdoms, are poor and destitute, Pakistan could accommodate a number of these countries in their need to develop in many fields, including military hardware and training. In fact, Pakistan with its nuclear prowess, despite adverse international conditions and and despite severe budgetary constraints, have proven that Third World solutions must come from within the Third World.

In the short term, this move by Pakistan will signal to the U.S. and the West to lift sanctions against Pakistan or the country might be put in a position to transfer its nuclear and missile know-how to the Middle East. The Israeli lobby in the U.S. would definitely not want this to happen. Consequently, this lobby will most probably want the U.S. administration and the Congress to repeal the Pressler amendment.

The results of this policy can be seen in the Pakistani Prime Minister's immediate visit to the UAE and Saudi Arabia and the Iranian Foreign Minister's visit to Pakistan soon after the Chagai blasts. Israelies are already rethinking their policy of transferring nuclear and missile technology to India.

In the long term, however, a host of smaller countries, especially the Middle Eastern countries, could become Pakistan's important bilateral allies and trade partners that could end their individual reliance on the industrialized North at least in some critical fields. This south to south trade route change could trigger a new era of prosperity for all and amelioration of poor and destitutes of India and Pakistan.

But Pakistan must choose its friends wisely. Three countries stand out as exceptionally important to Pakistan during its nuclear journey. These are Iran, Saudi Arabia and the United Arab Emirates. Pakistan must improve its bilateral relations with Iran and nurture them even further in all fields despite opposition by U.S. and a few religious political groups at home. Pakistan must fulfil Saudi Arabian peoples' desire to become self-sufficient in their own security.

Pakistan had provided defence forces to the kindom of Saudi Arabia in the past, the time to replace the American and Western alliance forces with Pakistani forces may have come. Eventually, the Saudis could become self sufficient in their defence needs. Immediately, however, they could save billions that they are remitting to the now 'unwanted' and embarrassingly expensive American forces. Now that the threat of the Iraqi nuclear (not proven) and other weapons of mass destruction has been removed, departure of the American forces seems fair and appropriate. It also removes friction between the U.S. and Iran.

In the wake of the Indian nuclear explosions of May 11, the Saudis are also beggining to think that the rapid increases in India's defence budget and types of weaponry, e.g. nuclear, and hydrogen bombs, ballistic missiles, aircraft carriers, and long-range Russian made SU-27 bombers may not be just for increasing leverage over Pakistan. They are realizing that the depth of Indo-Israeli nuclear and military connections and cooperation is not just directed at Pakistan alone. The ultimate aim of Indo-Israeli nexus could very well be the Mid East oil for India and water for Israel. The Saudis may,therefore, be inclined to send the Indian workers packing home as the reality sinks in that the remittances of expatriate Indians do help their government in the acquisition of Isreaeli nuclear and military hardware. In turn, Pakistan could benefit from increased recruitment of Pakistani workers for Saudi oil fields. The Sultan/President of the United Arab Emirates and his people are intelligent, progressive, and endowed with a special sense of pride as well as desire for scientific advancement. Pakistan must offer a special training wing for the UAE nationals in scientific fields of their choice.

The above three countries must remain at the base of Pakistan's Middle East policy. In turn, Pakistan's help to them will keep a steady flow of foreign exchange and oil and gas for the country's industrial advancement, on the one hand, and will make sure that Washington will listen to Islamabad's concerns due the Iranian connection, on the other.

Before the euphoria of Pakistan's scientific achievement dies down, Pakistan must immediately conclude long term energy, finance, and scientific exchange agreements with these countries. Initially, a number of proposed natural gas and oil pipelines between Central Asian Islamic states, Iran as well as Qatar and Pakistan should be built in the next few years. In return, Pakistan must pay them with training in military and other 'important' scientific and educational fields.

Fourth, Pakistan must solve the ongoing Afghan problem. It is essential to have Pakistan's western front quite now more than ever.

Fifth, despite an obvious set back to NPT since May 11, 1998, the core of the nuclear nonproliferation regime is still intact. Pakistan must strengthen this core by adhering to its principals, norms and standards as far as IAEA safeguards, technology transfer and observance of CTBT moratoriums, etc., are concerned.

There is no need for Pakistan to consider the Non-proliferation Treaty (NPT) as a dead letter. Let the Indians deal with this matter on their own and let them face the US and the nonproliferation community. Pakistan's NPT stand and her South Asian Nuclear Weapon Free Zone (NWFZ) proposals were fairly clear to the international community of nations, academics and diplomats. A concerted diplomatic effort is needed to highlight Pakistan's efforts in this regard.

Also, there is no need to sign NPT or CTBT at this stage, unless Kashmir problem is resolved and India signs as well as ratifies these treaties. Kashmir must now become corollary to Pakistan's nuclear disarmament. Pakistan should refrain from reiterating that it will sign any such treaties if India signs first and may want to reassess this strategy for two reasons. First, it could have worked against Pakistan had India signed CTBT days after detonating its nuclear devices. Tremendous pressure would have been put on Pakistan and India would have benefited from computer simulation and modelling data of nuclear detonation for future development of her nuclear weapons. Secondly, Pakistan need not insist on India to sign these treaties if she is willing to conclude an equitable agreement on Kashmir. It is cledar that Indian strategy is much more grandiose than just competing with Pakistan on the nuclear front. Obviously, this is a competition which India is bound to win if one compares Indo-Pakistani situations with the Cold war competition of the U.S. and USSR. Moreover, India may very well concede on Kashmir, if she sees that her regional and global ambitions are jeopardized by a nuclear Pakistan.

Sixthly, Pakistan must not sign a no first use of nuclear weapons with any state, especially India, as it was offered by her Prime Minister. With the offer of no fist use of nuclear weapons, India reaps the benefit of nuclear deterrence between the two countries and continues to disregard any solution on Kashmir, on the one hand, and claims its stake as a regional and possibly international power house, on the other. Pakistan's counter offer to India should be a treaty on no use of nuclear bombs on Indo-Pakistani cities.

On the military and strategic front Pakistan needs to take a number of policy and other measures as well. The most urgent need is to avoid an accidental or unauthorized nuclear war. A hotline between the Indian and Pakistani leaders, both at the armed forces and the political level, should be established immediately to minimize such a scenario. Pakistan must immediately adopt a nuclear deterrence doctrine and incorporate it into its forces' training and strategic as well tactical outlook even if it entails massive retaliation strategy against any major threat, nuclear or conventional.

Eventually, both India and Pakistan will want to go beyond first strike deterrence (also known as "use-it-or loose-it strategy"), which seems to be their current deterrence policy, to a second strike capability or the Mutual Assured Destruction (MAD) strategy. It means that the country can take an atomic hit and still retaliate with its nuclear weapons that have survived the first strike of the enemy.

Pakistan just does not have enough depth or places to conceal all its nuclear carrying missiles or warplanes from a surprise first strike of either India or any other nuclear armed country. Submarines are uniquely qualified to provide a second strike capability due to a natural stealth cover provided by many oceans and seas around the globe. The choice of submarines is crucial. Should they be diesel, nuclear, or hybrid? Should Pakistan manufacture its own or buy off the shelf somewhere? These questions have been addressed before; however, Pakistan may need to revisit them again in light of the changed geopolitical situation of South Asia.

Fortunately, the six boat submarine fleet of Pakistan that includes four Daphne and two Agosta class submarines is missile tested. There are three more Agosta class boats on order from France. Pakistan must accelerate its acquisition of the French Agosta class submarines. Next, their local assembly and construction should be speeded up from the current plan of action.

The current choice of French diesel subs is fairly sound and fortiuous for two reasons. One, these boats are much more quieter than their Soviet and German counterparts of the Indian Navy. Two, the French nuclear missile carrying boats with nuclear power engines are modelled on the Agosta design. Indeed, diesel subs are also quieter than their nuclear counterparts. However, the nuclear or a hybrid submarine with nuclear tipped missiles is considered a better guarantor of second strike capability due to its range and longer staying power at sea. For now Pakistan must immediately equip its existing fleet of Agosta and Daphne class French submarines with nuclear ballistic and cruise missiles as well as nuclear tipped torpedoes.

Moreover, the Chinese nuclear-diesel hybrid engine submarines are rumoured to be based on the Agosta model. Both these countries have time and again have proven to be reliable suppliers of arms and technology to Pakistan.[] Therefore, nuclear submarines' acquisition from these countries, especially China, by Pakistan at a future date of her choice will most probably not pose a major hurdle considering China did offer these boats to Pakistan recently.

In addition to ballistic missiles, Pakistan needs to develop cruise missiles for the following reasons. It is relatively easier to hide and move these weapons closer to the Indian borders. The technology is available within Pakistan. They are extremely difficult to detect during their flight. This technology provides greater length of time between launch and abandonment; if desired, such mechanisms could be incorporated with innovative sofware solutions and satellite based homing devices. This option could provid some flexibility of time and recall almost along the same lines as a piloted airborne carrier. Some technological problems will be faced by Pakistan in the fields of computers and software but it should not be impossible to overcome this problem.

It is imperative that Pakistan must let go its military reliance on the U.S., not so much out of spite but for strategic reasons. This country has never been reliable due to its global commitments and commercial interests. Pakistan's reliance on the U.S. can tantamount to suicide during the nuclear age, especially in light of the convergence of the U.S. and Indian strategic interests in South Asia and the Middle East. China, Germany and France[] have proven fairly reliable and can pretty much provide everything that Pakistan needs. Pakistan can forget about becoming self-sufficient in the production of high technology weapons now or for sometimes in the near or even far future. Instead of harping on this point, Pakistan should get whatever it can and transfer as much of technology as possible

Pakistan needs to have a reliable force multiplier in its airforce. Pakistanis have been fixated on the F16s and Mirage 2000 for all the wrong reasons. Both these planes have their own unique problems. The first has problem of supply and the second is very expensive. What about the Mig-29 or Sukhoi SU-27? It seems that Russia will sell to anybody with hard currency. Failing that one could approach Ukraine or Belarus[] for either technology as both these cuntries have most of these technologies and have been parading their military hardware in various air shows. In the long run, China is bound to induct these systems in her drive to modernize the PRC armed forces. That alone assures Pakistan of reliable supply of critical components and spares for these weapon systems.

Above all, Pakistan must improve its quilt-work of a radar system. A substantial investment in developing or acquiring AWACS is essential after Prithvis, Agnis and Shaktis have come to the neighbourhood. A better long term approach would be to develop and launch a couple of satellites, both low orbit and geo-stationery types in the near future, through two competing nuclear development establishments and three missile development organizations of Pakistan.

Last but not least, it is hoped that neither Pakistan, nor India will ever have to use the awesome power of the atom against their own kith and kin. Let's also hope that saner elements in their leadership will prevail and not test a futile attempt to test each other's nuclear preparedness. In the meantime, the U.S. and the most advance nations of the world may consider transferring C3I systems to these countries for possible unauthorized use of these weapons of mass destruction.

## PAKISTAN'S NUCLEAR TRAJECTORY

Pakistan's nuclear program has been at the center of attention for nonproliferation pundits for several decades for a variety of reasons. For them, the acquisition of nuclear technology, even for non-NPT states, both for peaceful and military applications (self-defense), is the divine right of the chosen few who are either unable or unwilling to recognize the legitimate security concerns of states in regions mired in a perpetual cycle of hostility. Faced with the traumatizing separation of its Eastern Wing in 1971, Pakistan resolved never to witness such an event at the hands of India again, and was forced to respond to India's nuclear challenge only three years later in the wake of Pokhran-1. Pakistan had taken the lead in calling for nuclear restraint in South Asia even before India's 1974 test when it first proposed a Nuclear Weapon Free Zone in 1972. This call was repeated twice, once after Pokhran-1 and again in 1978 when Pakistan proposed that both countries simultaneously renounce the acquisition or manufacture of nuclear weapons. The following year, Pakistan again offered India mutual inspection of each other's nuclear facilities and also proposed a simultaneous accession of India and Pakistan to the NPT and full-scope IAEA safeguards. In 1987, it expressed willingness to enter into a bilateral nuclear test-ban treaty with India and proposed a missile free zone in South Asia in 1994. None of these proposals were given any serious consideration. Since 2007, India has consistently rejected six nuclear-related Confidence Building Measures proposed by Pakistan on one pretext or another. Regrettably, India has rejected each one of these proposals in the past four decades even though there have been a few successful CBM's which have stood the test of time such as the agreement of non-attack on each other's nuclear facilities and the agreement of pre-notification of flight tests of ballistic missiles. However, proposals for a strategic restraint regime that would include a commitment not to build missile defences and include prior notification of cruise missiles were not accepted by India.

Therefore, when in the backdrop of a deep history of mistrust Pakistan resorts to indigenous efforts to build its nuclear deterrent, based on its own force goals and resources, it stands accused of following a "mistaken trajectory" and is seen as "punching above its weight." A dispassionate assessment of Pakistan's nuclear trajectory vis-à-vis India and the size of its nuclear fuel cycle in terms of the production capacities of various plants and facilities shows that while it has consistently built up its nuclear capabilities over time, there has been no abrupt or exponential increase in fissile material production comparable to India (for both existing or projected capacities). It is also a fact that Pakistan has reached this stage in its nuclear capability only after four decades of sustained effort and progressive indigenization in its nuclear and missile programs. It has learnt to brace sanctions, find solutions and improvise, and mastered all aspects of the fuel cycle at a fraction of the cost of producing any nuclear plant or facility of the same type or size anywhere else in the world (such as plutonium production facilities). A closer look at Pakistan's nuclear trajectory demonstrates that while India has been producing plutonium from CIRUS since 1963 and from Dhruva-I since 1988 and has a much larger infrastructure outside safeguards to produce more plutonium in addition to its considerable advantages in existing stockpiles of plutonium.

Pakistan is using infrastructure to produce plutonium from 1998 onwards which PAEC was able to build over a period of 25 years (1973 to 1998), save for second, third and fourth 50 MWt production reactors at Khushab (the fourth one nearing completion), all of which were initiated during the fifteen years after the 1998 tests. Thus, Pakistan's pre-1998 plutonium infrastructure comprises a fuel fabrication plant at Kundian (completed 1976-80); the New Labs reprocessing plant at PINSTECH (1973-1981); the 50 MWt Khushab-1 reactor, heavy water and tritium production plants (1985-1997); and the partially completed Chashma reprocessing plant (1978) which has recently been retrofitted and reportedly commissioned. After Khushab-1 was commissioned in 1998, Pakistan was able to add three additional reactors of the same type and size only because it was developing indigenous design and manufacturing facilities in parallel with work at Khushab Nuclear Complex in the 1980s and 1990s.

For comparison's sake, it would be useful to recall that Pakistan has built only two unsafeguarded reprocessing plants since the 1970s; one pilot-scale plant (New Labs) with 20-40 (completed in 1981-82) and the other commercial-scale plant (Chashma) with 40-100 tHM/yr capacity which the French had abandoned in 1978. At the same time, India has built five commercial-scale reprocessing plants (all outside safeguards); one at Trombay (50 tHM/yr) two at Tarapur (100 tHM/yr) and two (100 tHM/yr) at Kalpakkam (the second one nearing completion in 2014).

But Pakistan has no Fast Breeder Reactor and no unsafeguarded heavy water power reactors on its soil. India already has 100 MWt Dhruva-I in operation coupled with 125 MWt Dhruva-II nearing completion along with another 30 MWt reactor being planned. Its 40 MWt CIRUS reactor had already produced 500 kg of weapon-grade plutonium up to 2006 (IPFM 2006) and an additional 45 kg before it was shut down in 2010. Dhruva-I continues to produce 20-25 kg of weapon-grade plutonium every year. India's 8 heavy water power reactors kept outside safeguards under the Indo-US nuclear deal can produce 1250 kg of weapon-grade plutonium each year, even though India claims that the unsafeguarded reactor-grade plutonium produced by them during normal operations would be used as fuel (MOX) for its breeder reactor program (also unsafeguarded). India's 500 MWe EFBR can produce 145 kg of weapon-grade plutonium each year.

Comparisons in highly enriched uranium capabilities and stockpiles show a similar trend. Pakistan has not increased or expanded its uranium enrichment capacity in the past 20 years, where as India is doubling its existing enrichment potential (floor space) at its Rare Materials Plant (Rattehali) in Mysore. In fact, Pakistan's HEU stocks might be less than the known estimates since it is difficult to determine the precise SWU capacity of an enrichment plant and its UF6 feed production. That Pakistan is not engaged in, nor aims at entering into a fissile race with India, is exemplified by the following comparison of unsafeguarded fissile material stockpiles and production capabilities (existing and projected).

Curiously enough, Pakistan's plutonium quest has been at the heart of western non-proliferation efforts since the 1970s when the country was striving to complete the nuclear fuel cycle. It is intriguing that towards the late 1970s when Pakistan was completing research and development work on various plants and facilities for the enriched uranium route (uranium processing, conversion and enrichment) as part of the fuel cycle, and was also quietly building other unsafeguarded facilities for the plutonium route, the United States had used its full diplomatic pressure to secure a major non-proliferation objective in order to force France to cancel the deal for the safeguarded commercial-scale reprocessing plant in August, 1978 (which was never intended for Pakistan's weapons program anyway).

Only a year later, a June 6, 1979, a de-classified US State Department cable stated that Pakistan might be "allowed" to complete its gas-centrifuge program while the United States (in its misplaced opinion) had succeeded in stopping Pakistan's plutonium program in its tracks. This might have been so as the United States was probably not sure that Pakistan could build uranium processing, hexafluoride gas (UF6) production, and gas-centrifuge plants for the enriched uranium route anytime soon, but more significantly because plutonium was and still is the major non-proliferation concern for Pakistan since it provides the capability to develop miniaturized, boosted fission, tactical and thermo-nuclear warheads—the basis of a first-class operational nuclear deterrent.

Thermonuclear weapons is yet another area where Pakistan has shown restraint and has been punching below its weight, even though the capability exists to build these weapons, but perhaps boosted-fission warheads might suffice for existing force goals.

Pakistan's ballistic missile program was largely driven by the effects of the Pressler Amendment. Yet its missile development and testing trajectory does not reflect any arms racing with India in this field with both countries pursuing divergent pathways in the field. For instance, Pakistan's missile development and testing is solely geared towards the consolidation of its existing capabilities designed to achieve greater accuracy, reliability against increasing Indian ballistic and planned cruise missile defences and survivability of its strategic forces. This has been explained in a recent Carnegie study, which states that "*An analysis of aggregated missile test data since 1998 reveals that the armament dynamic is far more complex. The Indian and Pakistani nuclear programs are largely decoupled. The data show little correlation between the adversaries' testing behaviour contrary to what would be expected in a classic arms race. In fact, the types and ranges of missiles under development provide concrete evidence of the divergence in their nuclear objectives and security strategies. Pakistan is building weapons systems to deter India from conventional military operations below the nuclear threshold. India is developing systems primarily to strengthen its strategic deterrent against China....*"

This fact was reiterated when Pakistan did not respond to India's 5000-7000 km-range Agni-V ICBM. in kind, but conducted tests of improved versions of its 1000-1300 km-range Shaheen-1A ballistic missile as a potential substitute to the liquid-fuelled Ghauri. Pakistan also has no ballistic or cruise missile defense programs; no ICBM projects like *Agni*-V which is being armed with MIRVs and no SSBNs like India's *Arihant* armed with the 700 km-range *Sagarika* SLBMs. Pakistan's defense budget has largely remained static at around 2-3% of GDP ($5-7 billion) in the past decade compared to India's which has increased to around $ 40 billion. Similarly, a growing imbalance in conventional forces (which Pakistan can never bridge) is exacerbating with India becoming the world's largest net importer of conventional arms for several years in a row in the past few years.

This then brings forth the logic of Pakistan's recent development of battlefield or tactical nuclear weapons designed to deter limited conventional war below its nuclear threshold. TNWs would be used only as weapon of last resort in case of deterrence failure and collapse of conventional forces or the crossing of its perceived nuclear thresholds, whichever comes first. In case of deterrence failure, there would be no escalation control would become impossible and ineffective resulting in the employment of every means available to Pakistan to defend itself against aggression. Pakistan opted to build TNWs (presumably in limited numbers for deterrence only and not for war fighting) as means to supplement conventional defences.

Nonetheless, when Pakistan tested a 60-km range nuclear capable battlefield missile (Hatf-IX) *Nasr* in 2011, it caused considerable consternation in India and elsewhere. However, when India tested the 50-150 km-range *Prahaar* shortly thereafter,, and dubbed it a "tactical surface to surface missile capable of carrying *different types of warheads*, which operates as battle field support system to the Indian Army" or has recently added another 60-170 km tactical missile *Pragati,* to its missile arsenal, no one raises a finger. That is mainly because India has stopped short of declaring these systems nuclear capable and have declared them to carry conventional warheads only. But if India can develop unconventional warheads for the nuclear capable *Prithvi*-I and II, then it is only a matter of time before nuclear warheads for *Prahaar* and*Pragati* are developed, especially given their deployments against Pakistan and China.

So how many warheads would then suffice for credible minimum deterrence? Pakistan is being placed ahead of India in warhead count by a number of international publications and experts. What is astonishing is the basis of such estimates unless they have had the privilege of having done a warhead count themselves or been able to determine the exact amount of fissile material and the corresponding non-nuclear components developed to produce warheads. Warhead count and the amount of fissile material weaponized would invariable depend on various weapon designs (boosted fission, composite core, two-stage etc.) This in any case would be any nation's most classified information and neither India, nor Pakistan have declared their respective inventories of fissile stocks or warheads.

Since some of India's leading strategic analysts such as K. Subrahmanyam have called for the development of a strategic triad comprising a 400-warheads, Pakistan should settle for at least a triad consisting of a 200-250 warhead force that might include different types warheads required to maintain a credible minimum deterrent, designed to absorb an Indian first strike and respond—a capability needed for any country to maintain strategic stability with a nuclear armed neighbor.

However, any such force goals would depend on the availability of fissile material (especially plutonium and tritium for miniaturized warheads) whose production would be limited by the finite domestic reserves of natural uranium, unlike that of India who is being lavishly furnished by the NSG countries with the means of making the most optimum use of all its natural uranium stocks for weaponization.

When Pakistan attempts to consolidate its strategic forces and ramp up plutonium production—which has enabled it to operationalize its nuclear deterrent—it is accused of punching above its weight. It knows what it is doing within its capabilities and resources. Its force goals have been quantified and its fissile material production will continue till those targets are achieved so as to develop a triad-based assured second strike capability that can withstand massive retaliation and prevent the exploitation of strategic space at the tactical level.

Pakistan is in no way competing with India in pursuing regional and global ambitions through ballistic missile nuclear submarines, ICBMs or space weaponization or retaining huge stocks and production capacity of fissile material outside safeguards—a fact accepted by the NSG countries which accorded India the unique distinction of being the beneficiary of an NPT signatory state without any obligations and allowed it to retain a substantial part of its fuel cycle outside safeguards for producing more fissile material in the future.

Given these realities, if India today were to ask to sign the FMCT and the CTBT, it is most likely that it won't agree to be a part of either of these treaty arrangements and is conveniently taking cover behind Pakistan's stance on the FMCT at the CD. Some Indian scientists doubt whether all the Pokhran-II tests were successful, while many others question Pakistan's claims of having built a miniaturized nuclear warhead for*Nasr* without hot tests. So should both India and Pakistan jointly announce a second round of tests purely for technical reasons in addition to ensuring the reliability and "one-point safety" of their respective warheads and then unilaterally or jointly sign the CTBT, depending on their respective security calculus? Finally, Pakistan is accused of abetting terrorists and non-state actors when it has been fighting a war on terror on its soil for over a decade and has suffered more than 40000 casualties (including high-ranking civil and military officers) and incurred financial and economic lossesamounting to tens of billions of dollars. Such insinuations are used to justify India's appetite for limited conventional war in the region. So should the recent admission by India's former army chief, that it has been involved in sponsoring and abetting terrorist activities in Baluchistan be used by Pakistan to warrant its own version of Cold Start or proactive operations across the border?

Nonetheless, the silver lining is that a certain degree strategic stability in South Asia might be achieved in the foreseeable future when both India and Pakistan acquire assured second-strike capabilities. In fact, they are steadily moving on the path of technological maturation and once Pakistan is able to deploy a highly survivable triad-based credible minimum deterrent, then it would be irrelevant whether India adds to its capabilities for global reach and power projection beyond South Asia that might one day have the potential to target Europe, North America or Australia.

## PAKISTAN'S CIVIL NUCLEAR PROGRAM

Pakistan also has a civil nuclear power program, with two reactors currently operating—the Karachi Nuclear Power Plant, which went critical in 1971, and the Chasma Nuclear Power Plant, which went critical in 2000. Prime Minister Gilani announced May 12, 2011, that a second nuclear reactor at Chasma, constructed with Chinese assistance, had become operational. Beijing has also apparently agreed to construct two additional power reactors at Chasma, according to both Chinese and Pakistani officials. Pakistan Atomic Energy Commission Chairman Ansar Parvez stated May 12, 2011, that concrete has been poured for one of these reactors and that ground breaking for the other reactor would take place the next month. The first reactor is to come on line in 2016, with the next to follow 10 months later. Acting Assistant Secretary Van Diepen stated July 22, 2010, that such a sale would appear to be inconsistent with current Nuclear Suppliers Group (NSG) guidelines. Additionally, Pakistan and China are reportedly close to finalizing an agreement for Beijing to construct a third, larger, reactor in Pakistan. As noted, the NSG changed its guidelines in 2008 to allow nuclear trade with India. Secretary of State Clinton suggested July 20, 2010, that the United States does not currently support a similar change for Pakistan. Assistant Secretary of State Robert Blake reiterated Van Diepen and Clinton's positions March 18, 2011.

Pakistan is also operating two research reactors—Pakistan Research Reactor 1, which went critical in 1965,170 and Pakistan Research Reactor 2, which went critical in 1989. Pakistan Research Reactor 1, which was originally supplied by a U.S. firm, was converted from using highly-enriched uranium (HEU) to low-enriched uranium fuel in 1992.172 A "small amount" of the HEU fuel remains in Pakistan.

## Delivery Vehicles

Pakistan has two types of delivery vehicles for nuclear weapons: aircraft controlled by the Pakistan Air Force and surface-to-surface missiles controlled by the Pakistan Army. Pakistan could deliver its nuclear weapons using F-16 fighter aircraft purchased from the United States, provided that modifications are made. It is widely believed that Islamabad has made the relevant modifications to the F-16s previously sold to them by Washington.

Although concerns have been raised about the impact of these sales on the strategic balance in South Asia. the U.S. government maintains that the sale of additional F-16s to Pakistan will not alter the regional balance of power. The contract for provision of an additional 18 aircraft was signed in 2006, as was the contract for the weapons for those aircraft and a contract to perform the mid-life upgrade on Pakistan's F-16A/B model aircraft. Pakistan's F-16 fleet will, therefore, be expanded, but it is unclear what portion of the fleet will be capable of a nuclear mission. Mirage V aircraft may also be used as delivery vehicles.

DIA Director Burgess told the Senate Armed Services Committee March 10, 2011, that Pakistan is developing new missile systems which, when deployed and added to Islamabad's current ballistic missiles, will enable Pakistan "to strike a variety of targets at ranges of 200-2000 kilometers with both conventional and nuclear payloads." Islamabad has three types of ballistic missiles thought to be nuclear-capable: the solid-fuel *Hatf-III* (*Ghaznavi*), with a range of approximately 300-400 kilometers; the solid-fuel *Hatf-IV* (*Shaheen*), with a range of over 450 kilometers; and the liquid-fuel *Hatf-V* (*Ghauri*), with an approximate range of almost 1,300 kilometers; The solid-fuel *Hatf-VI* (*Shaheen-2*) missile, when deployed, will be "capable of reaching targets out to 2,000 kilometers," former DIA Director Maples stated March 10, 2009,72 adding that Islamabad has made "significant progress" on the missile.

A 2009 National Air and Space Intelligence Centre (NASIC) report appears to support this conclusion, stating that the missile "probably will soon be deployed." Pakistan's Inter Services Public Relations announced April 19, 2011, the first successful flight test of a "newly developed Short Range Surface to Surface Multi Tube Ballistic Missile Hatf IX (NASR)."

The missile has a range of 60 kilometers and "carries nuclear warheads of appropriate yield with high accuracy," according to the press release. Islamabad continues to carry out ballistic missile tests, but notifies India in advance in accordance with an October 2005 bilateral missile pre-notification pact. Maples also indicated that Pakistan is developing nuclear-capable cruise missiles: the Babur (ground-launched) and the Ra'ad (air-launched), both of which will have estimated ranges of 320 kilometers, according to the NASIC report. In an April 29, 2011, announcement of a successful flight test of the Ra'ad, the Pakistani government gave the missile's range as 350 kilometers; In an October 28, 2011, announcement of a flight test of the Babur, the Pakistani government gave the missile's range as 700 kilometers.

## Nuclear Doctrine

Pakistan's strategic doctrine is undeclared, and will probably remain so, but prominent officials and analysts have offered insights concerning its basic tenets. Describing the guiding principle as minimum credible nuclear deterrence. high-level officials' statements point to four policy objectives for Islamabad's nuclear weapons: deter all forms of external aggression; deter through a combination of conventional and strategic forces; deter counterforce strategies by securing strategic assets and threatening nuclear retaliation; and stabilize strategic deterrence in South Asia. .

Pakistani officials have also indicated that this nuclear posture is designed to preserve territorial integrity against Indian attack, prevent military escalation, and counter its main rival's conventional superiority.

Pakistan has pledged no-first-use against non-nuclear-weapon states, but has not ruled out firstuse against a nuclear-armed aggressor, such as India. Some analysts say this ambiguity serves to maintain deterrence against India's conventional superiority; the Foreign Ministry spokesperson stated May 21, 2009, that "there are acquisitions of sophisticated weaponry by our neighbour which will disturb the conventional balance between our two countries and hence, lower the nuclear threshold." Other analysts argue that keeping the first-use option against New Delhi allows Islamabad to conduct sub-conventional operations, such as support for low intensity conflict or proxy war in Kashmir, while effectively deterring India at the strategic level. Pakistan has reportedly addressed issues of survivability through pursuing a second strike capability, possibly building hard and deeply buried storage and launch facilities, deploying roadmobile missiles, deploying air defenses around strategic sites, and utilizing concealment measures.

## Command and Control

Pakistan's command and control over its nuclear weapons is compartmentalized and includes strict operational security. The government's command and control system is based on "C4I2SR" (command, control, communication, computers, intelligence, information, surveillance and reconnaissance). Islamabad's Strategic Command Organization has a three-tiered structure, consisting of the National Command Authority (NCA), the Strategic Plans Division (SPD), and the Strategic Forces Commands.

The NCA, established in 2000, supervises the functions and administration of all of Pakistan's organizations involved in nuclear weapons research, development, and employment, as well as the military services that operate the strategic forces. The prime minister, as head of government, is chairperson of the NCA. The NCA also includes the chair of the joint chiefs of staff; the ministers of defence, interior, and finance; the director general of the SPD; and the commanders of the Army, Air Force, and Navy. The final authority to launch a nuclear strike requires consensus within the NCA; the chairperson must cast the final vote. The NCA is comprised of two committees, the Employment Control Committee (ECC) and the Development Control Committee (DCC), each of which includes a mix of civilian and military officials. The ECC's functions include establishing a command and control system over the use of nuclear weapons. The DCC "exercises technical, financial and administrative control over all strategic organisations, including national laboratories and research and development organisations associated with the development and modernisation of nuclear weapons.

The SPD is headed by a director general from the Army and acts as the secretariat for the NCA. The SPD's functions include formulating Islamabad's nuclear policy, strategy, and doctrine; developing the nuclear chain of command; and formulating operational plans at the service level for the movement, deployment, and use of nuclear weapons. The Army, Air Force, and Navy each have their own strategic force command, but operational planning and control remains with the NCA. The SPD coordinates operational plans with the strategic forces commands. According to current and former Pakistani officials, Islamabad employs a system which requires that at least two, and perhaps three, people authenticate launch codes for nuclear weapons. On December 13, 2007, then-President Musharraf formalized these authorities and structure in the "National Command Authority Ordinance, 2007."89 The NCA was established by administrative order, but now has a legal basis. Analysts point out that the timing of this ordinance was meant to help the command and control system weather political transitions and potentially preserve the military's strong control over the system. The ordinance also addresses the problems of the proliferation of nuclear expertise and personnel reliability. It outlines punishable offenses related to breach of confidentiality or leakage of "secured information," gives the SPD authority to investigate suspicious conduct, states that punishment for these offenses can be up to 25 years imprisonment, and applies to both serving and retired personnel, including military personnel, notwithstanding any other laws. As a result, Pakistani authorities say that the ordinance should strengthen their control over strategic organizations and their personnel.

## Security Concerns

According to a 2001 Department of Defence report, Islamabad's nuclear weapons "are probably stored in component form," which suggests that the nuclear warheads are stored separately from delivery vehicles. According to some reports, the fissile cores of the weapons are separated from the non-nuclear explosives. But whether this is actually the case is unclear; one report states that the warheads and delivery vehicles are probably stored separately in facilities close to one another, but says nothing about the fissile cores. And, according to an account of a 2008 experts' group visit to Pakistan, Lieutenant General Khalid Kidwai, the head of the SPD, suggested that the nuclear warheads (containing the fissile cores) may be mated with their delivery vehicles. According to Kidwai, the report says, the SPD's official position is that the weapons "will be ready when required, at the shortest notice; [but] the Pakistani doctrine is not endorsing a USUSSR model with weapons on hair trigger alert." The 2001 Defence Department report says that Pakistan can probably assemble its weapons fairly quickly.

It warrants mention that, although separate storage may provide a layer of protection against accidental launch or prevent theft of an assembled weapon, it may be easier for unauthorized people to remove a weapon's fissile material core if it is not assembled. Dispersal of the assets may also create more potential access points for acquisition and may increase the risk of diversion.

As the United States prepared to launch an attack on the Afghan Taliban after September 11, 2001, President Musharraf reportedly ordered that Pakistan's nuclear arsenal be redeployed to "at least six secret new locations." This action came at a time of uncertainly about the future of the region, including the direction of U.S.-Pakistan relations. Islamabad's leadership was uncertain whether the United States would decide to conduct military strikes against Pakistan's nuclear assets if the government did not assist the United States against the Taliban. Indeed, President Musharraf cited protection of Pakistan's nuclear and missile assets as one of the reasons for Islamabad's dramatic policy shift.

These events, in combination with the 1999 Kargil crisis, the 2002 conflict with India at the Line of Control, and revelations about the A. Q. Khan proliferation network, inspired a variety of reforms to secure the nuclear complex. Risk of nuclear war in

South Asia ran high in the 1999 Kargil crisis, when the Pakistani military is believed to have begun preparing nuclear-tipped missiles. It should be noted that, even at the high alert levels of 2001 and 2002, there were no reports of Pakistan mating the warheads with delivery systems.

In the fall of 2007 and early 2008, some observers expressed concern about the security of the country's arsenal if political instability were to persist. Former Prime Minister Benazir Bhutto said in a November 5, 2007, interview that, although then-President Musharraf claimed to be in firm control of the nuclear arsenal, she feared this control could weaken due to instability in the country. Similarly, Michael Krepon of the Henry L. Stimson Centre has argued that "a prolonged period of turbulence and infighting among the country's President, Prime Minister, and Army Chief" could jeopardize the army's unity of command, which "is essential for nuclear security." During that time, U.S. military officials also expressed concern about the security of Pakistan's nuclear weapons. Then-IAEA Director General Mohamed ElBaradei also has expressed fears that a radical regime could take power in Pakistan, and thereby acquire nuclear weapons. Experts also worry that while nuclear weapons are currently under firm control, with warheads disassembled, technology could be sold off by insiders during a worsened crisis." However, U.S. intelligence officials have expressed greater confidence regarding the security of Islamabad's nuclear weapons. Deputy Secretary of State John D. Negroponte in testimony to Congress on November 7, 2007, said he believed that there is "plenty of succession planning that's going on in the Pakistani military" and that Pakistan's nuclear weapons are under "effective technical control." Similarly, Donald Kerr, Principal Deputy Director of National Intelligence, told a Washington audience May 29, 2008, that the Pakistani military's control of the nuclear weapons is "a good thing because that's an institution in Pakistan that has, in fact, withstood many of the political changes over the years." More recently, former DIA Director Maples stated March 10, 2009, that Islamabad "has taken important steps to safeguard its nuclear weapons," although he pointed out that "vulnerabilities exist." As noted, current DIA Director Burgess articulated a similar assessment in March 2011.

U.S. officials have also conveyed confidence in the security of Islamabad's nuclear weapons. General Petraeus stated on May 10, 2009, that "[w]ith respect to the—the nuclear weapons and—and sites that are controlled by Pakistan ... we have confidence in their security procedures and elements and believe that the security of those sites is adequate." Admiral Mullen echoed this assessment during a May 14, 2009, hearing before the Senate Armed Services Committee. More recently, Secretary of Defence Robert Gates stated in a January 21, 2010, interview that the United States is "very comfortable with the security of Pakistan's nuclear weapons." Then-State Department spokesperson P.J. Crowley told reporters April 9, 2010, that Pakistan "has demonstrated that it can secure its own nuclear weapons program." Similarly, Under Secretary of Defence Michele Flournoy stated during an April 29, 2010, hearing that "we believe that Pakistan has a very solid command-and-control system for their nuclear weapons," adding that "they have made a great deal of investment in the security of their nuclear arsenal." As noted, this confidence has continued into 2011. James Clapper, Director of National Intelligence, told the House Intelligence Committee February 10 that "our assessment is that the nuclear weapons in Pakistan are secure." General Petraeus told the Senate Armed Services Committee March 15 that "[t]here is quite considerable security for the Pakistani nuclear weapons." Asked about the security of Pakistan's weapons following a May 2011 insurgent attack on a military installation in Karachi, Assistant Secretary of State Robert Blake stated June 21 that "there is much more heightened security around" Pakistan's nuclear weapons facilities than at the Karachi installation. U.S. knowledge of Pakistan's arsenal, however, remains limited, according to U.S. officials. For example, Mullen stated that "we're limited in what we actually know" about Islamabad's nuclear arsenal. Leon Panetta, Director of the Central Intelligence Agency, similarly acknowledged in a May 18, 2010, speech that the United States does not possess the intelligence to locate all of Pakistan's nuclear weapons-related sites.

Other governments have also voiced opinions regarding the security of Pakistan's nuclear arsenal. For example, Indian National

Security Adviser M. K. Narayanan said that the arsenal is safe and has adequate checks and balances. Similarly, then-Secretary of State for Foreign and Commonwealth Affairs David Miliband told the *Charlie Rose Show* December 15, 2008, that Islamabad's nuclear weapons "are under pretty close lock and key." Furthermore, according to Director of the French General Directorate of External Security Erard Corbin de Mangoux, Pakistan's military and civilian leaders have a "sense of responsibility" to maintain control over the country's nuclear weapons; these leaders "know that the international status to which they aspire depends directly on their ability to exercise complete control over such an instrument of power," he argued in an interview published in spring 2010. Other non-U.S. officials, however, have sounded somewhat less optimistic. For example, Russian Deputy Prime Minister Sergei Ivanov said in a March 24, 2009, television interview that Moscow is "very much concerned" about the security of Pakistan's arsenal. Indian officials expressed concerns about the security of Pakistan's nuclear arsenal following the May 2011 insurgent attack on the Karachi military installation.

Pakistani officials have consistently expressed confidence in the security of the country's nuclear arsenal. Then-President Musharraf stated in November 2007 that Pakistan's nuclear weapons are under "total custodial controls." More recently, President Asif Ali Zardari told *CNN* December 2, 2008, that the country's nuclear command and control system "is working well."

Additionally, a Pakistani Foreign Ministry spokesperson stated May 21, 2009, that "there is simply no question of our strategic assets falling into the wrong hands. We have full confidence in our procedures, mechanisms and command and control systems."

Pakistani Prime Minister Yousaf Raza Gilani stated May 8, 2010, that Islamabad has "laid to rest" concerns about its nuclear arsenal's security. The May 2011 U.S. strike that killed Al Qaeda leader Osama bin Laden generated a public discussion in Pakistan as to whether a country such as India or the United States could successfully attack and destroy Pakistan's nuclear weapons.

Responding to these concerns, Prime Minster Gilani stated May 25, 2011, that the country's "strategic assets are well protected and our capability to defend our sovereignty, territorial integrity and liberties of our people, is very much in place." In addition to the above scenarios, the security of Pakistan's nuclear weapons could also be jeopardized by another conflict between India and Pakistan, Michael Krepon argued, explaining that an "escalating war with nuclear forces in the field would increase the probability of accidents, miscalculations, and the use of nuclear weapons."

This is because [w]hen tensions rise precipitously with India, the readiness level of Pakistan's nuclear deterrent also rises. Because the geographical coordinates of Pakistan's main nuclear weapon storage sites, missile, and air bases can be readily identified from satellites—and therefore targeted by opposing forces—the dictates of deterrence mandate some movement of launchers and weapons from fixed locations during crises. Nuclear weapons on the move are inherently less secure than nuclear weapons at heavily-guarded storage sites. Weapons and launchers in motion are also more susceptible to "insider" threats and accidents.

Such a war, Krepon added, would also place stress on the army's unity of command. Krepon has also pointed out that Islamabad faces a dilemma, because less-dispersed nuclear weapons may be more vulnerable to a disarming military strike from India."

## THE CHINA-PAKISTAN NUCLEAR "DEAL"

Others, such as Brad Glosserman, executive director of the Pacific Forum Centre for Strategic and International Studies, have gone further, arguing that the U.S.-India deal has in fact opened the floodgates for exactly such transactions as are now proposed by China toward Pakistan: "We all knew at the time that an agreement such as the India-U.S. one would have consequences for the non-proliferation regime and that's what you are seeing now.... The India-U.S. deal was a bad, troubling example to set, for proliferators, however justified the desire in Washington to improve ties with India." In other words, if the U.S.-India agreement had not been consummated, the currently proposed Chinese sale of new nuclear rectors to Pakistan would likely not have occurred.

These claims, however, are not persuasive. Whatever one's views of the U.S.-India civilian nuclear cooperation agreement, the accord reached between President George W. Bush and Prime Minister Manmohan Singh is fundamentally different from the proposed Chinese effort to export additional power reactors to Pakistan. *Pace* the recent claims of Maleeha Lodhi, the U.S.-Indian agreement is not "a fundamental violation of the [Nuclear Non-Proliferation] Treaty" because nothing in the treaty forbids agreements for peaceful nuclear cooperation—to include the export of reactors, other nuclear technologies, and nuclear materials—with states that are not signatories to it. All that the NPT requires is that every nuclear transaction with any non-signatory state be solely for peaceful uses and that all transferred items be fully safeguarded by the International Atomic Energy Agency (IAEA). The U.S.-India civilian nuclear cooperation agreement meets both these conditions and, therefore, cannot be considered a violation of the NPT by any stretch of the imagination.

The bilateral agreement between Washington and New Delhi, however, was clearly in conflict with the full-scope safeguards criterion encoded in the 1978 U.S. Nuclear Nonproliferation Act (NNPA) and adopted by the NSG at its Warsaw meeting in 1992 (which enjoined its members to refrain from any significant nuclear exports to non–nuclear-weapon states that had not adopted comprehensive safeguards). Consequently, the Bush administration expended enormous political capital in the U.S. Congress to amend the relevant components of American law, which previously had permitted nuclear cooperation agreements with non– nuclear-weapon states only after they had accepted full-scope safeguards. Thereafter, the administration, working in concert with the government of India, committed significant diplomatic resources to convince the NSG to accord India an exceptional waiver from the full-scope safeguards criterion that would have otherwise stymied international nuclear cooperation with New Delhi.

From the very beginning, President Bush always had the option of pursuing nuclear cooperation with India in the manner now pursued by China toward Pakistan. That is, the United States—after amending its own national laws— could have unilaterally begun nuclear trade with India, disregarding the sentiments of its NSG partners and abusing the normative character of the NSG's guidelines. Because maintaining the integrity of the global nonproliferation regime, however, was always important to the United States— and was perhaps even more important because of the exceptional treatment contemplated for India—the Bush administration spent considerable energy from October 2005 until the final extraordinary plenary in September 2008— consulting with its NSG partners *during eight meetings over four years,* not to mention the bilateral discussions that occurred in national capitals—to finally secure the special waiver for India that exempted it from the constraining condition of full-scope safeguards.

The current Sino-Pakistani nuclear transaction could not be more different.

For starters, the interstate agreement governing the potential export of the two Chinese reactors to Pakistan is a secret covenant, secretly concluded. Unlike the U.S.-India nuclear initiative, whose terms were public and vociferously debated in both countries starting with the initial announcement in July 2005, the conditions regulating the proposed Chinese sale (and any potential future transfers) are unknown to the international community.

Furthermore, the Chinese have sought to advance this transaction with Pakistan by subterfuge. By insinuating privately, but without any accompanying formal declaration, that the prospective sale of two nuclear rectors to Pakistan is grandfathered, in Maleeha Lodhi's masterfully equivocal formulation, "under the [Sino-Pakistani] agreement dating back to the 1980s that provided for an understanding in 2003 for further long-term collaboration," Beijing has sought to convey that all Chinese sales to Pakistan are *ipso facto* exempted from its obligation to uphold the NSG's requirement of full-scope safeguards because China joined the NSG only in 2004, well after the latest "understanding" reached with Pakistan.

This minor detail, however, eluded Chinese diplomats when they provided the NSG with a rendition of their outstanding commitments upon joining the organization. As Mark Hibbs has described it, "China then explained to the NSG that a longstanding framework agreement with Pakistan committed China to provide a second reactor, Chashma-2, more research reactors, plus supply of all the fuel in perpetuity for these units." Notice there is not a word about additional power reactors beyond the already contracted Chashma-2, which began construction in 2005, the year after Beijing joined the NSG.

Finally, and most conspicuously, unlike the U.S.-Indian civilian nuclear initiative, China has made no effort thus far—and is unlikely to make any in the future—to seek a specific NSG exemption for its nuclear trade with Pakistan.

The Bush administration campaigned for a waiver from the NSG's full-scope condition for India on two defensible grounds: first, India's nonproliferation record justified its progressive integration into the international nuclear regime and, second, its growing technological mastery over different nuclear fuel cycles made the international regime stronger through its inclusion rather than its continued exclusion. After long and arduous diplomatic efforts, these arguments finally carried the day—but not before the NSG wrested from New Delhi a strong reiteration of its disarmament obligations.

What is most pertinent, however, is that the United States made the investment over several years to persuade the NSG and, further, that the NSG's members took their time to consider the American proposal in all its complexity. To be sure, many were torn by the nature of the U.S. initiative; some were frustrated by what was perceived as strong American pressure; others had to balance their long-standing commitment to nonproliferation with their strong ties to India and/or the United States; and all had to struggle to figure out how best to integrate India into the global nuclear regime. When the consensus finally came, it did only after all the competing interests were weighed and adjudicated in 44 national capitals—which is exactly what the process was meant to do.

China, in contrast, has chosen a different route: seeking to short-circuit the NSG rather than appeal to its judgment. Knowing full well that Pakistan's poor nonproliferation record and its continuing reluctance to come clean on the activities of A. Q. Khan and his cohort will prevent the NSG from granting Pakistan any waiver from the full-scope safeguards requirement, Beijing appears committed to persisting with the course of action it has adopted thus far: namely, to attempt consummating various nuclear trades with Pakistan secretly if it believes it can get away with such dealings because of either diffidence or contrivance on the part of the international community. The glaring differences between the U.S.-Indian agreement and the proposed Chinese-Pakistani transaction thus say more about, in Hibbs' apt phrase, "China's growing nuclear assertiveness" than they do about any purported similarity between these two initiatives. Consequently, the United States can— and should—oppose China's current effort to sell new reactors to Pakistan without fear of "charges of hypocrisy." If duplicity is at issue on this question, it emanates only from Beijing and not Washington.

## *An Opening for China?*

But even if American nuclear cooperation with India is in fact fundamentally different in its structural characteristics from that between China and Pakistan, is there any truth to the charge that the former has engendered the latter? Many commentators in the United States seem to think so. Commenting on the Sino-Pakistani agreement, for example, Henry Sokolski, executive director of the Nonproliferation Policy Education Centre in Washington, has argued, consistent with Brad Glosserman's remarks quoted earlier, that "two wrongs make a wrong, but it was to be expected once we made the case for an exemption [involving India]."

Not so fast. In fact, the Chinese attempt to sell Pakistan additional nuclear reactors beyond the Chashma-1 plant agreed to in 1991 goes back to the first term of the George W. Bush administration—long before the U.S.-Indian civilian nuclear cooperation agreement was even contemplated. It is often forgotten that for over a decade now, Beijing has sought on various occasions to expand its civilian reactor sales to Pakistan. Sino-Pakistani discussions on this subject occurred even after China had joined the NSG in 2004. For most part, however, these efforts historically were stymied by Islamabad's lack of financial resources, although China's unwillingness to confront the international community through politically provocative transactions played some role as well.

In any event, whenever it appeared that a Chinese nuclear sale to Pakistan was in the offing, successive U.S. administrations reacted quite unfavorably. During the two terms of President George W. Bush, for example, the U.S. government démarched China formally or sharply queried it informally on several occasions, warning Beijing about American concerns regarding possible Pakistani diversion of Chinese-origin technology and materials to Islamabad's weapons programs while cautioning China not to violate standing NSG regulations on this issue. Similar démarches were issued in Islamabad, admonishing Pakistani policy makers about U.S. concerns regarding the potential circumvention of NSG guidelines.

Such complaints were leveled throughout the Bush years—*before, during, and after the civil nuclear cooperation initiative with India*. In every instance, the strong American remonstrations produced the desired effect: no Chinese reactor sale to Pakistan was consummated, even though it was obvious to U.S. policy makers that both Beijing and Islamabad were constantly testing the waters, probing the strength of American opposition.

The unvarying character of the conversations themselves gave the game away. Although intelligence alerts or news reports indicating a potential Chinese sale to Pakistan usually precipitated the démarches in both capitals, neither Chinese nor Pakistani officials would ever acknowledge the conclusion of any contract or confirm whether binding interstate agreements governing the contracts even existed to begin with. Rather, they would simply recite the facts about Pakistan's unsatisfied energy needs; assure the United States that any Sino-Pakistani nuclear energy cooperation—should it occur—would always be under IAEA safeguards and hence supposedly consistent with NSG guidelines; and, in the last years of the Bush administration, clamor for parity of U.S. treatment between India and Pakistan.

Whatever China is proposing to consummate with Pakistan today in regard to reactor and other nuclear sales, thus, has a long, repetitious, and even convoluted history that bears little *causal* connection to the U.S.-Indian civilian nuclear initiative. If nothing else, Lodhi's laconic explanation about Sino-Pakistani civil nuclear cooperation substantiates this conclusion fully. While there is no doubt that Pakistan's appeals for equal treatment with India have grown in intensity since the conclusion of the U.S.-Indian nuclear accord, the historical record equally corroborates the fact that China's desire to press forward with renewed nuclear cooperation with Pakistan predates the landmark agreement between Washington and New Delhi. As Hibbs noted—accurately— in a recent radio interview, the commercial contacts between China and Pakistan were very, very advanced indeed at the time that the United States and India made a separate nuclear deal and the Chinese were merely waiting for an opportunity to advance this project and they have that opportunity now because the U.S. has gone ahead with its project with India and the Nuclear Suppliers Group in 2008 has approved it. So China has had a few years to wait, they've waited and now the U.S.-India project is going ahead and China now sees this as their opportune moment.

The U.S.-Indian nuclear accord, then, cannot be held responsible for precipitating Sino-Pakistani civilian nuclear commerce—or its latest iteration. What the U.S.-Indian civilian nuclear cooperation agreement possibly contributed is a change in the psycho-political environment. This change encouraged China to test the prospects for forcing further change in the global nonproliferation system by implementing its own version of "exceptionalism" for its preferred strategic partners—in the hope that other states who acquiesced to the U.S. initiative would feel obliged to extend comparable courtesies to China.

Even if that were true, it only implies that Beijing and Islamabad ought to be held *a fortiori* to the same standards of endorsement for such cooperation, namely, securing an NSG exemption by China on behalf of Pakistan. The reasons for insisting on such a process are simple: even if the problematic character of Pakistan's nonproliferation record is discounted, the integrity of the global nonproliferation system requires an orderly and coordinated process for managing change—which the NSG currently provides—and China, as a member of that group, should be permitted to consummate its prospective deal with Pakistan only if it can first secure an NSG exemption from the current guidelines. In other words, China should be permitted to preserve its standing within the NSG only to the degree that it complies with the organization's existing rules.

### *U.S. Leadership Is Indispensable*

Whether China chooses to respect the NSG's guidelines and follow the process adopted in the case of the U.S.-Indian nuclear accord, however, will depend greatly on the U.S. response to Beijing's prospective sales to Pakistan. Although it is tempting to believe that the United States has few options and that the Sino-Pakistani deal could go through because China would simply disregard the NSG given its strategic interests in Pakistan, the historical record suggests otherwise.

For all of China's supposed nonchalance, Beijing is in fact quite sensitive to both American and international pressure on issues regarding proliferation, given its own past history with Pakistan, Islamabad's nonproliferation record, and the discomfiture associated with visible but awkward and undeniable transactions. Determined U.S. opposition to China's planned sales to Pakistan would engender caution in Beijing and energize resistance from other NSG members, most of whom are already apprehensive about Beijing's efforts to circumvent the existing guidelines.

This is especially relevant because the dramatic expansion of China's civilian nuclear power program has already made Beijing more dependent that ever before on international cooperation for its success; China's reliance on imported fuel, new reactor technology, and alternatives to the uranium cycle, in fact make it all the more important for Beijing to stay in the good graces of key NSG member states. As Hibbs has concluded succinctly, "... countries like Australia, the United States, Canada, countries that are in a position to support China's nuclear energy development, these countries are not powerless and would be in the position to engage China to restrain its behaviour."

In the NSG, as in any other international organization, however, a demonstration of robust U.S. leadership is indispensable. Resolute opposition by Washington will mobilize the pervasive international discomfort that might otherwise lie recessed and, in the case of Sino-Pakistani nuclear cooperation particularly, would be the single most important factor that makes the difference to whether China's plans in current form are realized or frustrated.

Unfortunately, the Obama administration's early response on this issue was hesitant and fumbling. T. P. Sreenivasan, formerly India's ambassador to the IAEA, has written about a closed meeting in Washington of nonproliferation experts in early June where a senior White House official despairingly remarked, "India imitates China, Pakistan imitates India. What can we do to stop their nuclear activities?" Further noting that Washington "did not want to displease China or Pakistan at this juncture," the official argued that American priorities today apparently cannot stray from "the economy and the war on terror." Commenting acidly that such observations reflect the attitudes of "a weak state, not a superpower," Sreenivasan chastised both U.S. policy makers and his own government for not standing up to China for its disregard of NSG processes.

It is indeed regrettable that many in Washington today conclude that the American "need" for China and Pakistan at this juncture in history prevents the administration from issuing a more tough-minded riposte toward their transgressions. This conclusion is certainly confounding because the United States arguably does not rely on China and Pakistan any more today than it has since 2001 and, consequently, has no reason to be more forgiving of their challenges today.

In any case, the mark of superior American diplomacy has always been its ability to integrate cooperation and resistance—depending on the issues—vis-à-vis a given state. Accordingly, pressing Beijing and Islamabad is by no means doomed to failure, especially since Washington *has* managed to successfully navigate complex competing pressures involving both countries in disparate issue areas during the last several years and because, at the end of the day, the United States still wields far more power than either or both of these countries combined.

Fortunately, the Obama administration is becoming more resolute than it was initially, thanks partly to the fact that the nonproliferation community within the U.S. Department of State has succeeded in slowly forcing change on this issue. As has often been the case in the past, internal divisions within the State Department have been largely responsible for the hesitant position initially adopted by Washington.

Thankfully, it appears as if the United States is gradually recovering both its wits and its fortitude. The State Department's spokesman, P. J. Crowley, for example, recently asserted publicly that the Sino-Pakistani plans regarding the Chashma-3 and -4 reactors "appear to extend beyond cooperation that was grandfathered when China was approved for membership in the Nuclear Suppliers Group," thus amplifying the position taken earlier by another State Department spokesman, Gordon Duguid, who had declared pointedly that the United States "expects Beijing to cooperate with Pakistan in ways consistent with Chinese nonproliferation obligations." The U.S. representative at the NSG meeting, Richard J. K. Stratford, also clearly reiterated this position at Christchurch.

# 7

# Small Arms Trade and Manufacture in Pakistan

In the case of South Asia and more specifically Pakistan, some very interesting aspects come forth. The source of weapons supply and acquisition has been myriad: ranging from illicit influx, transfer or trade to the local production facilities. Several countries in the region produce SA/LW in the government-owned or public sector enterprise, which is licitly regulated, with India and Pakistan possessing the most developed weapon manufacturing capabilities. But as such the predominant from of acquisition of LW by the state security forces continues to be the import or foreign technology transfer.

Although LW have somewhat always been available in the arms bazaars within the North West Frontier Province of Pakistan, such as Darra Adamkhel and Landi Kotal, the major impetus and free flow of modern light weapons has increased manifold after the Soviet occupation of Afghanistan. The December 1979 Soviet invasion resulted in Pakistan's proactive support to various Mujahideen outfits engaged in fighting the occupationist forces. This effort was practically driven by its own security interest but mainly on behalf of the US, which provided material and financial assistance to these Afghan guerrillas though Pakistan. The failure or ignorance of the incumbent government of the time to pay adequate attention to this dangerously spiraling trend of weapons accumulation and free flow in the hands of non-state actors aggravated this problem. In spite of the cessation of Soviet occupation, Afghanistan to date remains bitterly embroiled in a civil war, which has cast very severe shadows on the Pakistani civil society.

Before moving further the point to be stressed that when studying weapons proliferation, an important aspect is to keep in perspective the demand and supply factor. The motives for which suppliers and recipients engage in weapons transaction may be mixed. Suppliers may have political or commercial incentives or a combination of both. For this reason, excessive and destabilizing accumulation and transfer of small arms are closely related to the increased incidence of conflicts and high level of crime and violence. It is observed that sub-state or non-state forces make extensive use of such arsenal due to its merits of easy accessibility, storage and handling. Insurgent forces, irregular troops and freedom fighters, criminal groups and sub-state actors harbouring ethnic, religious and sectarian agenda use SA/LW for their particular motives with impunity. Generally speaking the most perturbing aspect of these conflicts is that more than 80% of the causalities are civilian, non-combatants-mostly women and children.

Market Trends and Origins of Arms Proliferation in Pakistan: The main focus with respect to weapons proliferation in Pakistan remains on the unorganized private enterprise at the Landi Kotal, where arms trade continues without any state supervision. In comparison to this, the POF as mentioned earlier creates mainly the military-specific ammunition, the production cost of is relatively expensive. Secondly, the POF manufactured ammunition has a very limited and restricted clientele. Another contributing factor is that POF sells only through designated distributors.

Secondly, the organized sector manufacturers are also bound to sell their products only to licensed buyers. This again limits their sale capacity. The overall number of licensed gun owners is not more than 80,000-90,000 people of the entire country's population. This makes the legal market a very small one, which is adequately served by the private producers

But recent trends indicate that the estimated number of weapons in circulation is much higher than tabulated. The rising ethno-sectarian strife, civil war in Afghanistan, and an enhanced sense of insecurity arising out of factors such as poor economic conditions, bad governance and deteriorating law and order situation, have given rise to a level of frustration and discontent. It is witnessed that this rising sense of apathy and social injustice has strengthened the appeal of SA/LW. Darra and its cheaper rates attract not only non-state actors, who purchase these weapons in bulk, but also a second category of buyers, such as officials, aw enforcing agents, influential politicians, feudal and tribal lords who regard possession of light weapons as a status symbol. Moreover the various governments too have contributed to exacerbating this situation by giving licenses for prohibited bore weapons to politicians and influential interest arming one (ethnic/ sectarian) group against another from time to time.

A principal source of weapons proliferation and supply to areas of regional and domestic conflict, the unorganized sector has a minimal manufacturing capacity of producing per unit a hundred weapons per day. With a very sudden and dramatic termination of the Afghan conflict, the political governments after Zia's military rule proved to be ineffective in solving this menace. Although attempts were made in the past and present to curb the proliferation and indiscriminate usage of small arms, they are very much an indicator of a dysfunctional state apparatus.

In Pakistan, the failure of governance-especially with regard to narcotics production and smuggling-coupled with the country's proximity to Afghanistan and involvement in the attempts to end the Soviet occupation of the country, has aggravated an already dire law-and-order situation. In many cases, access to light weapons has facilitated or intensified conflicts, often by emboldening the protagonists. Consequently, the ability of security forces has declined corresponding with the increased firepower enjoyed by the forces pitted against them. As regards the leakage of these illicit arms, the Soviet invasion of Afghanistan unshared in a new era in the light weapons trade in South Asia, with millions of tons of military material including SA/LW, being imported into the region.

Other countries also contributed in one way or indirect assistance in both material and finances. For example, China wary of Soviet designs contributed weaponary, while Saudi Arabia came forth with financial assistance. As a front line ally, Pakistan became the main conduit for this massive military assistance programme, with its top intelligence outfit, inter-services intelligence (ISI), managing the receipt and distribution and the American CIA coordinating the supply of weapons. With a bitter Vietnam experience still fresh in memory, the United States, at least initially, did not want to be seen as providing direct military assistance for the Mujahideen, and for these reason massive amounts of arms were purchased from the Chinese government. Interesting trends could be witnessed in this undercover arms pipeline; the CIA would procure through Egypt large amounts of antipersonnel mines originally produced in Italy. During this period, weapons even of Israeli and as Indian makes could also be found in circulation. The CIA would then arrange for the arms to be either flown to Islamabad or shipped, via Oman, to Karachi.

The US-orchestrated arms shipments had a fundamental impact on the war in Afghanistan. Moreover, the autonomy given to the Pakistan intelligence services in controlling the distribution of weapons was to have a profound effect on subsequent security conditions in the region. Washington's "hand-off" policy of allowing the ISI to control the arms pipeline was largely the product of Oakley's belief that the United States had failed in Vietnam because of excessive governmental interference and mismanagement.

One factor contributing to the availability of small arms and light weapons in many areas (of conflict) is their earlier supply by Cold War opponents. Much of the supply and acquisitions of arms in the regions of conflict dealt with by the UN has been conducted by Governments or by legal entities authorized by the Governments. Some states have exercised insufficient control and restraint over transfers and holdings of small arms and light weapons. Moreover, arms supplies associated with foreign interference in areas of conflict are still a feature of current realities. In general, the lines of supply often are complex and difficult to monitor, facilitated by the relative ease with which small arms and light weapons can be concealed.

Not surprisingly, the arms pipeline to the Mujahideen leaked significantly. By the time the weapons reached Mujahideen field commanders, they had been loaded and off-loaded at least fifteen times while transported over the distance of several thousand kilometers by trucks, ships, trains, and pack animals. How many weapons leaked out of the pipeline is unknown, but the estimates run into millions of unaccounted for weapons. One glaring proof of this is the April1988 Ojhri camp blast in the Rawalpindi metropolis, which claimed not less than 100 civilan lives. Although no official version of the inquiry conducted came out, it is generally speculated that the blast was engineered to cover-up for the undelivered and hoarded weapons, and there is also a major link between this incident and the Iran Contra scandal.

Another contributing factor, however diminutive is that Afghans returning to their country after months or years in the refugee camps in the North West Frontier Province have left their weapons behind in Pakistan. This again forms a cause for weapons proliferation. Under the Geneva Accord, it was agreed that any surplus weapons that were left off the pipeline would be handed over to the Afghans, and interestingly there was a frantic arms transfer to Afghanistan, before the agreement came into effect. Most of these were smuggled back into Pakistan and sold in arms bazaars of the tribal area.

Besides, Afghanistan has a significant number of small arms manufacturing units. The trade of these arms is a ready source of income for the war-ravaged Afghan population. With a long porous border that stretches the entire Pakistan-Afghanistan belt, coupled with corrupt and inefficient border control forces, the mechanism fails miserably in effectively checking and curbing the inflow of not only weapons but other forms of smuggling as well. This has made the availability of arms in the commercial market considerably high and in some cases prices have fallen, attracting buyers from all over the country and region to purchase unlicensed weapons. The various weapons on sale in this regard, can be grouped in to four categories;

1. Weapons that lecked from the US-supported arms pipelines.

2. The stocks of Soviet weapons captured by the Mujahideen during the conflict.
3. The third category of weapons is those manufactured by small-scale producers within the region.
4. Finally, the arms bazaars of the NWFP are full of miscellaneous weapons that must have arrived in the region though extremely circuitous and unpredictable routes-from Vietnam or the Middle East. For instance, G-3s have appeared from Iran, given that border controls between Iran and Pakistan were relaxed after the fall of the shah.

Though there is clear evidence that light weapons are proliferating at an alarming rate from the North to the South, there are also south-to-north movements from Sri Lanka, Singapore, and other starting points in Southeast Asia. There are also discernible east-to west and west-to east movements.

In Pakistan, it is not only the Afghan crisis alone that was instrumental in introducing the Gun Culture. Another very important but relatively ignored aspect was the Baluchistan insurgency of the 1970s, that witnessed a massive inflow of weaponry from the traditional leakage points

There is a dire need for the government to take control of the drug trade and prevent the proliferation and flow of weapons, domestically, regionally and particularly with the help of the international community. What will be difficult, if not impossible to implement is an effective gun control agenda-such as the present regime's Seven-Stage De-Weaponization Programmes. This 7- stage formula includes a ban on arms license, and a proliferation on carrying weapons in the first stage, which became effective from March 1, 2000. The other proposals or possibilities under the same action plan were to recover illicit/unlicensed arms, canceling of the prohibited arms licenses and also to regulate and bring under state control arms manufacturing units in the tribal areas. The problem is so acute that there is a need to implement such policies and reforms in their true spirit. Bringing Darra under the state umbrella is an issue that the governments past and present have seriously deliberated upon. As a necessary first step the tribal areas were awarded with the right to Adult Franchise as well, but the possibility of Darra manufacturers agreeing to any state supervision or taxation seems impossible an evidence of which is reaction faced by the government over its attempt to document and evaluate the economy. The government needs to stick to a given time frame and implement the necessary reforms, otherwise the situation could be one as identified by Pamela Constable, in one of her recent Washington post articles, "Pakistani Retreats in Battle for Reform"- that there is found a tendency on part of the Pakistani government to announce bold reforms, only to backtrack later when opposition surfaces.

At the practical level, this new de-weaponisation policy will face many problems, especially in the NWFP and tribal areas where it is part of local culture and tradition to carry a weapon and in fact it also forms a part of their attire. This plan will definitely discourage open display of weapons in major urban centers, but again this will not be able to redress the problem fully.

Efforts made by the past governments were inadequate for either they were not properly articulated or they failed to deal with the real root cause of the problem that is the illicit trafficking of weapons. Whatever measures enforced affected only the manufacturers, thus giving the illegal trading cartels a free hand to conduct their business with impunity.

Although light weapons have always circulated within Pakistan, the impact of the American-sponsored arms pipeline to the Afghan Mujahideen stands head and shoulders above any other adverse development in recent years. The flood of weaponry into the region has clearly played a major part in the erosion of low and order over the past decade. The growing proliferation of and access to small arms are increasing both the communal polarization and the incidence of violence. The very availability of weapons is providing a short-term solution for a long-term problem. At the very point when political discourse and sound governance are required to overcome these problems, the need is to harness our efforts together to combat this menace.

# 8

# Nuclear Power in Pakistan

- Pakistan has a small nuclear power program, with 725 MWe capacity, but is moving to increase this substantially.
- Pakistan's nuclear weapons capabilities of has arisen independently of the civil nuclear fuel cycle, using indigenous uranium.
- Because Pakistan is outside the Nuclear Non-Proliferation Treaty, due to its weapons program, it is largely excluded from trade in nuclear plant or materials, which hinders its development of civil nuclear energy. However, China is positive about nuclear cooperation with Pakistan.

Pakistan in 2010 produced 94.5 billion kWh of electricity, 33 TWh of this from oil, 26 from natural gas and 32 from hydro. Nuclear power makes a small contribution to total energy production and requirements, supplying only 3.8 TWh (3.8% of the electricity in 2011). Consumption in 2010 was about 77 billion kWh after 16% transmission losses. There was no import or export. Total installed capacity is about 20 GWe, but often only about 12 GWe is operable. In 2005 an Energy Security Plan was adopted by the government, calling for a huge increase in generating capacity to more than 160 GWe by 2030. Significant power shortages are reported, and load shedding is common.

In July 2013 the Executive Committee of the National Economic Council (ECNEC) approved 3.5 GWe of new power projects totalling Rs 1303 billion ($13 billion), comprising 2200 MWe nuclear, 425 MWe gas combined cycle, and 969 MWe hydro. These are designed to reduce the high reliance on oil and to reduce power costs.All depend on Chinese support.

## NUCLEAR POWER

The Pakistan Atomic Energy Commission (PAEC) is responsible for all nuclear energy and research applications in the country. The PAEC is reported to have two divisions which are responsible for nuclear power programs: Nuclear Power Generation (NUPG) and Nuclear Power Projects (NUPP). The NUPG directorate oversees the operational units, and the NUPP directorate is concerned with design and construction of planned units, and is closely aligned with the Nuclear Regulatory Authority (PNRA). PAEC's first nuclear power reactor is a small 137 MWe (125 MWe net) Canadian pressurized heavy water reactor (PHWR) which started up in 1971 and which is under international safeguards – KANUPP at Paradise Point in Sindh province, about 25 km west of Karachi. It is operated at reduced power, and is under review by PAEC because of its age.

The second unit is Chashma 1 in Punjab province in the north, a 325 MWe (300 MWe net) two-loop pressurised water reactor (PWR) supplied by China's CNNC under safeguards. The main part of the plant was designed by Shanghai Nuclear Engineering Research and Design Institute (SNERDI), based on Qinshan 1. It started up in May 2000 and is also known as CHASNUPP 1. Designed life span is 40 years. It, and the following 3 units, were built using international design codes and standards.

Construction of its twin, Chashma 2, started in December 2005. It was reported to cost PKR 51.46 billion (US$ 860 million, with $350 million of this financed by China). A safeguards agreement with IAEA was signed in 2006 and grid connection was in March 2011, with commercial operation in May.

The 2005 Energy Security Plan included intention of lifting nuclear capacity to 8800 MWe, 900 MWe of this by 2015 and a further 1500 MWe by 2020. Projections included four further Chinese reactors of 300 MWe each and seven of 1000 MWe, all PWR. There were tentative plans for China to build two 1000 MWe PWR units at Karachi as KANUPP 2&3, but China then in 2007 deferred development of its CNP-1000 type which would have been the only one of that size able to be exported. Pakistan then turned its attention to building smaller units with higher local content. However, in 2013 China revived its 1000 MWe designs with export intent, and made overtures to Pakistan for the ACP1000 design.

### *Chashma 3&4*

In June 2008 the government announced plans to build units 3&4 at Chashma, each 320 MWe gross and largely financed by China. A further agreement for China's help with the project was signed in October 2008, and given prominence as a counter to the US-India agreement shortly preceding it.

In March 2009 China's SNERDI announced that it was proceeding with design of Chashma 3&4, with China Zhongyuan Engineering Corp (CZEC) as the general contractor and China Nuclear Industry No.5 Construction Company as installer. In April 2009, a design contract with SNERDI was signed, and the government said that it had approved the project at a cost of $2.37 billion, with $1.75 billion of this involving "a foreign exchange component". In March 2010 Pakistan announced that it had agreed the terms for Chashma 3&4, whereby China would provide 82% of the total US$ 1.912 billion financing as three 20-year low-interest loans. It would also provide fuel for the reactors' lifetime nominally of 40 years.

The main construction contract was signed in June 2010, and the two 340 MWe CNP-300 (315 MWe net) units are to be completed in eight years. They will have a design life of 40 years and be under IAEA safeguards. Construction of unit 3 officially started at the end of May 2011, and unit 4 in December 2011. The dome of unit 3 was fitted in March 2013. Early in 2014 PAEC said they were several months ahead of schedule.

In April 2013 it was reported that the PAEC would receive a significant increase in budget appropriation to expedite construction of Chashma 3&4.

However, the Nuclear Suppliers Group (NSG) raised some questions about China's supply of Chasma 3&4. Contracts for units 1&2 were signed in 1990 and 2000 respectively, before 2004 when China joined the NSG, which maintains an embargo on sales of nuclear equipment to Pakistan. China argued that units 3&4 are similarly "grandfathered", and arrangements are consistent with those for units 1&2.

### Chashma 5

In November 2010 the PAEC is reported to have signed a construction agreement with China National Nuclear Corporation (CNNC) for a fifth unit at Chashma. In February 2013 a further agreement was signed by PAEC with CNNC for a 1000 MWe unit at Chashma. It was reported that China expected that this deal would be controversial under the NPT and guidelines of the NSG. Early in 2013 CNNC confirmed its intention to build a 1000 MWe class reactor, and said it would be an ACP1000 unit, though not necessarily at Chashma. The status of any continuing plan for Chashma 5 is very uncertain, and it may have been displaced by plans for a plant near Multan in southwest Punjab.

### Karachi Coastal Power Project

In June 2013 the Planning Commission said that two CNNC 1000 MWe class reactors would be used for Karachi 2 and 3 (KANUPP 2&3) near Karachi unit 1. Two coastal sites had been under consideration for the twin 1100 MWe units. CNNC in April 2013 announced an export agreement for the ACP1000, nominally 1100 MWe, apparently for Pakistan. This was confirmed in June by the PAEC which said that the next nuclear project would be 1100 MWe class units which it would build, the Karachi Coastal Power station, costing $9.5 billion.

In July 2013 ECNEC approved two units of the Karachi Costal Power Project with net generation capacity of 2,117 MWe. The total cost of this is estimated at Rs 959 billion ($9.595 billion), with $6.5 billion (68%) being vendor finance. PAEC also said that 82% of the total cost would be financed by China. At the end of August contracts were signed in Shanghai with CNNC, China Zhongyuan Engineering Co. Ltd. (CZEC), China Nuclear Power Engineering Co. Ltd. (CNPE), Nuclear Power Institute of China (NPIC), and East China Electric Power Designing Institute (ECEPDI). Ground breaking at the site near Paradise Point, 25 km west of Karachi, took place in November 2013, and first concrete is envisaged by the end of 2014. Construction is expected to take 72 months.

In the light of its inability to buy uranium on the open market, PAEC says that Pakistan has agreed with China to provide lifetime fuel supply for the reactors, this being specified as 60 years.

The Pakistan Nuclear Regulatory Authority has received the safety analysis of China's ACP1000 reactor from CNNC and is expected to take at least a year to complete the review before granting a construction licence.

### *Further Nuclear Capacity*

In August 2011 it was reported that Pakistan aimed for 8000 MWe nuclear at ten sites by 2030. PAEC has apparently selected six new sites on the basis of the Pakistan Nuclear Regulatory Authority (PNRA) and the International Atomic Energy Agency (IAEA) advice. These are Qadirabad-Bulloki (QB) link canal near Qadirabad Headworks; Dera Ghazi Khan canal near Taunsa Barrage; Taunsa-Panjnad canal near Multan; Nara canal near Sukkur; Pat Feeder canal near Guddu and Kabul River near Nowshera. Early in 2012 PAEC said that four reactors were planned for the Taunsa-Panjnad canal near Multan in Punjab.

In January 2014 PAEC announced its intention to build five further 1100 MWe nuclear plants to meet anticipated electricity demand, and have 8.9 GWe of nuclear capacity on line by 2030. "With more than 55 reactor-years of successful operating experience to its credit, the PAEC can confidently move from technology acquisition status to actually starting contributing sizable electrical energy to the system." Then PAEC was quoted as saying that eight sites would be chosen for a further 32 units, four 1100 MWe units at each, so that nuclear power supplied one quarter of the country's electricity from 40 GWe of capacity, this evidently presupposing more than a tenfold increase in electricity demand by a future date well beyond 2030. PAEC said an initial 1100 MWe plant would be built at Muzaffargarh, on the Taunsa-Panjnad canal near Multan in southwest Punjab. It was also reported that discussions with China were under way to supply three nuclear power plants for about $13 billion.

## *Fuel Cycle*

The government has set a target of producing 350 tonnes $U_3O_8$ per year from 2015 to meet one-third of anticipated requirements then. Low-grade ore is known in central Punjab at Bannu Basin and Suleman Range. A small (15,000 SWU/yr) uranium centrifuge enrichment plant at Kahuta has been operated since 1984 and does not have any apparent civil use. It was expanded threefold about 1991. A newer plant is reported to be at Gadwal. It is not under safeguards. It is not clear whether PAEC has any involvement with these plants.

In 2006 the PAEC announced that it was preparing to set up separate and purely civil conversion, enrichment and fuel fabrication plants as a new US$ 1.2 billion Pakistan Nuclear Power Fuel Complex (NPFC) for PWR-type reactors which would be under IAEA safeguards and managed separately from existing facilities. At least the enrichment plant would be built at Chak Jhumra, Faisalabad, in the Punjab and have a 150,000 SWU/yr capacity in five years – about 2013, then be expanded in 150,000 SWU increments to be able to supply one third of the enrichment requirements for a planned 8800 MWe generating capacity by 2030.

However, if Pakistan cannot obtain exemption for Nuclear Suppliers' Group trade sanctions in order to build more nuclear power capacity and obtain more uranium in the near future, there may be no point in proceeding with this civil Fuel Complex.

## *Wastes*

The PAEC has responsibility for radioactive waste management. A Radioactive Waste Management Fund is proposed in a new policy. Waste Management Centres are proposed for Karachi and Chashma.

Used fuel is currently stored at each reactor in pools. Longer-term dry storage at each site is proposed. The question of future reprocessing remains open.

A National Repository for low- and intermediate-level wastes is due to be commissioned by 2015.

## Regulation

The Pakistan Nuclear Regulatory Authority (PNRA) is responsible for licensing and supervision, and regulates the safety and security of all civil nuclear materials and facilities. In respect to the Chashma reactors, and presumably also the Karachi Coastal Power project, it works closely with China's NNSA. It was formed in 2001, superseding the Pakistan Nuclear Regulatory Board (set up by PAEC) and the Directorate of Nuclear Safety and Radiation Protection.

Pakistan is party to the convention on nuclear safety and two international conventions for early notification and assistance.

## R&D and other Activities

The Pakistan Institute of Nuclear Science & Technology (PINSTECH) near Islamabad is managed by the PAEC and is one of the largest science and technology research establishments in the country. It has conducted research into reprocessing used nuclear fuel, though today it claims to be focused on research in medicine, biology, materials and physics, including production of medical radioisotopes.

Pakistan has a 10 MW pool-type research reactor, PARR-1, of 1965 vintage, supplied by the USA under the Atoms for Peace program. It was converted to use low-enriched uranium fuel in 1991, and upgraded from 5 to 10 MW. PARR-2 is an indigenous 30 kW miniature neutron source reactor (MNSR) based on Chinese design and using high-enriched fuel operating since 1974. Both are located at the PINSTECH Laboratory, Nilore, near Islamabad. They are under IAEA safeguards.

New Labs is reported to be a reprocessing plant for weapons-grade plutonium production, and not under safeguards. It is run by PAEC and operational since 1981. This was apparently the culmination of a plutonium weapons program predating the Kahuta HEU weapons program.

A larger "multipurpose" reactor, a 50 MWt PHWR near Khushab, 200 km south of Islamabad, started operating in 1998 and is evidently for producing weapons-grade plutonium. A larger heavy water reactor was built at Khushab from about 2002, and appeared to be operational at the end of 2009. In 2006 building of a third reactor, similar to and adjacent to the second, started, with construction proceeding rapidly. A similar, fourth reactor has started construction a few hundred metres away, and was observed to be more than half complete late in 2013. These apparently add up to a substantial plutonium production capacity. Khushab is reported to be making demands upon the country's limited uranium resources. A small heavy water plant is nearby. Reprocessing of military material is reported to take place at Chashma, 80 km west, and a second reprocessing plant is apparently under construction there.

The Khan Research Laboratories (KRL) at Kahuta in Punjab is described as a weapons engineering R&D institute and research laboratory, focused on producing high-enriched uranium using centrifuge technology originally stolen from Urenco by Dr Abdul Q Khan. Set up about 1976 as the Engineering Research Laboratories it was a key part of Pakistan's weapons program, supported by the Army Corps of Engineers in competition with the plutonium program being pursued by PAEC. It was renamed in honour of Dr Khan 1981.

## Non-proliferation

Pakistan is not party to the Nuclear Non-Proliferation Treaty but does have its civil power reactors and two research reactors (PARR 1 & 2) under item-specific IAEA safeguards. An agreement for two further 340 MWe reactors came into force in April 2011. Pakistan has refused calls for international inspections of its enrichment activities.

Pakistan's Kahuta project (incorporating Project-706) to produce a uranium bomb was launched in 1972, following a disastrous war with India. It was partly financed by Libya to 1979. In May 1974 India exploded a nuclear test close to the Pakistan border, galvanising Pakistani efforts. The project was disbanded in 1983 after a successful cold test of weapon components.

In May 1998 Pakistan exploded five atomic devices in Baluchistan. At least one was evidently made from enriched uranium, but the Chagai II test in Kharan desert used plutonium produced by New Labs.

Pakistan is reported to be the sole nation blocking agreement of the Fissile Material Cutoff Treaty (FMCT) in Geneva negotiations.

Through the activities of Abdul Q.Khan, a centrifuge plant and nuclear weapons designs were supplied clandestinely to Libya from the late 1990s to 2003 to furbish a weapons program there. He also transferred centrifuge technology to North Korea in the 1990s, and to Iran. This is the main basis for the Nuclear Suppliers' Group (NSG) refusing to ease nuclear trade sanctions for Pakistan, as it has for India. China is the only country to act in defiance of trade sanctions, and appears to have deepened cooperation in response to the international US-led concessions to India in 2008.

## NUCLEAR POWER OF PAKISTAN'S ARMY

The Pakistan Army came into being as a result of the amalgamation of the Muslim troops of the pre-independence British Indian Army. The origin of many of its units dates back to the beginning of the British rule in the subcontinent.

This relation, however, is merely of historical nature. With the birth of Pakistan, a hotchpotch of the ill-equipped and ill-organized troops, breaking away from the old and established British Indian Army, had been transformed into a disciplined fighting force in consonance with the national ideals and aspirations.

On 3 June 1947, the British Government announced the plan for the partition of the sub-continent between India and Pakistan, and for the transfer of power to the two new states on 15 August 1947. On 30 June 1947, the procedure for the division of the armed forces was agreed upon by the Partition Council, chaired by the Viceroy of India Lord Mountbatten and consisting of the top leaders of the Muslim League and the Indian Congress.

Field Marshal Auchinleck, then C-in-C India, was appointed Supreme Commander under Mountbatten to ensure smooth division of units, stores, and so on.

It was announced on 1 July 1947, that both countries would have operational control of their respective armed forces by 15 August 1947.

## THE EARLY YEARS

Between 1939 and 1945, the strength of the Indian Army grew to a maximum of 2,018,196 personnel. On the eve of Partition in 1947, the figure had come down to about 11,800 officers, 450,000 other ranks plus about 50,000 of Indian Princely States' Forces. It is noteworthy, at that time (as per policy of the British Raj since 1857) there were only two completely Muslim combat units (1/15 Punjab Regiment and 3/16 Punjab Regiment), although there were several completely Hindu and Sikh units and regiments of the combat arms. The original agreement called for the armed forces and other assets to be divided to the ratio of 64% for India and 36% for Pakistan, but Pakistan was later forced to accept an 1/3 share of assets. Of the total 46 training establishments; only nine were located in Pakistan; all of the 17 Ordnance Factories were located in India, as were most of the Ordnance Depots and Engineer Store Depots. In addition to Pakistan receiving far less stores than originally stipulated, most of the stores received were of general nature, perishable, unwanted and obsolete. The move of 150,000 Pakistani personnel as well as 508 units and sub units of various sizes was to be carried out by rail through Indian Punjab and Sikh Princely States.

After 53 trains carrying personnel and their families were attacked, detailed and massacred by armed bands of Sikhs and Hindus in connivance with the railway authorities, the sea route from Bombay to Karachi was adopted. The Punjab Boundary Force consisting of five brigades under Major General Rees was created by Field Marshal Auchinleck's Supreme HQ in August-1947 to escort refugees from border districts of the two Punjabs across the international borders. Its area of responsibility covered 37,500 square miles and a population of 14.5 million. It was a gigantic task for a limited force manned largely by neutral British officers. About seven million Muslims migrated to Pakistan, and five million Sikhs and Hindus to India; a million perished.

Against an estimated requirement for about 4,000 officers, Pakistan had initially only about 2,300 - the gap being filled up on Quaid-e-Azam's appeal, to some extent, by 484 experienced and qualified British officers, who volunteered to stay and help

Pakistan and the Pakistan Army in difficult times. Many Polish and Hungarian officers also volunteered for the medical corps. Prior to August 1947, the most senior Pakistani (and Indian) officers were in ranks of brigadiers; after independence, the command of Army units had to be given to officers in their early 30s with eighteen years service, many of whom had combat experience and had won battlefield awards in World War II. Similarly, brigade commanders had 13-15 years service and division commanders 19-20 years.

By October 1947, guarding 5,000 miles of West and East Pakistan's frontiers were, about ten infantry brigades at less than 50% strength, and an armoured brigade with only 13 running STUART tanks. The Army has ammunition reserves for less than one week. In a Joint Defence Council Meeting, both Mountbatten and Supreme Commander Auchinleck had made it clear to Pakistan that in case of war with India, no other member of the Commonwealth would come to Pakistan's help. Field Marshal Ayub Khan, the first Pakistani C-in-C, was to recall in later years: "It would always be a matter of pride and glory for this army when history will recall how heavy a burden was placed on its young shoulders and how creditably it always rose to the occasion".

After the fraudulent accession of Kashmir by the Maharaja on 27 October, Mountbatten and Nehru air-transported the Indian Army into the Sri Nagar Valley. The Indian Army's offensive was halted at the Ceasefire Line (now Line of Control) Initially by Azad Kashmir Forces, and from April 1948 with support of the ill-organised Pakistan Army without adequate logistic support. At midnight on 30 December, GHQ India asked for a ceasefire to become effective on 1 January 1949. Pakistan accepted, as the fate of Jammu and Kashmir had been taken over by the UNO. Thus ended the six month war in Kashmir. By the end of 1948 five infantry divisions had been organised, but these were still lacking their full complement of supporting arms and services. The few artillery regiments received at partition were grouped into three Artillery Groups under independent headquarters to ensure maximum flexibility. By early 1949, the Pakistan Army had completed its formative stage and had been bloodied in battle experience, and continued its re-organisation. On integration of

Bahawalpur State in January 1949, the 6th (B) Division was created, but this was subsequently disbanded in 1956 on re-organisation of the army.

Back in August 1947, Quaid-e-Azam Muhammad Ali Jinnah, foreseeing the financial and military difficulties ahead, asked for US economic and military aid. Incidentally, the same request had also been submitted by New Delhi and Kabul.

After an evaluation of Pakistan's strategic location at the crossroads of South-, Central-and West Asia in proximity to both China and the Soviet Union, the USA acceded to Pakistan's request under the American Mutual Security Legislation.

In early 1954, Pakistan and the USA signed a Mutual Defence Assistance Agreement. Between 1954 -1965, Pakistan received US$650 million in military grants, US$619 million in defence support assistance, and US$ 55 million in cash or commercial purchases.

This aid enhanced Pakistani defence capability by increasing the firepower and mobility, and improving $C^3$1 facilities of five and a half divisions. The armed forces were modernised in keeping with the world trends; two Corps HQ were also catered for. Many senior and junior officers went for training and orientation to USA; new cantonments were built, and existing ones were expanded and modernised. By August 1947, the 7th Division (located in Rawalpindi with two brigades) was the Pakistan Army's only division. There also were static HQ designed "Areas" and "Sub-areas", having brigades and battalions at more than 50% below strength.

In the following months, as Pakistani personnel kept arriving from all over India, Middle East and South East Asia by rail and sea, the 8th Division was organised out of the Sind Balochistan Area, and the 9th (F) Division was created out of brigades of the Peshawar and Waziristan Areas. Similarly, the Lahore Area was re-organised as 10th Division, and the 12th Division was raised in November 1948. The forces in East Pakistan (now Bangladesh) were designated as East Pakistan Army, then as a Sub-area and finally in December 1948 as HQ 14th Division, initially with only two battalions that eventually were built up to brigade strength.

## KASHMIR WAR 1947-48

The 11 Cavalry equipped with armoured cars were the only unit employed in the war.

The GHQ assigned the unit an essentially defensive and passive role but the indomitable Colonel Tommy Masud commanding the unit was too resolute a man to be restrained 44. The unit thus took a prominent part in operations in Bhimbhar-Mirpur area under Tommy Masud, but its role remained limited since it was not allowed to conduct any major offensive operation to support the militia.The Pakistani GHQ finally moved 3rd Armoured Brigade near Bhimbhar, for a projected counterstroke at Indian communications to Poonch, when the Indians made a unilateral offer of ceasefire on 30 December 1947-1948.

## THE RANN OF KUTCH CONFLICT (APRIL 1965)

India and Pakistan became engaged in a short but sharp conflict into Pakistani claimed-area in the Rann of Kutch in April 1965. Both armies had fully mobilised. Pakistan eventually proposed a ceasefire, which India accepted; an agreement was signed, and the forces disengaged. The Award by the Arbitration Tribunal vindicated Pakistan's position. India then shifted the centre of gravity of operations to the Northern Areas.

## THE 1965 WAR

After several ceasefire violations, India attacked across the international border form Sialkot to Sind sectors. The attacks were halted on all fronts, and in a series of counterattacks the Pakistan Army penetrated inside Indian territory capturing more territory than the Indian Army. The biggest tank battle since World War II was fought at Chawinda, inflicting heavy casualties. India eventually asked for a ceasefire, arranged by the UN on 23 September 1965.

## THE THIRD EVOLUTION PHASE (1966-1970)

In 1966, commenced the third phase of the evolution of the Pakistan Army, which was able to at least partially enhance its defence capability over these five years.

The US embargo on military aid to Pakistan, and the continued Soviet heavy build-up of Indian forces, forced Pakistan to turn to China, North Korea, Germany, Italy and France for its defence procurement programmes. China, a time-tested friend and neighbour, enabled Pakistan to raise three fully-equipped infantry divisions with gun and vehicles, 900 Chinese tanks, and MiG-19F aircraft for the air force. France supplied MIR-AGE aircraft and submarines. In 1968, the Soviet Union offered US$30 million worth of aid to Pakistan and supplied 100 T-55 tanks, Mi-8 helicopter, guns and vehicles; in 1969, however, Soviet support was abruptly stopped under Indian pressure.

## THE 1971 WAR

1971 was the most tragic year in Pakistan's history, a year of political crises and conflict. Unable to resolve a political problem by political means, the then Martial Law regime resorted to military action in East Pakistan on the night on 25/26 March.

Widespread insurgency broke out, covertly aided by Indian trained infiltrators and India's Border Security Forces. In the first week of April, personnel of two infantry divisions and civil armed forces were airlifted in Pakistan International Airlines (PIA) planes with a 6,000-mile non-stop route via Sri Lanka - the longest operational air move by the army. Quick reaction by the Pakistani authorities restored 80% normalcy in the eastern wing of the country. Covert operations having failed, India concentrated about 400,000 regular army personnel in 12 divisions supported by five tank regiments, seven air force squadrons and Indian Navy. These forces, further strengthened by about 1,00,000 guerillas (Mukti Bahini) attacked from all directions on 20 fronts across the international border on 21 November, without a formal declaration of war. Intense fighting raged till 16 December in both Pakistan's wings; no town or battalion position could be overrun, till a ceasefire accepted by Pakistan was perfidiously changed into surrender by Indian-Soviet machinations.

## 1971-1979

After almost twelve years of clandestine efforts India exploded a nuclear device at Pokhran on 18 May 1974 not far from Pakistan's borders, as part of her coercive diplomacy, thus starting a nuclear arms race in the Sub-continent. By 1986, after only seven years of a crash programme, Pakistan had acquired her own nuclear capability to match and deter that of India. Thus was established a strategic balance in the region, 'striking terror into the hearts of the enemy' as enjoined by the Holy Quran. In 1976, the Higher Defence Organization was streamlined and revitalized. The western influenced strategic doctrine was critically analyzed and re-evaluated in the light of our geostrategic realities and operational environment. Core issues of Quranic concepts of warfare, regulated by laws like Jehad, checks and balances on use of force, prohibition of total unlimited war, humane measures to protect women, children and prisoners, encouraging negotiations for honourable peace and that enemies need not be permanent, and other fundamentals were highlighted in the re-evaluation.

## 1979 TO PRESENT

In December 1979, the Soviet Union invaded Afghanistan. The US offered US$400 million worth of military aid, which was however spurned by Pakistan as inadequate for a "frontline state".

Apprehensive of the two front threats to Pakistan, in 1981 the US again offered a package of US$1.5 billion worth of military aid. This was accepted and in five years provided 40 F-16 fighters, 100 M-48 tanks, 64 M-109 155mm SP howitzers, 40 M-110 203mm SP howitzers, 75 towed howitzers, and 1,005 TOW anti-tank missile systems, considerably enhancing Pakistan's defence capability. India and Pakistan are now engaged into a military conflict on the world's highest battlefield in 1982 resulting into more loss of lives due to harsh weather as compare to combat losses.

By 1989, the Soviet Union - having suffered heavy losses in men and material, and unable to withstand the Jehad - commenced withdrawing its forces from Afghanistan. Under the Pressler Amendment, the US again imposed an embargo on all economic and military aid to Pakistan, which continued for five years. In 1995, the Brown Amendment authorised a one-time delivery of US military equipment, contracted for prior to October 1990, worth US$368 million.

## OTHER SIGNIFICANT ACTIVITIES

### *Roles under UN Flag*

In addition to its main roles of repelling external aggressions and grappling with internal security issues, natural calamities, and nation-building projects, the Pakistan Army from 1960 onwards also played a heroic role as part of UN forces in peacekeeping, peacemaking and peace-enforcing, providing personnel to several different missions.

### *Military Missions Abroad*

Pakistani military missions were invited, during the last four decades by the governments of Libya, Saudi Arabia, UAE, Ghana, Zimbabwe, Jordan and others to organise and train their armed forces.

In the Gulf War of 1991, Pakistani ground forces played their role in Saudi Arabia's defence, and thereafter in prolonged mine lifting operations in Kuwait. In the medical field, Pakistan Army doctors have been working as personal physicians to Kings and Rulers in the Arab world.

### *Joint Exercises*

Periodically since 1955, first as members of collective security systems such as SEATO and CENTO, the Pakistan Army, Navy and Air Forces took part in exercises with forces of friendly countries, gaining valuable experience in latest systems and doctrines.

## TRAINING OF FOREIGN ARMY OFFICERS IN PAKISTAN

The numerous training institutions of various arms and services set up after 1947 have become such centres of professional excellence, i.e., the Pakistani Military Academy, School of Infantry and Tactics, Armour, Artillery, Army Air Defence, Engineer, and Signals Schools and Colleges, Command and Staff College, National Defence College, and others. These institutions are regularly visited by foreign army officers, who are trained alongside their Pakistani colleagues.

## PARA-MILITARY FORCES

Pakistan Army officers train and command the following para-military forces: National Guard (including Janbaz Force), Mujahid Force, National Cadet Corps and Women Guards (185,000), Frontier Corps (70,000), Pakistan Rangers (25,000), and Coast Guards.

### *Indigenisation & Modernisation*

The activities of POF Wah and Heavy Industries Taxila are described elsewhere in this issue.

### *Missiles*

To balance the threat posed by India's Integrated Guided Missile Programme, launched in 1983-84 to develop the PRITHIBI, AGNI, AKASH and NAG systems, the Pakistan Army has developed the capability of producing and deploying, at short notice, the indigenous HATF-3 ballistic missile with range of 800km. Pakistan has also developed and introduced into army's service the ANZA air defence and BAKTAR-SHIKAN anti tank guided missile system.

### *Army Vehicles*

To standardise the various types of vehicles of different origins in use in the army since 1947, the indigenous manufacture of the YASOOB series of military trucks (available in 3 ton and 6 ton medium and heavy duty versions) was launched in 1989 in collaboration with Pakistan Automobile Corporation. 1/4 ton jeeps named MILLAT and NISHAN are also being produced with civil collaboration. Re-engining (diesel) and refurbishment of the large fleet of M-34/M-35 trucks of US origin is also currently being implemented under the SHAHZORE project.

### *Communications*

To meet the challenge of the future battlefield, the Corps of Signals has completely revolutionised defence communications with the introduction of PASCOMS (Pakistan Army Strategic Communications) inaugurated in April 1995, DEFCOMM (Defence Communication) for inter-services communications, and PATCOM (Pakistan Army Tactical Communications). Under the latter programme, all corps have been equipped with hand-held radio sets, VHF vehicles radio sets, low and medium power radio sets, field exchanges and FAX machines. Work is in progress to have a real-time C4I System at all tiers of the Army.

## RECRUITMENT AND FORMATION

Since 1947, the Pakistani Armed Forces have grown into a national, highly professional, modern defence arm of the nation. Recruitment for officers and other ranks is open to all sections, classes, castes and tribes who meet the physical and educational standards. In 1972, the National Defence College commenced the first full fledged course to impart higher military education to senior officers. The National University of Sciences and Technology (NUST) was established in 1993 as a joint venture of the army and civil institutions, with links to the Michigan State University (USA) and Cranfield University (UK) for imparting graduate and post-graduate studies and PhD/MS programmes. It is based on the decentralised multi-campus concept and has the following affiliated colleges: Military College of Engineering (Risalpur), Military College of Signals (Rawalpindi), Military College of Electrical and Mechanical Engineering (Rawalpindi), Military College of Transport (Risalpur), Pakistan Navy Engineering College (Karachi), and PAF College of Aeronautical Engineering (Risalpur).

## THE ROLE IN THE SOCIAL SECTOR

The Pakistan Army, in addition to its primary responsibility of defence and security, is also playing its its role in the social sector and in nation-building activities through the Fauji Foundation, Army Welfare Trust, Frontier Works Organization, Special Communication Organization and the National Logistics Cell, and in assisting in alleviation of suffering and succour in natural calamities like floods, earthquakes, etc.

## NATION BUILDING PROGRAMME

The Founder of the nation extended full patronage to the Pakistan Army in particular and the allied services in general and asked the defence forces to defend not only the territorial integrity of the country but also its ideological frontiers. From the very outset, the Pakistan Army has been dedicated to the service of the nation. Through its innumerable services and excellent performance in the completion of nation-building projects, the Pakistan Army has won the confidence and respect of the nation with the grace of Almighty Allah.

Besides carrying out its basic duty of defending the country, the Pakistan Army has played a pivotal role in a number of nation-building projects. Some of these are; Building of road-networks in the inaccessible Northern Area, Azad Kashmir, Baluchistan. On a number of occasions, the army has conducted rescue operations during the great floods. Again it has also conducted anti-locust, anti-boar and anti-smuggling operations.

### *Earthquake - 2005*

Never before has Pakistan experienced such a big catastrophe as the earthquake of 8 October 2005 that shattered the vital areas of Azad Kashmir, NWFP and Islamabad. The overwhelming response of the Army had been admirable, this reflected the total devotion and commitment to uphold the flag of Pakistan at any cost within minutes after earthquake, Army Aviation Helicopters were in the air in order to assess damage and bring back injured casualties. All the main roads in Muzaffarabad were reopened after 36 hours of the earthquake. Fifty satellite phone PCOs in Kashmir and 60 in affected areas of NWFP had been installed for the convenience of people to make and receive calls free of cost. Around 72 average sorties were flown every day in areas' like Sortir, Lamina, Saropa, Chakothi, Garhi Dupatta, Pir Chinari, Billgra, Sawan, Pundu and Hatian Balla villages, while the areas in Neelum Valley where the rescue and relief operations were being carried out include Ghori, Dhani, Ging, Pangkot, Patikkka and Noseri. Relief items, including food, tents and blankets, were being dropped in Chakot, Sudhan Gali, Saropa, Neelum Valley and Gari Dopatta. Around 300 truck loads were distributed in Muzaffarabad almost every day.

The Pakistan Army medical staff continued to shift serious patients from quake-hit areas through MI -17, Chinook, Black Hawk, CH-53 and Sea King helicopters. Pak Army's medical teams were working day and night in Muzaffarabad, Rawalakot, Bagh,

Balakot and Batagram with a missionary zeal, our troops were working round-the-clock to mitigate sufferings of the millions of survivors. The foreign dignitaries and leaders of political parties who had been visiting the devastated areas were unanimous in lauding the role of our dedicated soldiers in alleviating human sufferings. Mercifully, Pakistan Army had done more than one could expect.

### Welfare Projects

The army's welfare projects and schemes contribute to the national development programme in a big way. The Army Welfare Trust, the Welfare and Rehabilitation Organisation, Armed Services ' Board and the Fauji Foundation all serve tens of thousands of nationals in service and after retirement. Besides, free medical services are provided to the citizens in the backward area of the country. The army provides educational facilities to the soldiers and officers. It encourages the servicemen to enhance their education and provides all necessary facilities in the regard. The army offers course in higher education like M. Phil and Ph.D. It runs the National University of Modern Languages which has, on its staff, a large number of foreign instructors. The army trains officers at this institute to further send them to foreign courses. The army has started own Medial College whose graduates will serve the armed forces. In the domain of national education, the army has also contributed in a big way bringing in, efficiency, order and discipline in so far as its management of schools and colleges in the Cantonment areas is concerned. There is a marked improvement in the performance of students and teachers of these institutions and the general administration has been improved remarkably.

# 9

# Nuclear Material Security of Pakistan

Nuclear material security is a concern for all states in the context of a terrorist threat. Physical security has long been considered a subset of international safeguards, but it has never been a prerequisite for placing nuclear material under international safeguards.

It can be a requirement of bilateral nuclear trade, however, and the United States requires physical security measures on some of the nuclear material it exports, mostly in conjunction with military programs. Often, physical security measures are implemented as a matter of course in implementing safeguards, since states have to account for missing material in their physical inventories.

India and Pakistan may provide particularly attractive targets because they have weapons-grade material on their soil, but terrorists' interest in a radiological dispersal device may make any or all radioactive sources potentially attractive to steal. India and Pakistan became parties to the Convention on the Physical Protection of Nuclear Material in 2002 and 2000, respectively. This Convention, which entered into force in 1987, was designed to protect nuclear material in transit between countries. The CPPNM defines a range of nuclear terrorist activities and requires parties to criminalize those activities. It does not cover physical protection of domestic nuclear material in storage or use, nor does it cover byproduct material. The United States and other members of the

Convention have been working for several years to expand the scope of the agreement, and agreed in September 2002 to extend physical protection to domestic use and storage. The IAEA has circulated proposed amendments to the convention, which may be considered in 2005. Both India and Pakistan have been active in discussions on expanding the Convention.

Since 1995, the International Atomic Energy Agency has conducted (although mostly outside of the regular budget) physical protection assessment programs, called International Physical Protection Advisory Service missions. States must request assistance, and then an international team conducts a confidential vulnerability assessment and recommends measures to address physical protection shortfalls. Neither India nor Pakistan has requested such a mission, and in the opinion of some observers, they are unlikely to do so because of the sensitivity of their facilities. However, in May 2002, the IAEA conducted a joint safety and security workshop in Islamabad. While Pakistan has participated in IAEA technical cooperation programs, India has not participated since the 1980s. In 2002, India requested a regional workshop on physical protection focused on security awareness and culture. India was among several states in which the IAEA conducted physical protection-related seminars in 2003.

## NUCLEAR WEAPONS SECURITY

Since the 1998 nuclear tests, India and Pakistan appear to have accelerated nuclear weapons development and, possibly, deployments. Most observers still believe that neither Pakistan nor India has deployed warheads mated with delivery systems. Fissile material components (pits) are thought to be kept separately from the rest of the warhead. Such a physical separation helps deter unauthorized use and complicates theft. In the early years of the U.S. nuclear weapons program, fissile material components of warheads were physically separated; in the earliest bombs, the two were mated in the bomb-bay of the aircraft. When nuclear missiles entered the U.S. inventory, the warheads were physically separated from the missiles. In addition to physical separation, however, there need to be rules and procedures for authorized use; it is not clear what those are for India or Pakistan. India and Pakistan have been moving towards more structured nuclear command and control authority, organization, and strategic planning. However, there is no information on whether they have implemented two-man rules (a requirement for the concurrent involvement of at least two people to be able to fire a weapon) or other procedures for ensuring no unauthorized use.

There is no reliable information on where fissile material is shaped or machined into components for weapons, or where fissile cores are kept if they are separated from other weapon components and delivery systems for India and Pakistan. Some observers believe that nuclear weapons parts are "probably distributed in a number of tightly secured facilities at different locations throughout Pakistan." Physical security in the case of Pakistan is provided by the military. India has kept strong civilian oversight of the weapons program, with the military kept predominantly at arm's length. However, the details of security in both cases are unknown. In April 2000, the Indian government ended independent safety oversight at BARC, the "nerve centre" of the Indian nuclear weapons program. Some analysts have interpreted this change as an indication of accelerated nuclear weapons work at BARC. On October 2, 2001, Pakistan's Foreign Ministry issued a statement that "Our nuclear assets are 100% secure, under multiple custody." Media reported that Pakistan had moved nuclear weapons components to several undisclosed locations. Subsequently, President Musharraf reorganized elements of the Pakistan Atomic Energy Commission (PAEC) and investigated several nuclear weapons scientists who reportedly had ties to Islamic extremists.

## *Personnel Security*

In terms of personnel security, concerns have focused mostly on Pakistan, and most recently, on the activities of Pakistani nuclear freelancer Dr. A.Q. Khan. At the end of 2003, evidence from Libya revealed that Khan had sold a variety of nuclear materials, technology, equipment, and even a bomb design, to Libya, Iran, and North Korea over two decades. Although there were reports that President Musharraf knew of improprieties regarding Khan in 1999, Musharraf took no steps to rein in Khan until 2001. At that time, Khan was "forced" to retire as director of Khan Research Laboratories and given a job as special advisor to President Musharraf. Before that, however, he had amassed millions of dollars in selling nuclear technology to rogue states. Pakistani officials claimed that they tightened controls on their nuclear weapons program with the creation of the National Command Authority (NCA) in February 2000. One of the features of those controls is the screening of key people in the Pakistani nuclear weapons program every two years by the Inter Services Intelligence Agency, Military Intelligence, the Intelligence Bureau, and the Strategic Plan Division of the NCA. However, "top-level people (including scientists) are controlled by their organizations and not psychologically screened." Much less is known about Indian personnel security. Although India set up a Nuclear Command Authority similar to Pakistan's in January 2003, there is little information on whether associated personnel screening measures have been implemented.

## Nuclear Material Safeguards: IAEA Safeguards

Most of the material and facilities in India and Pakistan is not subject to international safeguards. In India, there are safeguards on 6 reactors (Tarapur 1 & 2, LEU-fuelled power reactors; Rajasthan RAPS-1 and -2, which use natural uranium; and Koodankulam-1. and -2, LEU-fuelled power reactors). In addition, the Tarapur plutonium reprocessing facility (Prefre) is safeguarded when safeguarded fuel is used in the facility and the Tarapur MOX fuel fabrication plant has safeguards when it runs safeguarded material through it. The Hyderabad fuel fabrication plant has partial safeguards.

Key nuclear weapons-related facilities in India that are not subject to IAEA inspections include the Bhabha Atomic Research Centre (BARC) in Trombay, which houses the Cirus and Dhruva research reactors for plutonium production, plutonium reprocessing plants and a pilot-scale uranium enrichment plant. These sites, as well as storage sites for weapons-grade material or for weapons themselves could be highly attractive to terrorists because they may contain weapons-usable nuclear material.

Pakistan has IAEA safeguards on a few facilities. The KANUPP power reactor, which uses natural uranium, Chasma-1, LEU-fuelled power reactor, and two research reactors at Rawalpindi that have used HEU in the past are under international safeguards. The following facilities are not under safeguards: the Khan Research Laboratories at Kahuta, which include a uranium enrichment plant and facilities for fabricating HEU into weapons; centrifuge enrichment plants at Sihala, Golra and Wah/Gadwal, the Chasma reprocessing plant, and PINSTECH and SPINSTECH facilities related to reprocessing at Rawalpindi. These nuclear material production sites, as well as weaponization, storage and assembly sites (if separate facilities exist), could be high-value targets for terrorists.

## CHALLENGES FOR PAKISTAN'S NUCLEAR SECURITY

The attack last August against the Kamra military air base in Pakistan reignited concerns about the threat that terrorists could pose to the security of the Pakistani nuclear arsenal. There is no doubt that recent attacks on military targets in Pakistan have increased in number and boldness. So far, however, the targets of the attacks have not been military installations that contain nuclear weapons or components. Yet, the confluence of increased terrorist activity in Pakistan, the country's ongoing political instability, and the growing size of the Pakistani nuclear arsenal is increasing the challenge to Pakistan's nuclear security. The number of facilities and people that produce and use sensitive nuclear materials and technologies in Pakistan is increasing, raising the bar for personnel screening and infrastructure protection. Last summer, there was a reported threat by the Taliban to attack the nuclear complex at Dera Ghazi Khan, a remote town in southern Punjab, but the attack failed to materialize.

Since 2001, Pakistan, cognizant of the terrorist danger, has taken a number of steps to improve the command and control system for its nuclear assets and the screening and training of employees in its nuclear enterprise. As with all security systems, constant vigilance and a culture of continuous improvement are important to deter and, if necessary, respond to threats. The U.S. government has put forth a message of reassurance regarding

Pakistan's nuclear security. President Barack Obama and top administration officials have consistently said since 2009 that they have confidence that Pakistan takes its security mission seriously and that its physical protection and training are adequate and improving. This is in part a result of collaboration between the Pakistani and U.S. governments on best practices for the security of Pakistan's nuclear infrastructure. These interactions have led to better training and equipment.

Despite these assurances, a number of specialists around the world remain skeptical of the security steps that Pakistan has taken. There are several explanations for this perspective. One is that foreign experts and journalists have highlighted the danger when reporting on Pakistan's nuclear program. Also, within the country, the media, politicians, and anti-nuclear activists raised a number of questions about the ability of the Pakistani nuclear security establishment to protect and defend its nuclear assets against an intruding force in the wake of the Osama bin Laden raid at Abbottabad by U.S. special forces in May 2011.

In an article written after a 2009 visit to Pakistan, former U.S. Department of Defence official Lawrence J. Korb recounted various doomsday scenarios for Pakistan and argued that "given the strategic location of Pakistan and the fact that it has nuclear weapons, it's easy to see why some might embrace a worst-case scenario. But based on my visit, I don't buy it at this time." Although made four years ago, his point is still valid; the situation on ground is not as bad as it may appear to distant observers.

Yet, there is much that the U.S. and other governments do not know about the Pakistani nuclear arsenal, despite closer cooperation, especially between the United States and Pakistan, over the past decade. The overarching reason for the recurring concerns is the prevailing internal security situation in Pakistan. The nightmare scenario is that, in the event of a political collapse in Pakistan, things could spiral out of control and even the best training and equipment could not be relied on to keep terrorists away from Pakistan's weapons.

Understandably, distant observers will find it difficult to accept the notion that the nuclear installations in Pakistan are islands of stability and security in the midst of a generally chaotic security and political environment, especially when so little information on Pakistan's nuclear security regime is available. This is a major reason why the recent attacks on military bases have raised alarm about the security of Pakistan's nuclear infrastructure.

## THE KAMRA AIR BASE ATTACK

The Taliban attack in August 2012 on the Pakistani air force base at Kamra, northwest of Islamabad, made headlines in the international media and renewed concerns about the security of Pakistan's nuclear weapons. Many news reports speculated about the presence of at least a part of the Pakistani nuclear arsenal being at the base. Despite the reporting, the Kamra base does not have nuclear weapons. A Pakistani government spokesman denied that any nuclear weapons were stored at the base, and U.S. military and diplomatic officials ruled out the possibility that the attack on the base posed any threat to nuclear weapons.

The August attack was the third on the Kamra base and the most threatening so far. The target of the first attack, in December 2007, was a school bus carrying children of base employees on a public highway outside the base. In the second attack, a suicide bomber blew himself up at the main entrance to the base.

The August attack was carried out by nine militants who breached the perimeter fence but could not penetrate much farther due to timely response by the security forces. All of the attackers were killed during the ensuing shoot-out.

The base houses a major aeronautical complex with facilities for production of avionics equipment and the overhaul and assembly of aircraft, including jet trainers and the JF-17 Thunder, which China and Pakistan jointly developed. At the time of the August attack, some aircraft with airborne warning and control systems were parked on a tarmac that suffered some damage from rocket-propelled grenades fired by the militants. A recent attack by Afghan Taliban on Camp Bastion, a British military base in Afghanistan's Helmand province, has proven that even a facility located in a desolate area and protected with some of the most sophisticated sensors can be penetrated. The attackers destroyed five aircraft worth millions of dollars at a base that some have described as the safest place on earth.

Pakistani air bases cover a large area protected by barbed wire fences, which are not too difficult for an organized and determined attacker to breach. The aircraft parked on the runway are soft targets that can be observed from a distance and hit with relatively unsophisticated weapons. In addition, it should be kept in mind that the objective of the suicide bombers is to cause maximum damage, not to seize equipment or materials.

## PURSUING NUCLEAR SECURITY

In an address at the United Nations last September, Pakistani Foreign Minister Hina Rabbani Khar said that her country takes nuclear security "very seriously." Islamabad's efforts in the 15 years since its 1998 nuclear tests give some support to that claim. In February 2000, Pakistan announced the establishment of a National Command Authority (NCA), with the Strategic Plans Division (SPD) as its permanent secretariat. The responsibilities of the NCA include deploying and employing the nuclear force, coordinating Pakistan's strategic organizations, dealing with arms control and disarmament issues, and overseeing implementation of export controls and the safety and security of nuclear installations and materials.

The NCA has a three-tiered structure with two committees. The Employment Control Committee and the Developmental Control Committee constitute the first tier, the SPD the second tier, and the three services' strategic force commands the third tier. The SPD is responsible for the daily management of Pakistan's strategic assets, coordinating with all strategic organizations and overseeing the budgetary and administrative aspects of these organizations. The primary responsibility of the services' strategic force commands is to exercise technical, training, and administrative control over the strategic delivery systems. Operational control, however, rests with the NCA.

Islamabad also established the autonomous Pakistan Nuclear Regulatory Authority (PNRA) in January 2001. In 2004, comprehensive export control legislation was promulgated, with control lists meeting the guidelines of the Nuclear Suppliers Group, Missile Technology Control Regime, and Australia Group, which covers exports that are potentially relevant to biological or chemical weapons. Since then, rules and regulations and administrative structures have been developed for the effective implementation of the export control law. In late 2007, an NCA ordinance was issued to regulate the functioning of strategic organizations such as the Pakistan Atomic Energy Commission (PAEC) and the Khan Research Laboratories, which have played a central role in Pakistan's nuclear weapons program. The ordinance also specified criminal activities and the legal powers and procedures to deal with any infringements of the law. The ordinance was passed as an act of parliament in 2010.

From the perspective of nuclear security, however, the most significant organization is the security division of the NCA. The organization has grown exponentially over the years from a very modest beginning and is headed by a two-star general, who currently has 20,000 personnel under his command.

This strength is projected to reach a total of 28,000 men in the next few years. The division is responsible for the physical security of all sensitive nuclear sites through a layered system of defence with inner and outer perimeters augmented by electronic sensors and counterintelligence teams. It screens all personnel inducted into any component of the strategic program in concert with other intelligence agencies in the country. It also administers an improved and rigorous Personnel Reliability Programme.

It is useful to recount some of the most significant developments of the NCA Security Division. Initially, the division's security force comprised mostly retired military personnel. More recently, however, it set up a state-of-the-art training academy in Kalar Kahar, comparable to the U.S. Department of Energy's National Nuclear Security Administration's academy in Albuquerque, New Mexico. The new Pakistani academy provides specially selected Pakistani recruits with training similar to that given to the special forces. These recruits have become the backbone of the nuclear security force and gradually will replace most of the retired military personnel. Through field exercises and war games, Pakistan regularly tests the capabilities of the upgraded security force. The SPD training academy also is going to house a mock nuclear facility that is being designed and built in collaboration with the PNRA. This will become a "centre of excellence" for security forces training and, under the auspices of the International Atomic Energy Agency (IAEA), will offer training facilities to other countries.

The security division also has constituted an elite response force and an emergency response centre at its headquarters in Rawalpindi to deal with an emergency at any nuclear facility. It has installed radiation detection monitors at various entry and exit points. These portal monitors are in addition to the ones installed by the PNRA.

Pakistan also has taken steps to improve nuclear safety. In his address to the annual IAEA General Conference in Vienna last September, PAEC Chairman Ansar Parvez said Pakistan had been "actively engaged in absorbing lessons" from the March 2011 accident at the Fukushima nuclear reactor complex in Japan. The PAEC has "identified a comprehensive set of safety retrofits" that are "in various stages of implementation," he said.

The PNRA has set up the School for Radiation and Nuclear Safety, where it holds regular courses, workshops, and tabletop exercises to train first responders in handling a radiation emergency. It includes the customs service and other border control agencies. The PNRA also has established a National Radiation Emergency Coordination Centre at its headquarters in Islamabad and has put in place the national Nuclear Safety Action Plan to guide the organizations acting as first responders to a nuclear or radiological emergency.

The Pakistan Institute of Engineering and Applied Sciences has introduced master's degree-level courses with a specialization in nuclear safety, mainly, to train new PNRA personnel. Pakistan also has benefited from cooperation and exchanges of information on best practices with friendly countries, including the United States, and has maintained a vibrant, cooperative relationship with the IAEA.

## PARTICIPATION IN GLOBAL EFFORTS

Despite an impressive inventory of actions, Pakistani efforts to provide information about all these developments domestically and internationally have not been adequate. This has contributed to the continued skepticism about Islamabad's ability to protect its nuclear assets.

Yet, one avenue through which Pakistan has been able to play an active role in advocating for and taking action on global nuclear security issues is the nuclear security summit process, in which Pakistan is one of the more than 50 countries that have participated. There have been two nuclear summits, in Washington in 2010 and in Seoul in 2012. A third is planned for The Hague in 2014.

Participants at the summits endorsed a number of important steps, including President Barack Obama's goal of securing all vulnerable nuclear material in four years. The national leaders who attended the summits underscored the importance of maintaining effective security over all nuclear materials on their territory; encouraged the conversion of reactors that use highly enriched uranium (HEU) to low-enriched uranium; and recognized the importance of the International Convention for the Suppression of Acts of Nuclear Terrorism and the Convention on the Physical Protection of Nuclear Material and its 2005 amendment. (The amendment would extend protection requirements beyond the original agreement, which covers nuclear material while in international transport, by expanding the coverage to apply to nuclear facilities and to materials in peaceful domestic use and storage.) Pakistan has acceded to the convention on physical protection but not to the 2005 amendment or the nuclear terrorism convention.

Summit participants also supported full implementation of UN Security Council Resolution 1540, which requires all countries to enact legislation to prevent the proliferation of nonconventional weapons and their means of delivery, and recognized the continuing importance of the IAEA and its nuclear material security guidelines and activities. The participants also supported the actions of the Global Initiative to Combat Nuclear Terrorism (GICNT). Other ambitious objectives of the summits included the removal and disposal of nuclear materials no longer needed for operational activities and the minimization of the civilian use of HEU. The participants also agreed to consider plans to consolidate nuclear material at fewer national storage sites.

Pakistan has submitted four reports to the UN committee overseeing the implementation of Resolution 1540, thus meeting an international nuclear nonproliferation and security obligation that a number of countries have not met. Islamabad is an active participant in the GICNT, especially on issues related to nuclear forensics and efforts to upgrade the international community's ability to detect nuclear and other radioactive materials in order to prevent nuclear trafficking.

At the Washington and Seoul summits, individual countries made commitments to improving domestic regimes for nuclear security. Approximately 80 percent of these national commitments were fulfilled between 2010 and 2012. Pakistan did not make any unilateral commitments at the 2010 summit, but it did at the summit in 2012, when it pledged to open a nuclear security training centre and signed the Joint Statement on Nuclear Security Training and Support Centers. The centre is intended to serve as a regional and international hub for training in nuclear security; in the joint statement, Pakistan joined with 22 other countries in forming what will amount to an international network on that issue.

In Seoul, Pakistan also agreed to continue deploying portal monitors to detect special nuclear material as a means of impeding the illicit trafficking of nuclear and radioactive materials. In addition, it offered to provide nuclear safety and security assistance under IAEA auspices to interested states.

In its progress report at the Seoul summit, Pakistan noted its steps to improve export controls, secure radiological sources, and prevent nuclear smuggling.

In these areas, it revised its national export control lists and operates mobile laboratories for technical assistance to law enforcement and first responders.

Pakistan also reported that, under its renewed Nuclear Security Action Plan, originally established in 2006, it is upgrading the physical security at its 11 nuclear medical centers. Medical facilities utilize high-intensity radioactive sources that can be used in a "dirty bomb."

Pakistan has taken a number of actions related to nuclear security and safety beyond those it pledged at the summits. It has intensified collaboration with the IAEA by joining "collaborating centers," which are designed to standardize technology, disseminate information, and facilitate research and learning on a range of issues related to IAEA activities, including nuclear safety and security.

It also is participating in the development of the IAEA Nuclear Safety Action Plan.

It has incorporated some of the lessons of the Fukushima accident, including holding an international seminar on nuclear safety and security and developing a radiation emergency response mechanism and a Nuclear Security Emergency Coordination Centre. It also is considering a program for upgrading physical protection of civilian nuclear power plants. It is not yet clear how the Pakistani steps on nuclear security and safety should be seen. On one hand, if they represent the limits of Pakistan's movement toward transparency and cooperation, they are disappointing. On the other hand, they represent an evolution from Pakistan's previous opaqueness, and that may lead to further progress.

## Conclusion

Pakistan is located in a very dangerous neighborhood; it has a history of political instability; and terrorist activity in and around the country remains significant. Control of the nuclear program resides primarily with military authorities, which are not very transparent about nuclear security and weapons operations. There is only modest civilian oversight.

These distinguishing features make the security of the Pakistani nuclear weapons program and its infrastructure a global concern, which is unlikely to diminish anytime soon. As a result, all acts of terrorism in the country, especially those directed at military targets, are going to raise concerns and invite scrutiny and skepticism of official assurances of control.

Pakistan has taken its responsibility for nuclear security seriously. It has collaborated with the United States on best practices, training, and personnel screening. It is participating in international forums devoted to preventing nuclear terrorism and improving nuclear security. It has made strides domestically to improve the legal and regulatory system for preventing proliferation of sensitive materials and technologies. Not least, the authorities in Pakistan, the first Islamic country to possess a nuclear weapon, recognize that the nuclear weapons program is deeply intertwined with national identity and that security of its nuclear infrastructure is a top priority. Domestically or internationally, it cannot afford a loss of control. Yet, there is more that Pakistan can and should do to provide confidence to the international community that its nuclear program employs the highest level of safety and security.

First, there is the need to accept all international instruments that underpin the current nuclear security regime, including the nuclear terrorism convention and the 2005 amendment to the convention on physical protection. Also, as the Fukushima nuclear accident highlighted, the decision by any country, developed or developing, to remain insular and opaque on matters of nuclear safety and security can be harmful to that country and its neighbours.

Although the sovereign control of nuclear assets remains the dominant model at present, there is an increasing recognition that countries have an international responsibility to prevent the unauthorized release of radiation or the theft of materials from their facilities. Both dangers directly affect other countries. These concepts of sovereignty and international responsibility should not be in competition. Both are important and need to be balanced.

There should be a commitment to the highest levels of nuclear security at home and a willingness to provide nonsensitive information on these actions to the global community. This process could begin with the actions listed above, first as a voluntary activity and then evolving into a codified requirement for all countries over time. These steps offer the best combination of assurances and can improve international confidence in Pakistan's nuclear security.

## RESEARCH AND DEVELOPMENT OF ARMOUR

The manufacture of tanks and armoured vehicles, which started from zero in China, initially began with imitations but now has been replaced with our own designs and manufacturing. As early as the end of 1945, the PLA set up its first tank corps using tanks captured from its enemies during battles. By 1949, when the People's Republic of China was founded, the PLA already had two armoured divisions and two armoured regiments, and equipped these corps with 410 American or Japanese tanks and 367 armoured vehicles, all captured equipment. On the basis of this we started constructing and developing our own armoured weaponry.

On September 1, 1950, our Armoured Corps was officially established. To meet the needs of the tanks corps we bought over 400 tanks and mobile guns from the Soviet Union. Immediately after that, the tank corps made use of the equipment during the war to Resist U.S. Aggression and Aid Korea, and forcefully backed the infantry's operations. In 1956, we began to set up the tank industry. Until 1959, we copied designs to make medium-sized tanks (model 59) for our troops. Then, starting from the latter half of 1958, a magnificent stage in the history of the developing of our tanks began, a time when we designed and made our own tanks. After a hard struggle of 4 to 5 years, as we manufactured model 62 light tanks, we finalized the designs of model 63 amphibious tanks and model 63 armoured vehicles. Then four major series were gradually formed according to the requirements of our operations and capacities that would adjust to specific terrains and climates. They were medium-size, light, amphibious, and armoured carrier tanks. Step by step, they became the mainstay of our armoured weaponry.

During the Cultural Revolution, the research and production of tanks were seriously damaged. Though the scientists, technicians, officers and men in our defence industry worked hard to achieve some progress, and the design of the medium-sized model 69 tank was finalized along with a number of accessory automobiles during this time, on the whole, the level of technology and the quality of the equipment was not much improved, and the distance between the most advanced technology and ours grew.

Since the Third Plenary Session of the 11th Party Committee, the policy of reform and opening to the outside world has brought opportunities for the rapid development of science and technology in our national defence. In the wake of a strategic transformation in the guiding concept on the construction of our army, we have strengthened the strategic research about how to develop weapons and developed an overall plan of development. The plan and the policies we put into practice in developing weapons were constructive and reliable, so the research and development of tanks and armoured vehicles embarked on a steady and healthy road and achieved much progress. During this period, we did much research and finally manufactured over 10 new types of weapons, including the main battle tanks, caterpillar infantry battle vehicles, armoured carriers, mobile antiaircraft guns, antitank missile launchers, armoured command vehicles, tank bridge-making vehicles, tank rescue haulers, and tank transporters. Using advanced foreign technology, we actively improved our existing weapons, improving fighting capability and increasing the amount of equipment and weapons in every unit of the armed forces. Our armoured weaponry has played an important role in training and preparing to prevent war, as well as in self defence.

We have achieved great progress in the development of armoured weaponry after a tortuous experience. The many successes and failures have made us understand better the characteristics and rules of development:

- Strengthen research on developing weapons, and base macro decisionmaking on science. In the past, weapons development was much affected by political movements, the organizational system, and factors like personnel changes. We did not work according to scientific rules. In recent years we have, through wide discussion, decided upon an active and cautious policy for weapons development. We have formulated development principles with Chinese characteristics for the tanks and armoured vehicles and made long-and medium-term development strategy and plans. Therefore our weapons construction is done through long-term planning, good coordination, and priority development. The democratic and scientific method we adopt in our models and decisionmaking process is the important foundation for the constant and steady development of our weaponry.

- In weapons development, we should consult with the department that uses them. The armed forces are the direct users of weapons. In the making of set models, they should pay attention to the testing of these models. In recent years, we have verified our weapons models in actual battle and paid attention to the integration of tactics and technology as well. We have strictly carried out model testing according to testing standards, regional adaptation testing, and special testing under nuclear and chemical conditions. We have asked representatives from the armed forces to take part in the management of scientific research. This is of extreme importance for meeting the battle requirements of the armed forces and ensuring weapons quality. As reform of defence science and technology progresses, we should actively carry out contract systems under the guidance of the defence industry, respecting the decision of the chief engineer in matters of technology, and encouraging the initiative and creativity of the broad mass of scientists and technicians.
- We must uphold the policy of taking the initiative and actively importing technology, which is a shortcut for the development of weapons. Independence and self reliance comprise our basic national policy; this is also the policy we must follow in weapons development. But in the development of technology, we should try to create anew and be good at learning and inheriting these two are complementary. In the early days of our new Republic, we learned from the advanced experience and technology of the Soviet Union, jumping over the traditional technical development stage. This way the research and manufacturing of tanks were quickly on the track, and we were able to shift from copying to designing and manufacturing our own tanks. At the end of the 1970s,

through importing advanced technology, we were able to facilitate the quick development of our tanks and armoured vehicles and shorten the distance between the advanced-level and our own. Today we take the initiative with imported technology, stressing utilization and development and gradually form weapons systems that have our own characteristics.

- We need to step up innovation and expand the accumulation of technology, key factors in weapons development progress. The research of weaponry in the past followed the traditional way, that is, a model led the research work or even the production of accessories. This resulted in a lack of accumulation of technology, passive and insufficient research on models, a long research period, and many unnecessary repetitions. It should be a profound lesson for us. In recent years, we supported and directed innovation that correlates to the background of the models. We adhere to a principle that the component parts take priority over sets of equipment. In addition, we imitated the good points of advanced scientific and technological results from abroad and make use of them in some projects. We broke through the line of demarcation between the departments and the industries and encouraged competition. All the efforts produced a remarkable effect.
- The development of tanks and armoured vehicles must follow a process in which the vehicles are classified and grouped and put in a standardized series. If the army wants to enhance the overall operation capability of the armoured corps, there will be a variety of requirements for weaponry. Since the 1960s we have believed that all kinds of accessory vehicles should be derived from a basic model design that can be flexibly changed. In weapons research and manufacture, besides carrying out the principle of standardization from beginning to end, we tried every possible means to enhance the universality of the component parts. This universal concept is useful not only to help crate standardized products but also to lower the

costs of contract work, simplify the training of our army, and ensure logistics supplies.

- The development of weaponry needs a stable troop of scientists and technicians. In the early 1960s, along with the modernization construction of the armoured corps, we founded the Scientific and Technical Research Institute of the Armoured Corps and the Institute of Engineers for the Armoured Corps. We gradually had a team of scientists and technicians that combined theory with practice. They worked together with the national defence industry department and made contributions to our first generation of tanks. Because of the advent of the cultural revolution, the teaching system and research institute of the armoured corps suffered great damage and much talent was lost. Both the positive and negative experiences have made us realize that in order to develop weapons it is important to have a team of scientists and technicians rich in practical experience and full of creativity. Under the current new situation, we should take strong measures to ensure the stability of the team, and create favourable conditions for the upgrading of knowledge and the growth of talents.
- The organization that uses weapons should create a favourable technical system and environment for the development of new weapons. "Without technology there would be no armoured corps," these were the famous words that former Commander of the Armoured Corps General Xu Guangda used to say about the construction of the armoured corps. At the founding of our armoured corps, we established the department of technology and laid the organizational foundation for weapons development. When the first generation of new weapons was decided upon, documents for the use, repair, testing, and technology were edited, weapons were tested and their fighting capability, ease of use, and reliabilty were constantly improved. We created favourable conditions for the development of new types of weapons. Tradition and experience in this area should be upheld and carried forward.

We are facing new opportunities and challenges at a time when modernization is our central task and there is a new technological revolution going on. We should grasp the opportunity and gradually establish a weapons system that has Chinese characteristics and that meets the requirements of future anti-aggression war. The development of armoured weaponry should proceed from reality and in accordance with the actual conditions of our country and our army. We should go our own way and not follow the footsteps of the others. The future development of tanks and armoured vehicles should follow these principles:

- Pay attention to fire power, improve overall quality, and increase survival capability.
- Reform current weaponry in a planned way and strengthen combat capability.
- Take into account terrain and weather conditions and improve adaptability.
- Form modular sets with fewer basic models but higher standardization.
- Strive for advanced, reliable, economical, and easier-to-operate weapons.

These principles were established after summing up the experiences of developing armoured weaponry. In our future development work, we should put them into practice, strengthen test methods to ensure a weapon's long life, gradually certify, research, manufacture and equip for a complete set and arrange for advanced research, manufacture, production and improvement. At the same time, we should speed up the training of personnel and technical research so as to maintain good development momentum. Motorization and armoring our troops are the developing trends for the modernization of our army. Fast-reaction and quick-strike capabilities will be important factors for our armoured corps in winning future anti-aggression wars.

Weapons for our armoured corps in the year 2000 must meet the requirements of future warfare. Our armoured corps should improve the ability to strike deep, react fast, and coordinate well with the air force.

The overall efficiency and adaptability should be improved, and weapons systems with appropriate combinations of different levels of quality should be formed. At present, we should give priority to the development of new types of main battle tanks, infantry fighting vehicles, automatic battle command complexes, and anti-aircraft vehicles. At the same time, we should selectively improve our current weapons and improve their reliability and fighting capability.

We are confident that under the correct leadership of the Central Committee of our Party and the Central Military Committee, and with the great efforts of all people in the defence industry and armoured corps, the working capacity of our armoured weaponry will be greatly improved, and the capacity of combined-operations will reach a new level. It is a difficult and heavy task, however, as long as we persist in our efforts, we will definitely achieve our aim.

## SECURITY DISCOURSE OF PAKISTAN

Security has various components like national security, human security, food security etc with many dimensions like internal dimension and external dimension. The post colonialstate of Pakistan is faced with enormous security challenges related to all of the aboveforms and dimensions. The national security concern has remained dominant right from its creation in 1947 and the feeling of insecurity remained adamant. The partition created security constraint in Pakistan and such insecurity somehow strengthened Pakistani army. Pakistan needed to increase its military strength as a result of its rivalry with India and led to close relations with United States. Such unnecessary transfer of resources can be judged from the comparative military expenditure per head of population given by Stephen Cohen, which shows a figure of 212 dollars for Pakistan in 1981 against only 8 dollars for India. The consequences of maintaining armed forces at a 1:2 ratio against a hostile neighbour with a 7:1 superiority in population and for more developed industrial base naturally leads Pakistan towards underdevelopment and military dominance. However, Pakistan was able to maintain its national security though at the cost of development by implementing various policies taken by the state.

The overriding concern of Pakistan's national life is security both internal and external, country's defense from both internal and external threats. In past though ruled by military much of the time, yet Pakistan was able to measure its security threats but the last democratic government from 2008 failed to measure such threats and interests. From last several years Pakistan failed to compete with India and bring superpowers in tune with their security interests, for which Pakistan was successful in past. The increased role of India in Afghanistan and its emergence as economic giant, capturing attention from big powers (U.S.A, France, U.K) evident through different deals with India, again has caused feelings of insecurity in Pakistan and Particularly headache for military. Pakistan considers India as a growing challenge to its external security and interprets its active role in Afghanistan as a security threat to Pakistan. Pakistan is now faced with the looming threat from India's growing military might, numerical and quantitative imbalance in superior offensive capabilities on the sea and in the air.

However, though faced with many critical security issues, Pakistan is not able to implement security policies suited to its interests and accommodates itself with changing time and circumstances. Though Pakistan itself is insecure from others, yet Pakistan is considered security threat by international community. Its partnership with friendly countries is receding. The reason is the lazy security policies which often relent on military adventurist policies than on board security objectives and policies. From one side Pakistan tries to solve its problems and improve relations with India, yet on the other fights with the latter at Kashmir and Afghanistan front. Unlike India, Pakistan has not adopted soft security policies, which contain others, threat by attracting friends. The reason for Pakistan's receding relations with other countries is the double nature of policies adopted by it at different fronts and militancy operative in its landscape. With the result other countries policies towards Pakistan is that of 'use and throw' and might be left with open security challenges in future. Ironically, due to wrong security policies, Pakistan not only fails to coup up with changing geo-strategic reality but is sacrificing all its security interests for unimportant issues. At the end it is faced with hard realities of national security both at regional and international level.

Secondly, by not acting itself against terrorism, it gives other states chance to interfere with its sovereignty. The drone attacks from NATO led US forces are violating the sovereignty of Pakistan and it seems that post-colonial Pakistan is unable to prevent external attacks on its territory. Pakistan has become helpless on front of US led NATO drone attacks. For instance, attacks at Abbottabad, Gilgit Baltistan and tribal areas are open evidences of showing incapability of Pakistani state to guarantee security to its citizens. Thirdly, the presence of Taliban on its territory has worsened security concerns for Pakistan. There are growing attacks of cross border terrorism and suicide attacks by the Taliban and other militant groups against Pakistan who have launched jihad against it. Fourthly, there is a general perception in Pakistan about India's infiltration in Baluchistan, which may be true or wrong, yet a serious security concern for Pakistan.

On the other hand, the chief security concerns of international community particularly United States in Pakistan is political instability and due to it fear of a takeover of a government by terrorists and the falling of nuclear weapons into the hands of terrorists. There is a general consensus in Pakistan that Pakistanis adherence to the principles of peaceful settlement of disputes does not guarantee security to the Pakistan, thus are trying to develop nuclear capability in comparison with India, but US views Pakistan as involved in nuclear proliferation and is a cause of worry for them. Internally also, Pakistan is faced with problem of terrorism and its war on terror has severely damaged the country. What misfortune Pakistan had after 9/11 attacks upon U.S.A, no one could deny that, both externally and internally, its strength had declined. Pakistan's alliance with U.S.A over, "the War on terror" proved counterproductive as it itself has become the home of terror. The American policy towards Pakistan has shifted from cooperative alliance and Pakistan is looked as suspected ally. This proxy war has severely damaged Pakistani economy and peace, as it consumed millions of dollars.

The post-colonial state of Pakistan is insecure both externally and internally. For as long as there are disputes and conflicts in its territory as well as in south Asian region, latent threats to its sovereignty will continue to exist. The rise of India's power would be continuously seen to be as threat to Pakistan, though that made Pakistan to shed its previous positions and declare latter as the most favoured nation, yet unsettled claims on Kashmir will continue to be a conflict factor. Pakistan posse's most important geo-strategic location and its typical situation are both responsible for its survival as well as the problems. It has developed nuclear-capability but that has least strategic benefits for it. Its security is under threat from multiple fronts and integration under danger.

The second aspect of security is human security and again Pakistan has become the state which kills its people. The post-colonial state ofPakistan has failed to safeguard the rights of its people and human rights violations are at peak in Pakistan. The human rights violations mostly occur in the rural areas of Pakistan like Baluchistan and tribal areas. There are serious human rights violations problems in the citizen's life and authority throughout Pakistan, Such human rights problems include extra judicial killings, torture, disappearances commuted by security forces, as well as militant and terrorist groups, which affects citizen. The south Asian terrorism portal reports that during the year 2010, 542 civilians' students, teachers and human rights activists were victims of extra-judicial killings. Other human rights problems include poor prison conditions, instances of arbitrary detention, lengthy pretrial detention, and a weak criminal justice system, infringement on citizen's rights, harassment and censorship. Asian Legal Resource Center states that from October 2010 to may 2011 government agencies abducted and killed 120 persons. Human rights watch reports that between January to July 150 persons were killed and abounded their bodies outside Baluchistan under "kill and dump operation".

Some people are killed under custody through physical torture as reported by NGO, society for human rights and prisoners reports that 61 civilian killings occurred after encounter with police and 89 deaths took in jail. The number of persons missing from Jan-July in the judicial system increased to 228. The forced disappearances also continue. More than 14,000 persons had disappeared in Baluchistan since 2001. The dead bodies of 355 missing persons were found from June 2010- December 2011. Human Rights Watch reports that there were 45 cases of alleged enforced disappearances. Police tortured persons in more than 8000 cases during 2011-12 more than 2010,s record of 4,069 cases. The freedom of speech and press is also curtailed by Pakistani state. In May 2011 journalist Saleem Shahzad was abducted and later at the end of year was killed because of his article "linking navy with Al-Qaida". Many suspected of having hand of government agencies in his killings. It is Section 99 of the personal code allows the government to restrict information that might be prejudicial to the national interest. Thus, right to information is also restricted. These cases show that Pakistan is faced with severe human security crisis, and needs to take immediate steps to restore security of its citizens.

The third aspect of security is Food security, which reveals that the post colonial state of Pakistan is unable to provide food and all basic essential necessities to its all citizens. The food security of post colonial state of Pakistan is under constant threat from last several years. The inflation is very high, recorded at 34%. The inflation rate reported by economic survey during 2011-12 was 10.8%, with a food inflation is estimated 11.1% and non-food inflation 10.7%. Widely cited WFP data from 2008 concluded that 77 million Pakistanis-nearly half the country's total population-were going hungry, a 28 percent increase from the 60 million in March 2007. Ninety-five of Pakistan's 121 districts are faced with hunger and malnutrition-related diseases. Previously, this widespread food insecurity triggered civil unrest in many urban areas, and Pakistan's army was dispatched to guard grain supplies. According to figures from the UN Food and Agriculture Organization (FAO), the prices of wheat and rice-Paki-stan's two chief staple crops-were 30 to 50 percent higher than before the global food crisis. The prices of essential staples in Pakistan were nearly 40 percent higher than five-year cumulative averages.

Pakistan is at critical juncture and its security discourse might undergo change after 2013 elections. Pakistan need to have a re-look over its security policies and should take each and every part of security in to account, in order to guarantee its security from inimical forces both internally and externally. Further, in order to emerge as major power of the south Asian region, needs both soft and hard security policies, sometimes bargain and sometimes cooperate, to strength itself. The security situation though presents grim situation yet Pakistan will be able to handle all its mess, provided that it will mould security discourse interests and implement cautious security policies. However, it needs to maintain citizen's security with priority as the security of state also depends on the security of its citizens.

## PAKISTAN: NATIONAL SECURITY

Armed Forces Overview: The military is formally called the Pakistan Armed Forces, and as of 2004 consisted of approximately 619,000 active personnel in the army (550,000), air force (45,000), and navy (24,000), as well as 513,000 reserves. Under the 1973 constitution, the federal government controls the armed forces, and the president is the commander in chief. The Ministry of Defence has a permanent staff of civil servants headed by the defense secretary general, and the minister of defense is a civilian member of the prime minister's cabinet. The Joint Chiefs of Staff Committee deals with problems concerning military aspects of state security and is charged with integrating and coordinating the army, navy, and air force. The committee's secretariat acts as the principal link between the service headquarters and the Ministry of Defence. The Directorate for Inter-Services Intelligence (ISI) is of particular importance at the joint services level because it manages covert operations outside of Pakistan (and in internationally disputed areas) and because it has been involved in domestic politics, usually to keep track of the incumbent regime's opponents. The chief of the army staff (COAS) is the key power holder in the armed forces and is also one of the triumvirate that runs the country, along with the prime minister and president. The COAS usually operates from army headquarters in Rawalpindi. General Pervez Musharraf acts as both president and COAS.

Musharraf also heads a National Security Council composed of politicians and senior military officers.

Under the constitution, the military is responsible for defending the nation against external aggression and threats of war and is to aid civil authorities only when called to do so. The military is forbidden constitutionally from acting independently of the elected political leadership in domestic matters. However, from 1947 to 2004 military generals have acted as head of state for nearly 30 years, and in times of civilian government the armed forces have routinely intervened on domestic and foreign policy issues. The military justifies its consistent involvement in politics as protection from malign foreign interests and corrupt and incompetent politicians. Although public opinion surveys are rare, it appears that the public dislikes military rule, yet consistently has a more favorable view of the military than of elected officials.

Because the military conducts its affairs with carefully defended secrecy, the degree to which army officers and personnel are religiously motivated is debated. However, Western analysts tend to conclude that whereas the military increasingly sees itself as serving Islam, the institution's decision making is still largely secular. Military intervention in politics is designed to limit civilian involvement in sensitive matters, such as Kashmir, nuclear disarmament, internal military personnel decisions, and defense spending. The military also is extensively involved in the economy, and military enterprises produce approximately 3 percent of the gross national product. Military enterprises include the Army Welfare Trust (AWT), whose assets include the Askari Bank, one of the country's largest financial institutions, and the Fauji Foundation, which is the country's biggest conglomerate. These and other military financial institutions often are exempt from taxes and regulations covering the manufacturing sector and asset disclosure.

With regard to military strategy, the military's budget and personnel have reduced strategy to largely defensive objectives, such as limited offensive tactics in bordering areas (particularly Kashmir), use of irregular forces, and deterring and countering possible attacks from foreign powers (particularly India). The military's history of far lower military expenditures and capabilities than India has prompted the military to attempt to impose high costs on India to force its withdrawal from Kashmir. Furthermore, the military hopes that its nuclear capabilities can reduce the disadvantages of its conventional forces. However, the theoretical deterrence between nuclear powers has not limited military engagement between India and Pakistan—as exemplified by the 1999 Kargil War—and analysts believe that Pakistan's military strategy historically has suffered from overly optimistic assessments of potential success and underestimations of diplomatic and military losses, as well as a lack of contingency planning.

Foreign Military Relations: Pakistan has sought to become an important actor in international politics, but its foreign military alliances often are intended to address matters with bordering countries. Other countries have established alliances with Pakistan to address their own strategic interests in South and Central Asia, and these alliances have tended to be ephemeral. Pakistan's military relationship with China started in the 1970s as a way of countering India, but China has softened its relations since India's military strength has increased. Still, Pakistan and China maintain a military relationship, including periodic joint military exercises. United States aid in the 1980s was significantly reduced after the Soviet Union pulled out of Afghanistan in 1989 but resumed after the September 11, 2001, terrorist attacks. Moreover, in March 2004 the United States granted Pakistan status as a major non-North Atlantic Treaty Organization ally, which provides access to U.S. military equipment and cooperation. In fact, the United States is one of the largest suppliers of military equipment to Pakistan along with China and Russia. Pakistan's military relations with India have been contentious, and the two countries fought a limited conflict in Kashmir in 1999. However, under the 1999 Lahore Agreement the two countries provide each other with advance notification of missile tests, and in 2003 and 2004 they engaged in several high-level discussions that have eased tensions.

External Threat: The military and public generally view India as the nation's primary security threat, and opposition to India is often a greater source of social cohesion than either Islam or Urdu.

India's far greater military capabilities have been a source of both fear and frustration, and many suspect that this imbalance has prompted Pakistan to engage Indian forces indirectly through supporting insurgents morally, financially, or otherwise. Whether Pakistan has done so is debated, but it seems clear that the country's newly demonstrated nuclear capabilities have helped level military differences with its rival neighbor. Yet India is not the country's only security concern, as Pakhtun and Balochi irredentist movements in Pakistan's western provinces have contributed to sometimes-tense relations with neighbouring Afghanistan.

Defense Budget: According to World Bank figures for 1988 to 2003, Pakistan's military expenditures represented 25–29 percent of central government expenditures and 6–7 percent of gross national income. In fiscal year (FY) 2004, military expenditures constituted 18 percent of government expenditures. Historically, Pakistan's governments have used defense spending to stimulate economic growth.

Major Military Units: The army, with 550,000 active personnel and 500,000 reserves, is organized into nine corps located at Bahawalpur, Gujranwala, Karachi, Lahore, Mangla, Multan, Peshawar, Quetta, and Rawalpindi. The Northern Area Command is headquartered at Gilgit and is directly responsible to army general headquarters. The army has 2 armoured divisions, 19 infantry divisions including 1 area command, 9 corps artillery brigades, 26 independent brigades (7 armoured, 1 mechanized, 6 infantry, 5 artillery, and 7 engineer), 3 armoured reconnaissance regiments, 1 special forces group, and 1 air defense command. The navy has 24,000 active personnel—including 1,400 marines and 2,000 in the Maritime Security Agency—and 5,000 reserves. The navy has four commands: fleet, logistics, naval installations in the north of Pakistan, and fleet headquarters at Karachi, the nation's only major naval base. Two bases are under construction at Gwadar and Ormara. The air force has 45,000 active personnel and 8,000 reserves. Air force headquarters in Rawalpindi has directorates for operations, electronics, administration, and maintenance. The air force has three regional air commands: Northern (in Peshawar), Central (Sargodha), and Southern (Faisal).

Major Military Equipment: In 2004 the army had an estimated 2,461 tanks, 1,146 armoured personnel carriers, 1,829 tube-launched optically-tracked wire-guided "TOW" missiles, 260 self-propelled artillery, 52 multiple rocket launchers, 2,350 mortars, 165 surface-to-surface missiles, 10,500 antitank guided weapons, and 1,900 air defense guns. The army also had 80 observation aircraft, 45 liaison aircraft, 2 survey aircraft, 22 attack helicopters, and 131 transport helicopters. The navy had 8 anti-surface warfare submarines, 3 inshore submarines, 7 frigates, 6 missile craft, 3 coastal patrol craft, 6 combat aircraft, and 9 armed helicopters. The air force had 415 combat aircraft and no armed helicopters. Pakistan became a nuclear state in 1998 and periodically tests nuclear-capable short- and medium-range missiles.

Military Service: Military service is voluntary, and active-service personnel are liable for duty eight years after active service ends. Officers are obligated to serve until 50 years of age, other ranks until 45 years of age. Women serve in the military but are a numerical minority.

Paramilitary Forces: The central government (specifically the Ministry of Interior) controls the coast guard, paramilitary forces, and numerous specialized police agencies, such as the Federal Investigative Agency and railroad and airport police forces. However, provincial governments organize paramilitary forces, which often act as an extension of the army to assist provincial police in internal security matters.

In addition, senior government officials often have strong control over security forces and have at times established personal security forces. The largest paramilitary organization is the 185,000-member National Guard, which comprises the National Cadet Corps, the Women Guards, and the Janbaz Force. The Frontier Corps reportedly has 65,000 members and is responsible for Balochistan and the North-West Frontier Province. The Pakistan Rangers has 35,000 to 40,000 members and deals with unrest in Punjab. The Northern Light Infantry has an estimated 12,000 members, and the Maritime Security Agency, which is under the navy's direction, has an estimated 2,000 personnel.

Foreign Military Forces: Pakistan hosts 45 military observers from nine countries stationed in Jammu and Kashmir under the United Nations Military Observer Group in India and Pakistan (UNMOGIP). U.S. military forces occasionally work with Pakistan's military against insurgents supporting the Taliban and al Qaeda in areas of Pakistan bordering Afghanistan.

Military Forces Abroad: In 2004 Pakistan's military participated in United Nations peacekeeping missions in Burundi, Côte d'Ivoire (9 personnel including 3 observers), the Democratic Republic of the Congo (1,092 personnel including 26 observers), East Timor (78 personnel including 5 observers), Georgia (8 observers), Liberia (2,762 personnel including 16 observers), Sierra Leone (3,865 personnel including 15 observers), Serbia and Montenegro (1 observer), and Western Sahara (7 observers).

Police: Provincial governments are charged with police administration in their respective jurisdictions, and provincial police forces operate independently. The federal government is largely uninvolved in provincial police administration but controls police in federally administered and tribal areas. The federal minister of interior supervises police nationwide, and the Police Service of Pakistan (PSP) selects, trains, and assigns senior officers to provincial or central government agencies. Although service in the PSP is competitive and well paid, lower-ranking police personnel often have far lower education, skills, and motivation. Police often are accused of routine extortion, violating civil liberties, and acting to preserve the tenure of government officials rather than the rule of law. The quantity of overall crime and various types of crime (such as murder and banditry) increased steadily from 1992 to 2003, and the extensive availability and use of automatic weapons in Pakistani society is often referred to as the "Kalashnikov Culture." Furthermore, the population generally does not perceive the police to be effective against crime or publicly accountable.

Internal Security and Terrorism: Pakistan has numerous categories of terrorism and internal threats, with most insurgent groups identifying themselves as religious or ethnic separatists. Some political parties represent distinct religious and ethnic communities, and rivalries among these parties have been violent. Violence between religiously identified groups is rarely based solely on differing religious doctrines but rather the different social, political, and economic statuses that correlate with religion. Some Islamic militias have connections to the Taliban and al Qaeda, which was linked to two assassination attempts on President Musharraf in December 2003. Militant organizations have some influence on Pakistan's foreign policy, and militants in Pakistan (such as Harkat-ul-Ansar) have assisted militant organizations in countries whose governments are perceived as oppressing Muslims. There are also concerns that Pakistan's nuclear arsenal could be seized by insurgents in an event such as a coup or assassination of the nation's president. However, the government claims that it has enacted security measures to prevent such a threat and that the numerical and political superiority of religious moderates over religious extremists is a substantial obstacle to the latter's access to Pakistan's nuclear weapons.

The most significant violence between religious groups is between Islamic militias, the Shia militia Sipah-e-Mohammed Pakistan (SMP, "Army of Mohammed") and the Sunni militias Sipah-e-Sahaba Pakistan (SSP, "Army of the Friends of the Prophet") and Lashkar-e-Jhangvi (LeJ, "Army of Jhangvi").

The violence has, at times, disrupted both civil order and the economies in areas of Sindh and Punjab provinces. The violence has resulted in large part from the influx of weapons and returning mujahideen from Afghanistan, as well as financial support from large landowners, drug lords, and some political parties. Tensions between ethnic groups often stem from perceptions that other ethnic groups dominate politics and economics to the detriment of minority ethnicities.

The Muhajir Quami Movement (MQM) was involved in substantial conflict in the 1980s and early 1990s but has since been far more quiescent as a result of internal factionalism and an apparent lack of motivating doctrine. The only other significant ethnic violence involves secessionists in Balochistan, who contend that the government is appropriating the province's mineral wealth while providing little economic benefit in return. There are also long-suspected connections of foreign-sponsored subversion, such as Indian support of Sindhi dissidents and Iranian ties to Shia and Balochi militants.

Human Rights: The government's human rights record is generally regarded as poor by domestic and international observers, although there have been some improvements since 2000. Security forces use excessive and sometimes lethal force and are complicit in extrajudicial killings of civilians and suspected militants. The police and military have been accused of engaging in physical abuse, rape, and arbitrary arrest and detention, particularly in areas of acute conflict. Although the government has enacted measures to counter these problems, abuses continue. Furthermore, courts suffer from lack of funds, outside intervention, and deep case backlogs that lead to long trial delays and lengthy pretrial detentions. Many observers inside and outside Pakistan contend that Pakistan's legal code is largely concerned with crime, national security, and domestic tranquility and less with the protection of individual rights. Provincial and local governments have arrested journalists and closed newspapers that report on matters perceived as socially offensive or critical of the government. Journalists also have been victims of violence and intimidation by various groups and individuals. In spite of these difficulties, the press publishes freely, although journalists often exercise self-restraint in their writing. In 2002 citizens participated in elections for the National Assembly, but those elections were criticized as deeply flawed by domestic and international observers.

Societal actors also are responsible for human rights abuses. Violence by drug lords and sectarian militias claims numerous innocent lives, discrimination and violence against women are widespread, human trafficking is problematic, and debt slavery and bonded labor persist. The government often ignores abuses against children and religious minorities, and government institutions and some Muslim groups have persecuted non-Muslims and used some laws as the legal basis for doing so. The Blasphemy Law, for example, allows life imprisonment or the death penalty for contravening Islamic principles, but legislation was passed in October 2004 to eliminate misuse of the law.

Furthermore, the social acceptance of many these problems hinders their eradication. One prominent example is honor killings ("karo kari"), which are believed to have accounted for more than 4,000 deaths from 1998 to 2003. Many view this practice as indicative of a feudal mentality and as an anathema to Islam, but others defend the practice as a means of punishing violators of cultural norms and view attempts to stop it to as an assault on cultural heritage.

## "NUCLEAR SECURITY IN PAKISTAN: REDUCING THE RISKS OF NUCLEAR TERRORISM"

Today's frightening instability in Pakistan comes in a world in which global terrorists are actively seeking nuclear weapons and the materials and expertise needed to make them, a quest that has been underway for more than a decade. Rapid action is needed to keep the Taliban's advances in Pakistan from creating new opportunities for these deadly adversaries.

Yet, assessing nuclear security in Pakistan should not be viewed in isolation. The challenges faced by Pakistani authorities must be seen in their broader context to be properly understood and effectively countered.

All countries in possession of nuclear weapons are concerned about the possibility of losing control over a bomb or weapons-related material. Consequently, states must pay utmost attention to securing these means of mass destruction. Recent years have seen increased international cooperation on nuclear security, improvements in international material protection control and accounting procedures, and increased funding for nuclear security-related initiatives. Despite increases in the scope and sophistication of security measures, much work remains to be done in order to lock down all nuclear materials to a Fort Knox standard. The fact remains that missing weapons-usable material turns up regularly on the nuclear black market. The most worrisome aspect of these recurring incidents is that facilities from which the materials originated did not report them missing. In addition, there have been some notable lapses in warhead security, even in the United States.

Despite such troubling developments, global security efforts until now have been good enough to avert a nuclear catastrophe. The bad news is that nuclear threats are growing.

According to former CIA analyst Bruce Riedel, "Pakistan is the most dangerous country in today's world."

## DAUNTING SECURITY TASK

Ensuring complete control over nuclear equipment, material, and technology is more difficult now than at any time in the past. There is a burgeoning global interest in all things nuclear. More states are seeking nuclear technologies, power, and weapons. Production, transportation, and storage of nuclear materials will expand throughout the 21st century. The presence of more material in more places increases the odds of a security breach leading to the loss of a bomb or the theft of materials to make a bomb. The anticipated global renaissance in nuclear energy will pose new challenges in this regard unless the associated proliferation risks are fully taken into account in decisions on materials processing, transportation, and storage. In this light, it is essential to secure not only weapons-grade plutonium and uranium from military programs, but also plutonium, highly enriched uranium, and other materials from civilian programs. Materials that would not meet the standards required for a nuclear weapon developed by a state might be usable in a terrorist's yield-producing bomb.

Thus, a zero tolerance standard must be adopted for the loss of any nuclear weapon or of materials that may be fashioned into a bomb. Terrorists know that they can exploit any vulnerability to their advantage. In December 1998, Osama bin Laden expressed al Qaeda's intent when he stated in an interview, "Acquiring weapons [of mass destruction] for the defence of Muslims is a religious duty." In November 2001, he added, "I wish to declare that if America used chemical or nuclear weapons against us, then we may retort with chemical or nuclear weapons. We have the weapons as deterrent."

In its efforts to achieve the stature of a state, a terrorist group is most interested in producing a nuclear yield-a mushroom cloud. Consequently, a terrorist group would improvise a nuclear device or essentially build a crude nuclear bomb, one that has a low yield and may be unpredictable, inefficient, and unsafe in comparison with the complicated weapons systems in a national nuclear arsenal. To counter this qualitatively new threshold of nuclear-related threats, states must ensure that terrorists do not acquire any nuclear materials. This risk increases the demands that must be placed on security measures for materials at all stages of their use, i.e., production, processing, transportation, and storage, in research reactors as well as weapons facilities. The bottom line is that it is not enough to preclude terrorists from getting their hands on a bomb. States must eliminate any possibility that terrorists will acquire sufficient materials to build a bomb or successfully attack or take over a facility containing weapons or materials.

After the September 11 attacks, for example, the United States raised the level of the security for nuclear weapons and nuclear materials. As a centerpiece of this effort, President George W. Bush signed a National Security Directive in August 2006 establishing the U.S. government's Nuclear Materials Information Program. This program directed the consolidation of all U.S. information pertaining to all nuclear materials worldwide, in all forms and at all levels of enrichment. It included radioactive sources that could be fashioned into a dirty bomb. Every country was considered as a potential source of a crude terrorist weapon, including the United States. The directive prescribed a systematic approach to assessing the security status of all nuclear materials in facilities and in transit. It required the construction of a forensics database containing all U.S. holdings.

In addition, substantial new investments were made in upgrading security throughout the U.S. nuclear establishment. To that end, security planners in the Department of Energy and the Nuclear Regulatory Commission made assumptions about the likelihood that malicious insiders at nuclear sites would work with outsiders to allow access to facilities and materials. The Energy Department and the FBI dramatically increased intelligence and counterintelligence efforts to mitigate threats posed by malicious insiders. Defence in depth-multiple, reinforcing layers of security-was strengthened to catch any leakage of materials or information that could enable an outside group in its pursuit of a bomb.

In spite of such upgrades, serious security lapses have occurred in the U.S. nuclear establishment over the past several years. Others will surely happen in the future because no security is perfect. Thus, constant vigilance is required; it is important to strive continuously toward the elimination of nuclear threats, knowing that it may never be possible to achieve this ideal standard. The surest way to fail is to become complacent, to believe it cannot happen here.

That is certainly true in Pakistan. Nevertheless, all signs indicate that the professional and disciplined Pakistani military establishment that maintains control over the nuclear arsenal understands the dangers of a breakdown in nuclear security. Senior Pakistani military officers have consistently expressed a high degree of confidence that they are prepared to counter a range of plausible threats in this regard.

These officers have a lot to worry about, notwithstanding high-level reassurances from Pakistani authorities that everything is under control. Three worrisome trends are exerting mounting pressure on the Pakistani military's ability to secure its nuclear assets and prevent a nuclear catastrophe. First, growing extremism in Pakistan increases the odds of insiders in the nuclear establishment collaborating with outsiders to access weapons, materials, or facilities. Second, the rapid expansion of Pakistan's nuclear weapons program will introduce new vulnerabilities into the security system. Finally, growing instability within the country could lead to unanticipated challenges to nuclear command and control procedures, resulting in a "loose nuke" scenario, a takeover of a facility by outsiders, or, in the worst case, a coup leading to Taliban control over the nuclear arsenal.

## COLLABORATION SCENARIOS

The greatest threat of a loose nuke scenario stems from insiders in the nuclear establishment working with outsiders, people seeking a bomb or material to make a bomb. Nowhere in the world is this threat greater than in Pakistan. Pakistani authorities have a dismal track record in thwarting insider threats. For example, the network run by the father of the Pakistani bomb, Abdul Qadeer Khan, channeled sensitive nuclear technologies to Iran, Libya, and North Korea for years under the noses of the establishment before it was taken down in 2003, to the best of our knowledge. The Umma-Tameer-e-Nau (UTN), founded by Pakistani nuclear scientists with close ties to al Qaeda and the Taliban, was headed by Sultan Bashiruddin Mahmood, who had been in charge of Pakistan's Khushab reactor. He discussed al Qaeda's nuclear aspirations with bin Laden. According to Mahmood, bin Laden asked him how he could construct a bomb if the group already had the material. It is stunning to consider that two of the founding fathers of Pakistan's weapons program embarked independently on clandestine efforts to organize networks to sell their country's most precious secrets for profit.

Although the UTN network apparently was neutralized before it had a chance to fulfill al Qaeda's long-held aspirations to obtain what bin Laden has called a "Hiroshima bomb," this was the first known case in which a "WMD for hire" network had been created specifically to provide weapons of mass destruction to terrorist and extremist groups. In this context, members of the UTN group represented the broad set of scientific-and engineering-related capabilities necessary to construct an improvised nuclear device. They had an international reach. Most importantly, some prominent members of the group had once held positions in the Pakistani establishment and had connections to people on the inside with access to nuclear materials. It is not certain that this group had the wherewithal to have succeeded in its desire to enable al Qaeda's quest for a bomb, but it is encouraging that resolute Pakistani and U.S. follow-up action apparently nipped in the bud a potentially serious threat.

There are troubling indications that these insider threats are not anomalies. In the Khan and UTN cases, the rogue senior officers and their cohorts in the nuclear establishment were not caught by Pakistan's security establishment. It would be foolhardy to assume that such lapses could not happen again. The Pakistani military, intelligence, and nuclear establishments are not immune to rising levels of extremism in the country. There is a lethal proximity between terrorists, extremists, and nuclear weapons insiders. Insiders have facilitated terrorist attacks. Suicide bombings have occurred at air force bases that reportedly serve as nuclear weapons storage sites. It is difficult to ignore such trends. Purely in actuarial terms, there is a strong possibility that bad apples in the nuclear establishment are willing to cooperate with outsiders for personal gain or out of sympathy for their cause.

### *Relying on Secrecy*

Pakistani authorities certainly recognize the gravity of this problem. One of the ways they are coping is to emphasize secrecy and clandestinity over the more visible manifestations of nuclear security. The U.S. and Russian model of nuclear security relies on redundant layers of high walls, gates, and guards at sites in order to produce a highly visible image of impenetrability that will deter those seeking to gain access to them. Essentially, Pakistan has sacrificed some of the advantages of the traditional approach to security in favour of reducing unique vulnerabilities and threats arising from the circumstances in which it finds itself.

The thrust of the Pakistani military's strategy is to reduce its vulnerability to a nuclear security incident by systematically denying outsiders opportunities to gain illicit access to nuclear weapons. Consequently, the nuclear establishment is distributed geographically: Materials processing and weapons production facilities are consolidated in sites near Islamabad in areas under tight government control. Special nuclear material is reportedly stored apart from the weapons themselves. Warheads are reportedly stored separately from delivery systems.

Another precaution taken by the Pakistani military is to maintain strict secrecy over the location of storage sites and to transport and deploy weapons clandestinely rather than in convoys that have a stronger, highly visible security profile. These security precautions produce fewer visible signs of movements, thereby lowering the risks associated with possible theft of or attack on weapons at their most vulnerable point, in transit.

Paradoxically, this dependence on secrecy over physical security could backfire in the event a malicious insider gained access to locations of weapons storage sites, transportation routes, and similar insider information, especially because more moving parts are involved in assembling weapons when they are being deployed. In such a case, there would be fewer barriers between an outside group and the bomb.

The emphasis on maintaining clandestinity and secrecy in nuclear activity may hold other unintended consequences. For instance, Pakistan's development of indigenous weapons-use controls-permissive action links (PALs)-for partially disassembled weapons systems is more challenging than for PALs built into a fully integrated weapons system. Moreover, although unpredictability in nuclear-related movements and activity is good from the standpoint of frustrating would-be attackers, it could conceivably increase the chances of a dangerous miscalculation of Pakistan's actions by India, especially in a crisis in which Pakistan's archrival interpreted a nuclear terrorist incident as a threat against its security.

Another trend that militates against achieving perfect nuclear security is the rapid expansion of the Pakistani nuclear program. Pakistan's nuclear arsenal roughly doubled from 1998 to today's total of a hundred weapons, in round numbers. In the coming years, as new plutonium-production capacity at the Khushab site comes online, the total number of nuclear weapons could increase dramatically. Using plutonium as the nuclear-explosive material also would allow Pakistan to build smaller nuclear weapons.

The expansion of the nuclear weapons program will mean more material, more construction of facilities for processing material and manufacturing weapons and delivery systems, and more demands for waste storage and transportation. More of everything means more vulnerabilities, more places for something to go wrong.

Finally, Pakistan's expanding nuclear program and the insider threat that accompanies it is taking place in the context of the broader trend of increasing instability in the country. In terms of assigning probabilities to a potential nuclear meltdown, the most likely scenario that Pakistan may confront is not a loss of control over one of its nuclear weapons, although that risk certainly must be addressed. Rather, threats are more likely to emerge from the increasing number of potential pathways to a bomb, specifically, the increasing threats posed by a slow hemorrhaging over time of technology, design, and construction knowledge and materials that might ultimately cross the threshold and produce a terrorist bomb. This phenomenon is more complicated and subtle and more difficult to counter than the scary, well-hyped scenarios involving loose nukes stolen by terrorists from a storage site or in transit.

# Bibliography

Akbar S.: *Jinnah, Pakistan, and Islamic Identity: The Search for Saladin*, 1997.

Alam, Aftab : *US Policy Towards South Asia: Special Reference to Indo-Pak Relations*, Raj, Delhi, 1998.

Allana, G.: *Pakistan Movement: Historic Documents*, Karachi, Department of International Relations, University of Karachi, 1967.

Allison, Graham: *Nuclear Terrorism: The Ultimate Preventable Catastrophe*, New York: Times Books, 2004.

Anil, K.C.: *Military and Democracy in South Asia : Challenges, Politics and Power*, Sumit Enterprises, Delhi, 2009.

Barber B.R.: *Strong Democracy. Participatory Politics for a New Age*. Berkeley, University of California Press, 1984.

Bearce, George D.: *British Attitudes Towards India 1784-1858*, Oxford, University Press, 1961.

Bhat, T.P. : *Pak and China : Trade Complementarities and Competitiveness*, Bookwell, Delhi, 2008.

Brooks, Constance : *Disaster Preparedness*, Washington, DC, Association for Research Libraries, 1993.

Chitkara, M.G. : *China-Pak Relations Challenges Before New Millennium*, APH, Delhi, 2001.

Das, Bharti : *Irritants in China-Pak Relations*, Kilaso, Delhi, 2005.

Digumarti Bhaskara Rao: *Military Conversion : Impact on Science and Technology*, Discovery, Delhi, 2003.

Friedman, G.: *The Future of War of Cyber Crimes*, N.Y., Random House, 1996.

Gao, Mobo: *The Battle for China's Past: Mao and the Cultural Revolution*, London, Pluto Press, 2008.

Ghosh, Ajoy : *China-Pak Conflict : Threat to South Asian Security*, Reference Press, Delhi, 2003.

Hoffman, Bruce, *Inside Terrorism*, New York: Columbia University Press, 1998.

Hurewitz, Jacob C.: *Diplomacy in the Near and Middle East: A Documentary Record 1535-1914*, Princeton, New Jersey, 1956.

Imtiaz, A.: *State and Foreign Policy: India's Role in South Asia*, New Delhi, Vikas, 1993.

Jagannath P. Panda: *China's Path to Power : Party, Military and the Politics of State Transition*, Pentagon, Delhi, 2010.

Jha, Prem Shankar : *India and China : The Battle Between Soft and Hard Power*, Penguin Books India, Delhi, 2010.

Kunju, N. : *Indo-Pak : Nuclear Cold War*, Reliance, Delhi, 2002.

Laquer, Walter, *The New Terrorism: Fanaticism and the Arms of Mass Destruction*, Oxford: Oxford University Press, 1999.

Nevile, P.: *Lahore: A Sentimental Journey*. New Delhi: Penguin, 1993.

Posen, B.R.: *The Sources of Military Doctrine*, Ithaca, 1984, Cornell Univ. Press.

Prabir De: *Pak and China in an Era of Globalisation : Essays on Economic Cooperation*, Bookwell, Delhi, 2005.

Rhodes, Richard, *The Making of the Atomic Bomb*, New York: Simon and Schuster, 1988.

Selden, S.: *The Promise of Representative Bureaucracy: Diversity and Responsiveness in a Government Agency*, New York, M. E. Sharpe, 1997.

Shaun Narine, *Explaining ASEAN: Regionalism in Southeast Asia*, Boulder, CO: Lynne Rienner Publishers, 2002.

Spindlove, J. R.: *Terrorism today: The past, the players, the future*, Upper Saddle Creek, NJ: Prentice Hall, 2000.

Thomas Arnold: *The Spread of Islam in the World, A History of Peaceful Preaching*, Goodword Books, 2001.

Whitaker, D. J.: *The Terrorism Reader*, New York: Routledge, 2001.

Winston, Mark L.: *Travels in the Genetically Modified Zone*, Cambridge, Harvard University, 2004.

# Index


**A**

Arms Trade, 241, 242.

**C**

Cold War, 31, 48, 54, 77, 86, 149, 153, 176, 180, 244.

**D**

Defence Doctrine, 23.
Delivery Systems, 30.
Diplomacy, 70, 109, 110, 139, 143, 208, 239, 262.

**E**

External Threats, 7, 289.

**I**

Internal Threats, 5, 298.

**K**

Kashmir War, 260.

**M**

Manufacture, 98, 161, 182, 185, 212, 215, 241, 264, 282, 285, 287.

**N**

National Defence Economy, 98, 100, 102.
National Security, 21, 23, 24, 34, 48, 49, 51, 52, 54, 55, 68, 145, 156, 168, 177, 186, 288, 290, 300.
Nuclear Deterrence, 29, 30, 31, 32, 40, 51, 85, 105, 172, 220, 221, 222, 226, 227, 239.
Nuclear Diplomacy, 109, 139.
Nuclear Doctrine, 1, 24, 27, 201, 206, 207.
Nuclear Infrastructure, 38, 39, 199, 273, 274, 281.
Nuclear Material Security, 268, 278.
Nuclear Posture, 66, 161, 224.
Nuclear Power, 19, 25, 37, 47, 49, 50, 51, 111, 169, 170, 198, 200, 202, 212, 222, 238, 248, 249, 252, 253, 280.
Nuclear Program, 2, 3, 8, 16, 20, 28, 29, 34, 44, 52, 55, 60, 66, 67, 138, 145, 168, 177, 187, 212, 214, 216, 230, 301, 308.
Nuclear Proliferation, 17, 21, 22, 27, 36, 43, 48, 49, 50, 52, 53, 54, 55, 56, 57, 149, 185, 186, 290.
Nuclear Security, 3, 18, 35, 46, 47, 48, 84, 139, 228, 272, 273, 274, 275, 276, 278, 279, 280, 281, 301, 304, 306, 307.
Nuclear Strikes, 156.

Nuclear Tests, 30, 35, 58, 59, 98, 139, 140, 146, 154, 162, 186, 196, 197, 202, 269, 275.
Nuclear Threat Reduction, 84, 90, 187.
Nuclear Trajectory, 214, 215, 216.
Nuclear Weapons, 1, 3, 4, 8, 13, 14, 17, 20, 21, 22, 23, 29, 30, 31, 32, 33, 34, 35, 36, 37, 38, 39, 40, 41, 42, 43, 44, 45, 46, 47, 48, 49, 50, 51, 52, 53, 54, 55, 56, 57, 58, 60, 61, 62, 63, 65, 66, 67, 68, 84, 86, 87, 91, 92, 93, 94, 95, 96, 97, 98, 105, 109, 111, 112, 136, 155, 166, 167, 168, 169, 170, 171, 172, 173, 176, 177, 180, 182, 183, 184, 185, 186, 187, 188, 189, 191, 192, 193, 194, 195, 196, 198, 213, 214, 215, 216, 218, 219, 221, 223, 224, 225, 228, 229, 230, 231, 232, 234, 235, 236, 241, 242, 245, 250, 254, 256, 257, 258, 260, 261, 262, 263, 280, 295, 307, 308.

**P**

Policy, 10, 20, 23, 24, 25, 41, 45, 49, 50, 51, 52, 54, 55, 56, 57, 63, 65, 67, 69, 70, 72, 73, 75, 83, 86, 90, 92, 93, 94, 104, 108, 111, 113, 116, 136, 139, 140, 141, 142, 143, 144, 145, 146, 147, 150, 151, 152, 153, 154, 155, 158, 168, 173, 174, 176, 177, 178, 179, 180, 186, 187, 188, 190, 207, 208, 210, 211, 212, 224, 226, 227, 235, 236, 239, 244, 247, 253, 257, 283, 284, 290, 294, 299.

**S**

Small Nuclear Force, 201.

**T**

Terrorism, 15, 18, 24, 56, 57, 61, 67, 70, 71, 73, 92, 109, 112, 113, 114, 134, 135, 142, 153, 158, 161, 180, 189, 200, 278, 280, 281, 290, 291, 298, 301.

**W**

Weapons Development, 56, 100, 102, 103, 108, 269, 283, 284, 285, 286.

❑❑❑